LB
2837
.P38
2001

Perlmann, Joel.

Women's work?

$32.00

DATE			
WITHDRAWN			

BAKER & TAYLOR

Women's Work?

Joel Perlmann &
Robert A. Margo

Women's Work?

American Schoolteachers, 1650–1920

The University of Chicago Press
Chicago & London

JOEL PERLMANN is a senior scholar at the Jerome Levy Economics Institute of Bard College and Levy Institute Research Professor at the College. He is the author of *Ethnic Differences: Schooling and Social Structure among the Irish, Italians, and Blacks in an American City, 1880–1935.*

ROBERT A. MARGO is professor of economics at Vanderbilt University and a research associate of the National Bureau of Economic Research. He is the author of *Race and Schooling in the South, 1880–1950: An Economic History* and *Wages and Labor Markets in the United States, 1820–1860.*

THE UNIVERSITY OF CHICAGO PRESS, CHICAGO 60637
THE UNIVERSITY OF CHICAGO PRESS, LTD., LONDON

10 09 08 07 06 05 04 03 02 01   1 2 3 4 5
ISBN: 0-226-66039-7 (cloth)

Library of Congress Cataloging-in-Publication Data

Perlmann, Joel.
    Women's work? : American schoolteachers, 1650–1920 / Joel Perlmann and Robert A. Margo.
        p.   cm.
Includes bibliographical references (p.   ) and index.
    ISBN 0-226-66039-7
    1. Women teachers—United States—History. 2. Women teachers—United States—Social conditions. 3. Elementary school teachers—United States—History.   I. Title: American schoolteachers, 1650–1920.   II. Margo, Robert A. (Robert Andrew), 1954–   III. Title.
    LB2837 .P38 2001
    372.11'0082—dc21
                                                    00-011053

To my aunt, Rose (Eti) Field, New York City
schoolteacher 1930–1970, who taught me to read;
and to Sheri Donovan-Smith and Joe Russo,
my children's first-grade teachers —JP

To Daniel and Lee —RAM

CONTENTS

PREFACE

The value of interdisciplinary work is a cliché in American colleges and universities. But such work remains exceptional in the social sciences, perhaps because bridging disciplinary gaps in perspective and technique is far more difficult than most deans or provosts care to admit. In our own fields of social history and economic history there have been few if any such collaborations. We shared common substantive interests, especially in educational history, and common methodological interests as well, but working across disciplinary assumptions proved to be challenging as well as repeatedly illuminating. The issues the book addresses, and the formulations with which it discusses them, would have differed considerably had either of us tried to carry out the research, or write the book, alone.

Joel Perlmann supervised the collection of national samples of teachers from nineteenth-century census schedules, Robert Margo the collection of samples of city teachers; Elyce Rotella assisted Margo in the initial collection and analysis of the Houston teacher lists (discussed in chap. 5). Perlmann was primarily responsible for the research and writing through chapter 4, Margo for chapter 5, both authors for the conclusion. Nevertheless, we discussed research strategies, results, and chapter drafts very extensively with each other. When exploring the issues discussed in chapter 2, for example, we discovered that most of our initial expectations needed drastic revision; the related e-mail correspondence between us was probably longer than that long chapter is now.

In the course of this research, we collected a great deal of evidence from nineteenth-century manuscripts and publications. Such work could not have been undertaken without financial support. In addition, such support also enabled both authors to spend many months of full-time research on this project. We are glad to finally have the chance to acknowledge the support (and patience) of grantors: the Spencer Foundation, the National Science Foundation, and the U.S. Department of Education. Additional support of various kinds was given by the Harvard Graduate School of Education, the University of Pennsylvania, Colgate University, Vanderbilt University, and the Jerome Levy Economics Institute of Bard College. We owe a special debt to John Collins, the librarian of Harvard's Gutman Library, and to his staff, for helping us in every way to draw on Harvard's superb collection of state and local school reports. The actual data collection, from hundreds of microfilm rolls and hundreds of old publications, was the work of well over a score of students; we cannot thank them all individually, but we must express our admiration for and gratitude to several doctoral students who spent months or years coordinating this work with good sense and good cheer: Victoria Macdonald, Kathy Roberts, Sylvana Siddali, Julie Sun, Geoff Tegnell, and Keith Whitescarver. And, finally, over the years we have accumulated intellectual debts to many colleagues, including Susan Carter, the late Lawrence Cremin, Thomas Dublin, Stanley Engerman, Claudia Goldin, Carl Kaestle, Michael Katz, Mark Lytle, Richard Murnane, Elyce Rotella, Stephan Thernstrom, David Tyack, and Maris Vinovskis. Versions of the material in this book have been presented to audiences at many different institutions and conferences, including Brandeis University, the City University of New York Graduate Center, the Harvard Graduate School of Education, the Jerome Levy Economics Institute of Bard College, the University of Pennsylvania, the Social Science History Association, Wellesley College, and the Western Economic Association, and we are grateful to those in attendance for their comments.

INTRODUCTION

During the course of the nineteenth century, teaching in American primary schools came to be regarded as women's work. In the 1920s, when the figure peaked, over 90 percent of primary schoolteachers were women; and by the 1990s—after decades of transformation in schools, families, women's education, and women's work—that percentage had changed but little. Before teaching became women's work on a national scale, other widespread and enduring regularities influenced the relative use of female teachers. Whether the teacher would be a man or a woman varied from country to city, indeed from summer to winter; and, most fundamentally, it varied by region. Moreover, while these earlier, regional patterns endured for decades, they did change over centuries. In this book we describe these regional gender patterns of employment in teaching; we try to explain how these patterns came about, evolved, and eventually declined— declined so fully that today they are all but unknown, except to a few specialists who have observed one or another part of this history.

In order to try to make sense of the subject taken as a whole, across time and region, we have found ourselves looking in new ways at the history of education and of women's work; at views of women in different cultural settings; at economic, demographic, and social structural differences that affected women's roles; and at the ways in which the politics and organization of schooling would have affected who would teach. The theme of feminization in American teaching has been long familiar to both the history of education and of women's work, but the long sweep, with careful attention to institutions and to patterns of hiring in different regions, especially in the countryside (where such large majorities lived for so long), has forced us to recast the subject.

1

We begin by showing, in this introduction, that by the time of the American Civil War, and in fact long before that, the teaching arrangements of the northeastern and southern states differed starkly, with far higher proportions of women teachers employed in the Northeast compared with the South. Moreover, this regional difference was reproduced across much of the continent, as the settlers moved into what we call today the Midwest. What explains the creation of these divergent regional arrangements in the East, and what explains their western re-creation in a new social situation? These subjects comprise our first three chapters, the first on the evolution of a New England pattern in which the role for women came to be central; the second on how and why the southern pattern came to be so different; and, finally, the third on the migration of social, cultural, and institutional patterns into the new communities of the Midwest.

Thus the first three chapters are concerned with the puzzle of how these regional disparities could have developed, survived, and even migrated across so long a period and such a vast area. In the fourth chapter, we turn from this puzzle to the explanation for the subsequent uniformity in the triumph of the female elementary school teacher everywhere in the half century before 1920.

Finally, the fifth chapter considers a special, important, group we consider only tangentially in the rest of the work: the teachers in urban school systems at the end of the nineteenth century. Because some of these systems annually published remarkably rich information about their teaching forces, we can study the careers of men and women in the cities. We focus on understanding the extent of the gender gap in salaries and on the likelihood of promotion to a role in administrative work.

■■

Throughout we have relied on a rich array of evidence, on the arguments of school reformers and the discussions of school administrators, on colonial school records and town histories, and even on letters to editors. However, because our subject is ultimately about patterns of "more" and "less," about the proportions of women teachers in various situations, our argument is primarily based on quantitative evidence about American teachers drawn from several key sources. Often, especially after statewide administrative structures for education were created, we found data in state and city school reports and, later, in federal education reports as well. But these published reports would not have allowed us to understand how local areas differed and would not have taken us far enough back in time to answer our questions—especially in the South. We have therefore relied extensively on evidence of a sort that was simply unavailable not long ago, namely, large samples drawn from the manuscript schedules of the United States censuses, the enumerations undertaken every decade. The manuscript schedules, the actual sheets that the census takers filled out as they went from house to house across America, tell us a good deal about specific individuals. Of course they do not tell us everything we wish we could have asked, but access to the schedules is a giant advance over reliance on the publications of the Census Bureau that followed each enumeration, for we are no longer dependent on the tabulations that the compilers of those old volumes chose to provide. What is more, on a personal computer we can perform in seconds classification of individuals that would have quickly dried up the entire federal census budget had such explorations been turned over to an army of nineteenth-century census clerks.

The census schedules of which we speak—records about individuals that list information on matters such as age, sex, occupation, race, place of birth, literacy, place of residence—are available for every census beginning in 1850 (except 1890; those were destroyed in a fire). Moreover, during the past decade, a remarkable endeavor among American historians and social scientists has created gigantic samples from each of these censuses—nationally representative samples of hundreds of thousands and even millions from each census. And a second generation of effort in this direction has found ways of arranging these unique data sets so that they are now remarkably simple to use. These data sets are known as the Integrated Public Use Microdata Samples (IPUMS). We rely on them extensively in the discussions that follow. None that we use existed fifteen years ago, several crucial samples did not exist when we first began to write about our findings, and indeed at least one very important sample has been available for less than a year. Thus the way we frame our questions and the way we search for answers simply could not have been undertaken much earlier.

To these national samples of the population, drawn from census schedules, we have added our own efforts at data collection from the census schedules, namely national samples *of teachers* drawn from the census schedules of 1860 and 1880, samples that include even more teachers than the corresponding IPUMS samples, in fact many times more teachers. The 1860 census was chosen as the earliest reliable enumeration for our purpose (the only earlier census schedules to record information on individuals did not systematically include women's occupations; by 1860 the instructions were detailed and unambiguous on the need to do so). We rely especially on the

1860 sample of teachers in the work that follows, along with the IPUMS national samples of the population; both are drawn from manuscript records of enumerators from the decennial censuses.

In addition to the census records, we have exploited, in chapter 5, the remarkable set of city records mentioned earlier, namely the annual lists of urban teachers which include biographical information about each teacher as well as salary level and title in the school system. Such lists, of course, varied greatly from one city to another, as well as over time. We focus on some especially detailed late nineteenth- and early twentieth-century lists for four cities from across the country.

Those readers who are not familiar with the work of recent social or economic historians may well find the availability of so much detailed information about ordinary people of the past astonishing. Many of the topics we explore, far from being buried hopelessly in the daily life of a prestatistical era, can be very well documented; and consequently not every speculation concerning these topics need be treated as equally well founded—evidence to confirm or deny these speculations is often available. Nevertheless, as our analyses drove us farther and farther back in time, the earliest census schedules of 1850 and 1860 could no longer help us. Reports in published state and local records also became scarcer—less uniform in coverage and often less detailed about what we wanted to know. All these problems became greater still as our subject forced us back into the colonial era. We do offer some original research from that period too, nearly all from New England, and we were occasionally able to draw on relevant work by other recent historians of that era. But the colonial and early Republican history of country schools for the masses is neither well developed nor sustained; we were driven back to a search of old institutional histories of education, histories of very uneven quality from our perspective. Nevertheless, we found a great deal of material, some from historians long gone who anticipated some of the issues we raise today.

Thus our evidence is from many sources, differing in detail and quality as well as in its nature as enumeration data or narrative history or discussion of issues by contemporaries. Some hypotheses we can formulate and then confidently accept or reject; others turn out to be new speculations that we must leave hanging; we hope that we have made it clear to the reader where the evidence is strong and where it is weak. And we seriously do hope that this book will stimulate others to extend the research where the evidence is weak. It takes the overview of the long-term patterns across the geographic expanse as far as we know how to take it with the evidence before us.

We should also stress explicitly what the foregoing discussion has left implicit. Our explorations are not meant to provide a general social or economic history of schoolteaching nor even a general history of gender in American schoolteaching. We are attending to a few key interrelated issues that we believe are interesting and important.

Our focus on the quantitative record is partly dictated by the nature of the problem we are addressing. If we want to explore regional differences in the prevalence of a phenomenon, the choice of quantification is a matter of logic, not taste. We have tried hard to make the argument in the text relevant to all who are interested in the substantive questions; for example, the tables found in the text generally are limited to proportions and averages; the underlying statistical work has been relegated to footnotes and appendixes.

At the same time, we would have been delighted to find more discussions by contemporaries comparing gender and schoolteaching across regions. We found very few such references that were directly on the subject and we cite nearly all we found. The phrase "directly on the subject" deserves elaboration. There were, for example, quite a number of mid-nineteenth-century school reformers, especially in New England, who discussed the advantages of hiring female teachers (Horace Mann is an example of such a reformer); such writings have been examined extensively by historians of education and gender, and we draw on that historical research. However, it is a long way from the arguments of Horace Mann to understanding why the same arguments were not compelling in the South in that period (but would be compelling later). Would the unpublished correspondence of Horace Mann with southern educators deal with this regional difference in the use of female teachers? We made a brief foray into that correspondence, but to no avail.

Still, another reason for our concentration on the quantitative record is that our comparative advantage as scholars is the collection and analysis of such materials. We are convinced that the local picture can be fleshed out, and perhaps such work will challenge our formulations. In particular a more detailed saturation in discussions of education, and particularly in local unpublished records, might yield revealing qualitative material of relevance— about views of women's abilities, about their "proper" functions, and about the motivations of school authorities.

Although our approach is that of quantitative history, we are led, in the end, to cultural and institutional explanations of the gendered character of teaching in American life and of its evolution. Thus we believe that our findings will resonate with a wide variety of readers, regardless of whether they would have struck a different balance between quantitative and qualitative research methods had they written this book. Readers interested in the history of education, for example, should find our results of interest, because the evolution of the gendered character of teaching is inextricably tied up in the history of school organization. Readers interested in women's history should find interesting the discussion of an occupation gendered throughout American history but gendered differently across regions in the same period, and then evolving in all regions into an occupation gendered differently than it had been in any region before. We hope anyone interested in the sociology of occupations or in labor economics will find the case of gender and schoolteaching interesting as well, not least because of our conclusion that the dynamics of the case cannot be divorced from the initial cultural and institutional settings—thus, "history matters." Finally, the supply of teachers is a perennial topic in educational policy, and it is widely believed that the dramatic widening of job opportunities for educated women since 1970 has made it far more difficult for school boards to fill their classrooms with the "best and brightest" women. Although we do not offer specific policy formulations, we hope that by reading this book, those involved in educational policy will achieve a deeper understanding of the historical factors that once made teaching the overwhelming occupation of choice for educated women.

We have not addressed one sort of question in the analysis that follows, namely what difference it made to the lives of children in different regions to have had a woman teacher. We know the arguments that contemporaries offered for hiring (or not hiring) the female teacher, and these are discussed as part of the relevant intellectual background to our social history. But it is quite another thing to ask, from the perspective of our own time, what if anything we believe of these earlier arguments, based on ways of distinguishing between the sexes that will seem quaint or simply prejudiced today. Still, if women were socialized to hold and exhibit different characteristics than men, it may not have been entirely irrelevant that the teacher was a woman. At the same time, when women were hired more cheaply than men, the savings may have translated, as one historian has argued, into the expansion of the educational system out of the exploitation of women teachers. Yet some of those savings may have also gone into hiring more intellectually talented and better-prepared individuals, because when women were hired for lower wages, some of the savings could go to increasing the quality of the pool of teachers hired. We try to describe and explain the evolution of certain long-forgotten teaching patterns. We leave to others, who will use different tools, to explore how these regional differences in staffing the schools may have affected the pupils of each region.

■■

We can introduce the subject of our first three chapters as it first struck us with force. When we explored the prevalence of female teachers in the national sample we had drawn from the census manuscript schedules of 1860, we observed the patterns presented in table 1.1.[1] The table distinguishes between rural and urban teachers (urban defined here as incorporated places of 4,000 or more residents).[2] In urban areas, it is clear, the regional differences were not so great; between 65 percent and 80 percent of teachers were women in the urban areas of every region. Why urban school systems recruited a female teaching force long before rural schools did so is a subject to which we return in chapter 4. Briefly, however, we can pause to note that fewer older children stayed in school in the urban economy, and these students attended different schools (grammar or high school as opposed to primary, e.g.); as such, these older students did not present a discipline problem for female teachers. Also urban areas were most likely to be influenced by the latest pedagogical opinions, and in the 1840s these opinions stressed the nurturing value of female teachers for young children, as well as the economic good sense in hiring women for lower wages than men could command. The urban patterns in our table reflect the fact that in the larger urban communities educational leaders were in touch with each other. Henry Barnard, for example, helped advise Charleston and New Orleans on the choice of a superintendent of schools and on school practices; indeed, in Charleston, many young women from the North were recruited as teachers in the late 1850s. Finally, the urban economy may have made supplemental work less valuable for prospective male teachers than it was in the seasonally based rural economy.

However, in 1860 only one American in five lived in an urban area (of 2,500 or more), as did a comparable fraction of our teachers (17 percent of the sample lived in places of 4,000 or more residents, the criterion available

1. Page 22. See also app. 1 on sources.
2. On coding of places by population, see app. 1.

to us). In the rural areas, where the great majority of people lived, the contrasts in arrangements for teaching were much greater than in the larger towns and cities. In New England, 84 percent of all rural teachers were women; in New York, the number was nearly as high, 79 percent. It was notably lower in the other Middle Atlantic states (59 percent), and dramatically lower still in the South, where 36 percent of all rural teachers were women on the eve of the Civil War. Among the New England states, Connecticut had the lowest proportion of female teachers in the sample (75 percent); in every other New England state at least 83 percent of the rural teachers were women. In the South, Virginia had the highest fraction of women teachers, 54 percent, three other states had between 33 percent and 40 percent women among their teachers, and in the other nine states of the South the number was below 33 percent.

In order to understand midwestern patterns, it is important to distinguish the northernmost tier of that region from the rest: in Michigan, Wisconsin, and Minnesota, 86 percent of all rural teachers were women; in the other seven states of the region, 58 percent. It is these regional patterns that we seek to understand more fully.[3]

Most teachers were young everywhere, and most of the youngest teachers were women everywhere, as later tables will show. By no means all of the great regional difference in the prevalence of female teachers was due to the age structure of the teachers, however. The regional differences in the prevalence of female teachers were clear within age groups, especially in the difference between the Northeast and the South.

Understanding these regional differences in the prevalence of female teachers is the task of our first three chapters. In chapter 1 we explore how the pattern of the Northeast came about (focusing chiefly on New England for reasons that will become clear). The story has roots in the earliest colonial arrangements and evolves over two centuries of growth and transformation, from colonial outposts to established rural communities and into the age of industrialization. Obviously school arrangements changed a good deal, as did views of women and their roles, over such a long social history. However, the stages of change were distinctive to the social history of that area; in the South, the evolution followed a different course, as we show

3. This grouping of the states into subregions is confirmed by published census data from 1870, and from published state data in the antebellum era, some of which we will encounter in the following pages. See especially U.S. Office of the Census, *Ninth Census of the United States* (Washington, 1872), vol. 1, table XVII A and B.

in chapter 2. Across these chapters, the analysis proceeds on two different levels. One level may be called institutional, exploring why certain kinds of schools developed in each region, and why schools of different kinds encouraged the presence or absence of female teachers. For example, if the "dame school" (a sort of seventeenth-century nursery school) was more prevalent (for whatever reason) in New England than it was in the South, this institutional difference would have created more teaching roles for the earliest American women in one region of the colonies than in the other.

The other level on which the analysis proceeds is the exploration of the wider social context; on this level we ask whether there were reasons *other than* institutional reasons why women might have been more likely to teach in one region than in another. For example, if women were relatively more likely than men to be illiterate in the South than in New England, it would have been harder to staff southern than New England schools with women. Of course, this distinction in levels of analysis is imperfect; for example, this sort of regional difference in a gender gap in literacy might have been expected to encourage certain kinds of institutional arrangements, arrangements less reliant on literate women, in the South. Nevertheless, it matters a good deal whether one thinks such a literacy gap helped create an institutional arrangement (perhaps a half century earlier) or whether this putative gender gap in literacy was still operating directly on the selection of teachers at a certain moment in time. To put this latter possibility more vividly, we might say that the institutional arrangements could be ignored—the internal life of the school considered a black box—and the gender gap in literacy would still explain why teachers in one region were more likely to be women than teachers in the other region. Readers will find it helpful to bear in mind these two levels of analysis—of institutions and of the wider social context—in the next two chapters. While the chapter division is based on geographic region, the internal divisions within the chapters (especially in chap. 2) reflect this conceptual distinction between levels of analysis.

In particular, we argue that the simplest economic understanding of behavior will not adequately explain our evidence. Such an explanation suggests that we could learn a great deal about employment choices—about who sought work as a teacher and about who was hired as a teacher—if we knew how much competing demand there was for women's time in other work within each region. Economists can often measure this competing demand by exploring the ratio of female to male wages for the same kinds of work in different places. And so, following this method, we thought that if we had evidence of the 1860 female-to-male wage ratio in locales across the United States, we could explain much about why women were more attractive to hire as teachers in some regions than in others. As it happens, we were able to construct just such wage ratios for hundreds of locales. Yet the female-to-male wage ratios we constructed do not adequately explain the prevalence of female teachers across these locales; we were obliged to turn to a fuller, more subtle, explanation, that draws on the way in which economic decisions were embedded in the web of institutions and perhaps also in the larger milieu of cultural norms.

In chapter 3, the last of the chapters dealing with regional differences, we approach these variations in another way. We were fortunate to have evidence from the hiring decisions in communities across the Midwest, both communities settled by Yankees and communities settled by Southerners. When these settlers entered new labor market conditions, what explains their decisions to hire the teachers they did?

New England:
The First Two Centuries

THE COLONIAL INSTITUTIONAL BACKGROUND

On the whole, the standard histories of colonial schooling are limited in scope and out of date; and given the changing interests of historians over the generations, because they are out of date they also contain relatively little material on women pupils or even women teachers. A certain irony marks this historiographical situation. Before the 1960s, American educational historians routinely produced histories of colonial schools (although the gender-related aspects of the topic were never their central focus). Then, in 1960 Bernard Bailyn published a celebrated critique of this earlier literature, arguing that its limited focus on public versus private institutions was misguided, and indeed that its exclusive focus on the school was inappropriate for an era in which education occurred as much (or more) through other institutions as well, such as the family. Bailyn's essay, fascinating in itself, also served as a major stimulus to the study of the colonial family. Yet an unfortunate by-product of Bailyn's essay was that historians tended to turn away from the study of the colonial school as an institution (an outcome Bailyn certainly did not mean to encourage, for his essay stresses the increasing importance of the school over the course of early colonial history).

A second development in American historical thinking also tended to lead historians away from concern with colonial schools. The revisionist movement of the 1960s and 1970s stressed the role that schools played in creating and sustaining the unequal class and race relations of modern America. This revisionist literature was debunking in tone, exposing the falsities in myths of equal opportunity for all American children. Given such a focus, it is hardly surprising that the focus of revisionist history was on urban industrial America rather than on earlier periods. In the face of Bailyn's critique of earlier colonial schools and the revisionist emphasis on modern America, it seemed that only an intellectual slouch would care about the institutional history of colonial schools.

Yet now we find ourselves in the curious situation of needing a better understanding of colonial institutional realities in order to answer the questions of our own time. We rest on a small number of historical studies, most quite old, for most of the discussion in this section; we draw especially from two such works. The first is an unpublished doctoral dissertation about seventeenth-century Massachusetts school law by Geraldine Murphy (completed the same year Bailyn published his critique and written partly under his guidance) that historians have come to recognize over the years as an invaluable repository of information about much more than the law. The other is much older still, a 1914 study of colonial school arrangements in New England drawn by W. H. Small, a school superintendent in Providence, Rhode Island, for whom, as he tells us, "curiosity became a disease"; thanks to that disease, we have an immense collection of citations on all aspects of colonial schooling that interested Small.[1] Our discussion centers on Massachusetts, with but few examples from towns elsewhere in New England. Nevertheless, in other parts of the region the institutional evolution we describe was apparently similar to that of Massachusetts. A fuller treatment might seek to take account of these intraregional differences, but it would not change the direction of the narrative.[2]

1. Our discussion of the institutional evolution draws especially on the work of Walter Herbert Small, *Early New England Schools* (Boston, 1914); Geraldine Joanne Murphy, "Massachusetts Bay Colony: The Role of Government in Education" (Ph.D. diss., Radcliffe College, 1960); and Jon Teaford, "The Transformation of Massachusetts Education, 1670–1780," *History of Education Quarterly* 10 (fall 1970): 287–307. See also Walter Herbert Small, "Girls in Colonial Schools," *Education* 22 (May 1902): 532–37; Harlan Updegraff, *The Origin of the Moving School in Massachusetts* (New York, 1908); Kathryn Kish Sklar, "The Schooling of Girls and Changing Community Values in Massachusetts Towns, 1750–1800," *History of Education Quarterly* 33 (winter 1993): 511–42; E. Jennifer Monaghan, "Literacy Instruction and Gender in Colonial New England," *American Quarterly* 40, no. 1 (March 1988): 18–41; and David Tyack and Elisabeth Hansot, *Learning Together: A History of Coeducation in American Public Schools* (New Haven, Conn., 1990).

2. The Massachusetts law served as a model for several other parts of the region as well, although the development of the Latin grammar school was probably less widespread in other colonies. The one colony that seems to have had somewhat different arrangements was Rhode Island. Small, *Early New England Schools;* Sheldon Cohen, *A History of Colonial Education, 1607–1776* (New York, 1974); Robert Middlekauf, *Ancients and Axioms: Secondary Education in Eighteenth-Century New England* (New Haven, Conn., 1963).

Lawrence Cremin summarizes the school arrangements that Massachusetts settlers knew from England: "The principal outcome of the Tudor educational revolution was an unprecedented availability of schooling in early seventeenth-century England, though there was no school system in any latter-day sense. This schooling proceeded on two levels which were clearly distinguishable, both institutionally and in the literature that emerged after 1580: there were the petty schools, which concentrated on reading, but which also offered writing [and] ciphering . . . and there were the grammar schools which stressed the reading, writing and speaking of Latin." Nevertheless, the differences blurred in reality as each institution offered some of what the other taught. Cremin continues, "Most of the petty schools were presided over by a single dame or master; most of the grammar schools were presided over by a master."[3] The Massachusetts Bay Colony, in passing its renowned School Law of 1647, probably envisioned re-creating institutions that divided functions in a similar way. The colony required that towns of fifty families provide for instruction in reading and writing and that towns of one hundred families provide also for a Latin grammar school.

Nevertheless, as Murphy showed, in responding to this law, most seventeenth-century towns did not faithfully re-create the institutions Cremin describes. In particular, outside a few large centers of population, true Latin grammar schools—if by that we mean schools that focused principally on classical languages—probably were not common at any time. Rather, most towns seem to have responded to the law with a variety of strategies, from outright noncompliance to ways of complying with the letter of the law but compromising on its spirit. Some towns had already begun to use the most important of these strategies during the second half of the seventeenth century, and others typically did so during the first two or three decades of the eighteenth century. The strategy was to hire a Latin master, a schoolteacher with a knowledge of Latin, as the town teacher— but to arrange for him to spend most of his time teaching English language skills, notably writing, advanced reading skills, and often ciphering. If a demand for teaching Latin arose, the master could meet it.[4]

A more cynical seventeenth-century strategy for compliance was to

3. Lawrence A. Cremin, *American Education: The Colonial Experience, 1607–1783* (New York, 1970), 173–75.

4. Nathaniel B. Shurtleff, ed., *Records of the Governor and Company of the Massachusetts Bay in New England* (Boston, 1853), 203; Murphy, "Massachusetts Bay Colony," esp. chaps. 5 and 7.

designate as schoolmaster a man who knew Latin and pay him a small sum with the understanding that he would rarely if ever be asked to teach anyone anything. However, at the close of the seventeenth century, the terms of the colony law were strengthened in a number of ways—chiefly by stiffening the fine, making it impossible to hire a Latinist who was not teaching, and providing a mechanism for scrutiny and reporting of town practices. Consequently, by the early eighteenth century the most glaring subterfuges that had been used for noncompliance with the law became impossible; every town with a hundred families now made some meaningful provision for a Latin master, most commonly by hiring him to teach the English curriculum. In Boston and a handful of other locales, the concentration of population permitted institutional differentiation sufficiently great to permit schools that actually concentrated on the Latin language to flourish at public expense. However, in considering New England towns generally, we should be careful about confusing the terminology for schools (Latin grammar schools) with the actual subject matter that was taught there.[5]

In any case, the arrangements in the countryside created an institution that offered English instruction beyond the level of basic reading skills, that met the minimal demand for classical instruction, and that satisfied the terms of the colony law to "provide for" a Latin teacher. And, as Murphy stressed, the legal requirement that teachers know Latin may well have provided towns with teachers whose mastery of the English curriculum was surer than would otherwise have been the case. The drawback, of course, was that the teacher who knew Latin commanded a relatively high salary, which the town had to raise: by direct taxation of the entire town, by taxing all those with boys of school age (typically ages six to twelve), by charging tuition, by selling some town land, or by some combination of such measures.

All this, one must remember, was a common way to comply with the Massachusetts legislation requiring most towns (those with over one hundred families) to provide Latin grammar instruction. Still other towns in Massachusetts simply did not comply with the law for short or for long stretches of time. They might have hoped to avoid presentment for the penalty, or at least hoped to do so during the course of enough years to make noncompliance cheaper than compliance. It is quite possible that the nature of advanced instruction was not so different in the complying and noncomplying towns. In both cases, the advanced English curriculum was

5. Murphy, "Massachusetts Bay Colony."

what all boys studied most of the time and what most boys studied all the time. In the noncomplying towns, the school might be called a reading and writing (rather than a Latin grammar) school, and the skill level of the schoolmasters (as measured by their training) might have been lower. Moreover, in the other parts of New England, there may well have been fewer institutions designated as Latin grammar schools, relative to population size, than there were within Massachusetts, whether due to less demanding legislation, weaker enforcement, or lower population density (and lower density resulting, in turn, in fewer towns required to support such an institution).[6] In some cases, the legal provision was reflected in similar but weaker statutes and only the largest towns were likely to have a Latin grammar-school master. Elsewhere, advanced town-supported instruction was probably similar to that in the noncomplying Massachusetts towns. We will return later to the evolution of this institution after 1730.

The town schools we have been describing did not teach rudimentary literacy. Rather, they required that a child have a rudimentary knowledge of reading before enrolling. A child could obtain that rudimentary knowledge at home, but increasingly children obtained it at a dame school. As the name implies, the institution was universally regarded as the province of women. The schooldame provided something between day care and primary instruction in reading. This first schoolteaching function for women, as many have noted, grew out of child-care functions within the home— first, in the sense that the instruction offered was initially offered in the dame's home, and, second, in the sense that the dame school replaced instruction that families had originally provided for their own children (indeed, the dame may often have taught her own along with other children). This process had been evolving in English society and continued in New England.[7]

These dame schools were not mandated by the school law of 1647. Nevertheless, even during the course of the seventeenth century, some towns did work the dame schools into the pattern of compliance with that law. The law of 1647, it will be recalled, obliged small towns (fifty to one hundred families) to provide for instruction in English reading and writing. Some of the towns soon claimed to be in compliance with the law by simply

6. See Small, *Early New England Schools,* 14–29, 47–57.
7. E. Jennifer Monaghan, "Noted and Unnoted School Dames: Women as Reading Teachers in Colonial New England," in Giovanni Geliovesi et al., eds., *History of Elementary School Teaching and Curriculum, International Series for the History of Education* (Hildesheim, Germany, 1990), 1:47–53.

designating a dame-school mistress as town teacher. Woburn, Chelmsford, Sudbury, Andover, and Haverhill did so in 1679, Groton and Weymouth in the early 1690s. Also, in the early eighteenth century some towns began paying the women who ran the dame schools directly, rather than relying on private payment by parents. In other words, a formerly private institution, a traditional dame school, eventually came to be viewed as a public enterprise. One reason for doing so was to subsidize literacy instruction for the children of the poor (as in Marblehead in 1700, Charlestown in 1712, and Salem in 1729).[8]

An additional reason for the town's support for the dame schools, and for the incorporation of these women into the arrangements for town-supported schooling, had to do with the growth of New England towns and the dispersal of their populations into hamlets at some distance from the town centers. The interests of the families in these hamlets were different from the interests of families in the town center: the hamlets needed their own roads and their own schools. After 1680, the issue of how to provide for the needs of outlying areas became pressing. In the second quarter of the eighteenth century, this pattern began to yield a formal division of many towns into separate school districts that eventually determined aspects of school policy for themselves (an arrangement that was fundamental to American educational development until at least the middle of the nineteenth century).

Typically, a town initially sought to provide only the most basic and inexpensive instruction in the outlying districts and relied on the single schoolmaster (in many Massachusetts towns, as we have seen, a Latinist) to offer instruction in the advanced English curriculum. Payment for the schoolmaster might be divided evenly among all districts; or the outlying sections might be deemed unable to utilize the educational services at the town center and freed from contributing all or part of the costs of the schoolmaster; or, finally, the schoolmaster might spend some time in each of the town's hamlets (teaching a "moving" school). The tendency to delay establishment of more advanced schools in the outlying hamlets must often have been strengthened by the towns' obligation to pay the relatively high salary of the schoolmaster who had been working at the town center (a salary especially high if the schoolmaster was a Latinist). This process of population dispersion and accompanying demands for services in the outlying

8. Small, *Early New England Schools,* 166–67 and passim; and Monaghan, "Noted and Unnoted School Dames," 50.

areas had a profound impact on the institutional arrangements. In the outlying districts women were often supported as the town teachers, where they offered the rudiments of reading and occasionally somewhat more. Thus, Framingham voted in 1713 "to settle school dames in each quarter of the town." Plymouth in 1725 supported a grammar school in the center of the town and permitted the hamlets at "each end of town, which for some years past had a woman's school among them" to deduct the costs of the woman's schools from their contribution to the grammar school. Brookline in 1727 arranged to have two schoolhouses, each with a woman's school operating at the time the master was in the other schoolhouse. Dudley in 1743 supported a schooldame for three months at each end of the town and a schoolmaster for three months in the center of the town. And Westminster in 1766 allowed that "a woman's school be kept seven months in the outskirts of town."[9]

In sum, the nature of compliance with colonial school law, the need to provide elementary instruction for the poor, and the need to provide inexpensive schooling following population dispersal are among the reasons why women who provided instruction in reading moved from having informal, private roles to being town-supported teachers. While the preponderance of women teachers taught only reading, there is no doubt that some colonial women schoolteachers taught writing as well as reading in town schools. In Sudbury in the 1690s a "widow Walker" taught both reading and writing. In 1746 Wenham supported a dame "to teach children and youth to read and write." Other women taught in Boston in 1737 and in Braintree from 1758 to 1760. When schooldames were the only teachers operating in an outlying hamlet, the incentive for the woman teacher to teach more than the rudiments of reading may have increased. Thus the dame school evolved into one tier of a two-tier system of schools supported by the New England towns.[10]

Just when the schools taught by dames came to be associated with the summer season is unclear and is not important to our purposes here, but this feature too can be found quite early. The need for the older boys to work on their families' farms during the summer helps explain why their schooling would be concentrated in winter. However, quite apart from the agricultural cycle, there are, as Walter Small noted, other reasons that the school terms would have followed the seasons, and reasons why the seasonal

9. Small, *Early New England Schools*, 179–80, 69–70.
10. Murphy, "Massachusetts Bay Colony"; and Small, *Early New England Schools*.

pattern reflected the needs of the youngest as well as of the oldest pupils:
the need for lighting (without artificial illumination), the need to heat the
winter schoolhouse, and the difficulty of travel in the winter. The hardship
of winter life in particular would help explain why the youngest children
would more easily be sent out in the summers; women taught the youngest.
This association between summer and the women's schools is found as early
as 1702, when the records of Waterbury, Connecticut, speak of "a school
dame for to keep school in the summer," and Small cited similar remarks in
records of Lexington, Weymouth, Amherst, and Windsor and in Norwich,
Connecticut, before 1750; they also existed in Dedham, Framingham, and
Weston and in Sutton, New Hampshire, before 1770.[11]

We cannot say just how prevalent the combination of all these features
together was in the New England towns at particular points in time, but
there is no reason to suspect that the examples cited from the available
records were unusual precursors. By 1750, women teaching in a lower tier
of town-supported schools may not yet have become the norm; however,
such an arrangement was probably common enough to be recognized by
contemporaries as an acceptable way for a town to provide reading instruction. One crude measure of the presence of female teachers comes from the
history of Middlesex County compiled by Samuel Adams Drake in 1880.
Among the histories of the fourteen Middlesex towns that had been incorporated by 1750, support for female teachers is mentioned as having occurred by that date in eight of the towns—two of the references are to
supporting a woman's school (Framingham and Lexington), one to a summer schoolmistress (Stow), two to schooldames (Chelmsford and Hopkin-
ton), and three provide the name of the woman supported (Woburn, Biller-
ica, Westford). Moreover, these references are surely a low estimate of the
prevalence of women in town-supported teaching; historians of other towns
may simply have omitted mentioning the presence of women discussed in
the sources.[12]

The character of more advanced instruction was evolving too. The pressure for educational services in the outlying hamlets led not only to more
town support for women to teach rudimentary reading, but also to a demand

11. Small, *Early New England Schools*, 379, 162–86; Carlos Stafter, *The Schools and
Teachers of Dedham, Massachusetts, 1644–1904* (Dedham, Mass., 1905), 64.

12. Samuel Adams Drake, ed., *History of Middlesex County, Massachusetts* (Boston,
1880). First tabulated by Kris Bentley, "Women and Education in Middlesex County in the
Eighteenth Century" (seminar paper, Harvard Graduate School of Education, Cambridge,
Mass., April 1991).

for schools that taught writing and more advanced English subjects: "reading and writing schools." The writing schools' curriculum focused on the skills that were of value in commerce, including double-entry bookkeeping. Nearly always, a man was hired to teach such a school both because men were more likely to have possessed the writing and ciphering skills and because a male teacher would seem more consistent with the identity of the upper-tier teacher at the town center. In any case, the schools for writing and advanced reading in the outlying areas were freed from any need to comply with the law requiring Latin instruction. Only one school in a town needed to offer Latin, even in Massachusetts towns, and even in those that complied with the law.[13]

Thus, the advanced English curriculum often came to be offered not by one schoolmaster in each town (in many towns a Latinist) but by one man in each district. The district schoolmaster, generally, was less well educated than the schoolmaster at the town center, but he was cheaper to hire. As the population of the outlying areas increased, the pressure must have grown to disperse teaching funds among both women teachers in the lower tier and several male reading-and-writing teachers, instead of concentrating the funds in the salary of an especially well-trained teacher at the town center.

Several other factors facilitated that change. Jon Teaford has shown that the courts and the colonial legislature, which had been crucial in compelling town support for the Latin schoolteachers, apparently began to forsake the task. In Middlesex County, for example, in the two decades between 1700 and 1720, twenty-nine presentments were made against towns. In the two decades between 1760 and 1780, however, only two presentments were made, both before 1764. The wars and dislocations beginning in the 1760s probably further reduced the willingness to support such an expensive teacher. And the ideals of the revolutionary era may have contributed to a diminution of support for elite, classical learning at the expense of more basic learning for the people.[14] Finally, in response to these tendencies, a

---

13. Teaford, "The Transformation of Massachusetts Education," 298–303; E. Jennifer Monaghan, "Readers Writing: The Curriculum of the Writing Schools of Eighteenth-Century Boston," *Visible Language* 21 (spring 1987): 167–213.

14. "Provincial legislation also displayed a flagging commitment to the grammar school since it ceased to increase the penalty for noncompliance after 1718. As the salaries of grammar schoolmasters rose in the eighteenth century, it became cheaper for towns to pay the fine for noncompliance (if indeed the courts would compel them to do so) than to hire the masters." Teaford cites the evidence on Middlesex county presentments and the general court's failure to raise fines for noncompliance ("The Transformation of Massachusetts Education," 295–96). In addition to wars and dislocations, Robert Middlekauf stresses an increased resistance to tax

new movement developed during the 1790s to reformulate modalities for more advanced education: the widespread founding of academies (male and, in the new spirit of the time, female).

The new arrangements for town-supported schooling, involving winter schools taught by men and summer schools taught by women, are familiar from many nineteenth-century memoirs. An oft-cited example is Warren Burton's memoir, *The District School as It Was*, portraying the many summer and winter sessions the author attended, and the many different teachers he encountered, by turns loving or ferocious. However, James G. Carter's description of school arrangements, written in 1826, is more systematic, and Carter knew as much about these schools as anyone. He was a leader of early school reform efforts in the 1830s, and, when it came time, in 1837, to appoint the first secretary of the Massachusetts Board of Education, many were surprised that Horace Mann, and not Carter, had been selected; Carter instead became a member of the board. Carter's description of schools in the New England countryside in 1824 is useful to us for its explanation of the distinction between summer and winter sessions.

> Appropriations are expended a part in the summer months for the advantage of the younger children, and a part in the winter months for the accommodation of those who are more advanced in age and whose labor cannot be spared by their poor and industrious parents. The summer schools are taught by females; and children of both sexes, of from four to ten years of age attend, females often much older. In these schools from twenty to forty, and sometimes twice that number of children, are taught reading, spelling, and English grammar by a single instructress. In the more improved of this class of schools writing, arithmetic and geography are added to their usual studies. In the leisure time between lessons, the female part of the school are devoted to the various branches of needlework. . . . The whole expense of a school of this kind, taught by a female, exclusive of the house, which in the country costs but a trifle, does not

---

burdens after 1783, which would have centered attention on the expensive Latin teacher (*Ancients and Axioms*, 137). The new Massachusetts school law of 1789 reduced the scope of the legal compulsions by declaring that towns of two hundred families must support a Latin master. Yet it was changes other than those in the wording of the law that counted most; at the dawn of the nineteenth century, only thirty of over one hundred larger towns seem to have complied with the legal requirement to maintain a Latin master. See Middlekauf, *Ancients and Axioms*, on the preservation of the old tradition through 1783 (29–30); on its rapid decline thereafter (129–30); and on the academies (136); and, on the law of 1824, see George H. Martin, *The Evolution of the Massachusetts Public School System: A Historical Sketch* (New York, 1894; reprint, 1915), 116.

exceed from two to three dollars per week. . . . In the winter months an instructor is employed, and arithmetic, geography and history are added to the studies of the summer schools. These schools bring together for instruction those children and youth, whose labor is too valuable to be dispensed with, in the season which gives the agriculturalist most employment. The total expense of a school of this kind amounts to from six to ten dollars per week; and it contains from thirty to eighty, or a hundred scholars.[15]

Thus there existed an association between the gender of the teacher, the season of the year, the age and sex of the pupils, and the level of the curriculum. Summer sessions were taught by women for the younger children and the girls; winter sessions included the older boys who typically could not be spared in the summer, "which gives the agriculturalist most employment." The summer schools concentrated on reading, while the winter schools also offered more advanced subjects. Summer school cost about two-thirds less than winter school.

THE CHANGING EDUCATION OF NEW ENGLAND GIRLS, CA. 1730–1820

The early history of New England schools provided the context out of which a two-tier system of instruction developed, in which women taught the lower tier. The system had evolved greatly in the century after 1730; however, the two-tier character of the arrangement, and its relevance to the gender of the teacher in each tier, persisted.

That women teachers were used especially for the young in the summer session might well have made it possible to generally hire women who were somewhat younger than the men teaching the winter sessions. The later stages of this pattern are probably reflected in table 1.1, in which the youngest teachers in New England and New York were most likely to be women. By contrast, a male teacher in the winter session who had to control the older boys would probably have found it advantageous to be somewhat older

---

15. Warren Burton, *The District School As It Was by One Who Went to It*, rev. ed. (Boston, 1850). Carter's description appeared in a series of newspaper articles (which were soon published) on the condition of New England schools. On Carter, see the article in Allen Johnson et al., eds., *Dictionary of American Biography* (New York, 1929), 3:538; and Lawrence A. Cremin, *American Education: The National Experience, 1783–1876* (New York, 1980), 135–36, 154–55. James G. Carter, *Letters on the Free Schools of New England* (Boston, 1824; reprint, New York, 1969), 31–32 (quotation).

TABLE 1.1 Percentage of Women among Teachers in the
         United States, 1860

Regions[a]	Urban Areas[b] % Female (N =)	Rural Areas % Female (N =)
New England	81 (198)	84 (409)
New York	78 (193)	79 (472)
New Jersey, Pennsylvania	79 (62)	59 (370)
The South	65 (71)	36 (723)
Michigan, Wisconsin, Minnesota	70 (27)	86 (236)
Other Midwest	67 (73)	58 (757)
Total	76 (625)	61 (2,997)

Source: A national sample of teachers selected from the 1860 U.S. census manuscript schedules. See appendix 1 on sources.
    [a] The South includes 14 states: DE, FL, GA, MD, NC, SC, VA, AL, KY, MS, TN, AR, LA,
TX (and DC). Other Midwest includes 7 states: IL, IN, OH, IA, KS, MO, NE. The total includes
31 teachers in the Far West not included above.
    [b] Urban = incorporated places of 4,000 residents or more. See appendix 1 on sources.

(and perhaps also his age meant that he had more formal schooling so that
he could in fact teach the more advanced content of the winter session).[16]

   Later, especially between 1830 and 1860, the predominance of women
in the teaching force would become much greater—as women took over
the winter schools, the upper tier of instruction. Given the long involvement
that New England women had in teaching the lower tier of schools prior to
that time, indeed throughout the preceding two centuries of New England's
history, one might, in fact ask why it took so long for women to be recruited
as teachers for the upper tier of schools. One reason, of course, is that for
a long time the upper tier was tied to the knowledge of Latin, at least in
order to meet legal requirements—and Latin was rarely taught to women
in the schools, and never at the colleges.

   Still, during the late eighteenth century some towns' outlying districts
established schools to teach English writing under a master who did not
know Latin, and other towns simply replaced a Latin master with one or
more less expensive men who did not know Latin but could handle the
English writing curriculum. Why didn't women get most of these upper-
tier teaching jobs? Probably part of the answer turns on the education girls
were receiving in New England. Paralleling the changing function of the

---

   16. The age structure also reflects, of course, the impact of marriage, after which women
were more likely to stop working than men. Also, by 1860, the age structure even in the rural
areas may reflect the beginnings of high schools (or the prevalence of academy teaching) or
supervisory roles which were more typically given to men.

upper-tier school was the changing prevalence of girls' enrollment in the upper tier of schools, and their eventual suitability, through this preparation, to teach the curriculum of those schools. An important part of the answer is probably bound up with the gradual shift, over a long period of time, both in the function of the schools and the schooling that New England women received in the late eighteenth century.

We know that girls were generally excluded from the upper tier of the town schools throughout the early history of that institution. The first step for girls into most town-supported schools may well have been through the woman's (later, summer) school. With that first step accomplished, the magnitude of the second step—girls moving into the upper tier of the town's schools—may have seemed less great to contemporaries. Still, there is something of a puzzle buried within this description. The dame school of the seventeenth century apparently catered to very young children only, whereas in the summer school of the early nineteenth century, "children of both sexes, of from four to ten years of age attend, females often much older," as Carter put it. When did the older girls begin attending these schools? Typically, they began to do so as soon as the woman's school moved out of the dame's own house and into a separate town building: it must have been easier to accept a wide range of ages when the schooldame was only teaching and not simultaneously caring for other household responsibilities.

If, in outlying hamlets, only the woman's school existed, that fact may have encouraged longer utilization of the institution by boys than would have been the case if a Latin grammar school had been available. Further, if the woman's school was already used by both sexes, once its male pupils extended their stay, its female pupils may have done the same. In these ways, the increasing prevalence of the summer school may have entailed longer school attendance by girls than had been the case in the seventeenth-century institutions that concentrated on basic reading literacy. This development, to repeat, would have been familiar, although probably not the norm, in 1750.[17] On the other hand, we can assume that relatively little writing instruction occurred at these schools. Occasionally, however, the

---

17. Sklar, "The Schooling of Girls," suggests that the increasing funding of summer schools might serve as a measure of increasing prevalence of girls in the town schools, and of changing town commitments to girls' education. However, we suspect that, unfortunately, the budget devoted to each cannot be a good measure either of town commitment to female schooling or even of female prevalence in the schools.

enterprising schooldame may have tackled rudimentary writing. Also, it is plausible that if girls were being instructed for longer and longer periods in reading, that sturdier foundation in reading may have encouraged more extensive informal instruction in writing at home, either during their school years or later in life. For town-supported schooling in writing, girls generally needed to await admittance to the upper tier of the town schools. Certain institutional changes that we described earlier would have encouraged this entry of girls into the upper tier of schools. It seems reasonable to assume that where Latin was actively taught, the entry of girls seemed especially pointless since Latin was far from the future callings of the girls. A possible corollary is that where the town schoolmaster was a Latinist, whose special claim to high salary was his mastery over the classical languages, the use of his time for the girls seemed inappropriate. If so, as Latin usage diminished in the schools, and as Latin masters themselves became less common, and as more humble writing teachers became more prevalent, the chances of girls' entry into the upper tier of schools rose. Once again, the boundaries may have been more fluid in the outlying areas, especially when reading and writing schools, as well as woman's schools, prevailed there. Also, to the extent that the attendance of girls of ten years old or more (not merely toddlers or four-year-olds) was becoming more common in the lower tier of schooling, the attendance of girls in the upper tier would have appeared a more obvious next step. The entry of older girls into the woman's (summer) school was probably accomplished with little fanfare or struggle, given the prior dame school arrangements.

The entry of girls into the upper tier of schools was a similar matter, although this step is reflected in some late eighteenth-century town records discussing girls in town schools. Small noted that "until well toward the close of the eighteenth century" exceedingly few mentions of girls' admission can be found.[18] Then the topic becomes more common; most of his examples are from the 1780s and after, although a few date from the 1760s and 1770s (these early cases typically involved special arrangements for girls, not admission to the same schooling as boys). Joel Perlmann, Sylvana Siddali, and Keith Whitescarver tried to supplement Small's narratives by choosing a sample of towns whose records are available today for the period 1760–1810, surveying these records for mentions of, or debates about, girls in the upper tier of schools over many decades of the eighteenth century. A great many school issues were discussed in these records; yet they contain

18. Small, *Early New England Schools*, 278.

no mention of girls' entry into town schools. This silence very strongly suggests that in most towns this change did not spark a struggle.

While girls generally did not attend the upper tier of schools in the seventeenth and early eighteenth centuries, it does not follow that their absence required formal town action. Rather, girls may simply have stayed away: they were not sent by their families. There were a few exceptions to such behavior, but most families who wanted to send a girl could be dissuaded by ridicule or argument, and perhaps a few exceptional girls did attend the town schools in the early years. In any case, loud challenges that made their way into town records were exceedingly rare. Later, as institutional structures and attitudes changed, girls began to attend the upper tier of schools—often at first through the exceptional arrangements so often described (attendance after the regular hours for boys, and so on). Eventually, however, girls did come to attend the regular sessions of the upper-tier schools—not all at once, but rather in growing numbers as the years passed. This shift often passed without challenge, if enrollment were not increasing too quickly and if the perceptions of townspeople were changing with the attendance (because attitudes were changing and because the structure of schooling had been evolving in the numerous ways described earlier). These changes did not overturn formal regulations but altered custom—custom that must have seemed increasingly antiquated.

In any case, since the sources in most towns are silent on the issue, we cannot precisely date the admission of girls to the upper tier of schools. Our suspicion, however, is that the process might have begun in the less prestigious reading and writing schools (perhaps typically in smaller towns or hamlets) during the last half of the eighteenth century, and no doubt accelerating, so that most change came in 1770 or later.

Because the town records are so mute on this aspect of institutional change, historians have also sought some evidence from another quarter, the changes in female literacy. The ability to write, rather than only to read, is key, since writing was more fully the province of the upper-tier school; and, fortunately, our evidence of colonial literacy, evidence from the precensus era, in fact pertains to writing rather than to reading, since that evidence comes from examining who could sign as opposed to merely make their mark on various documents. Recent work by William Gilmore, Gloria Main, Perlmann and Dennis Shirley, and others suggests the following chronology for new female literacy levels. In the first decades of the eighteenth century, 30 to 40 percent of all women could write at least at a rudimentary level; in the 1760s it is likely that 60 percent of all women could write at this level; and by the 1790s the percentage of women with the ability to write, at least minimally, had increased to 80 percent or more.

A tight link between signature data that cover a primitive measure of writing ability (by signers of widely varying ages) on the one hand, and the institutional evolution we sketched earlier on the other hand, should not be expected. Some girls must have learned to write well enough to sign rather than mark a document, even in the lower tier of town schools. Others learned to write at home (as children or as adults). Still others learned at private schools. Nevertheless, as girls' attendance at the upper tier of schools grew, the ability to write would have become still more prevalent. And there is a rough consistency between these narratives, so that by the end of the eighteenth century girls must have formed a far higher fraction of those who had mastered the curriculum of the upper-tier schools than was the case at the beginning of the century.

After about 1730, as the Latin mission of the upper tier of schools became less salient, the argument for excluding girls from these schools weakened; and when the teacher was himself unable to instruct in Latin, the rationale for excluding girls because the schools taught Latin disappeared altogether. Nevertheless, there remained the rationale that English writing was not essential for women, and that view apparently continued to keep girls out of the town schools. Just when and why this argument lost its force is something historians have yet to understand fully. We suggest that it had a long and slowly evolving history; but that evolution may also have been accelerated by the American Revolution. Women may have been thrust into roles that encouraged self-reliance and assertiveness then, and in turn training for such roles may have seemed more appropriate to the future. Moreover, the particular nature of the Revolution had ideological implications for women's education: a republic required a virtuous citizenry to survive, and a virtuous citizenry was in turn dependent on the morals and intelligence of mothers. While the core of this argument was old—that the virtue of mankind rested on the nature of mothers—the argument took on a new urgency because republican institutions were regarded as especially fragile and especially dependent on the virtue of subjects, rather than on despotic coercion.[19]

19. For a fuller discussion of the historiography of New England female literacy, as well as the relation between historians' claims concerning changing views of women and changing female schooling, see Joel Perlmann, Sylvana Siddali, and Keith Whitescarver, "Literacy Schooling and Teaching among New England Women, 1730–1820," *History of Education Quarterly* 37, no. 2 (summer 1997): 117–39.

To 1860: Women Prevail in the Winter Sessions

In sum, by the earliest years of the nineteenth century, the winter schools had shifted away from whatever Latin had been part of the curriculum, and girls were attending those schools in New England in increasing numbers. All this made it possible that women would become more prominent in the teaching of those winter schools, but of course these developments did not necessitate such an outcome. Indeed, even in training men may have had an edge for some time. Men alone had some chance of university training, and they were probably more likely to have had rigorous academy training before about 1820. But other factors in addition to the supply of educated women may also have influenced the timing of the shift to female teachers in the winter sessions of New England schools between 1830 and 1860. Those who hired teachers in the towns may have been impressed by the argument about discipline, the view that women could not control the older boys; or their awareness of women's mastery of the English writing curriculum may simply have lagged behind the rise in that mastery.[20] Also, as we discuss later, women may have been freed from household production in the early industrial revolution, making it easier for more of them to seek employment and for others to seek longer employment than a summer term. Given the state of our evidence on their instruction, we cannot fully determine whether adequate numbers of New England women were academically prepared to take over winter session teaching a generation before they did; certainly the revision of their literacy levels makes it understandable why they were able to run the summer sessions for over a half century before they took over the winter sessions.

Whatever the reasons, women were typically hired for the summer sessions and men for the winter sessions until between 1830 and 1860. Nevertheless, some women were already teaching in the winter sessions in 1830, well before Horace Mann or other reformers of the common school era began to call for that change. The first systematic data that show the number of teachers by gender and session appeared in Mann's report of 1842, which showed that 33 percent of winter and 95 percent of summer school teachers were women, for a total of 62 percent of all district teachers (table 1.2). By comparing this evidence to less detailed figures from 1829 we can press back

---

20. Also, at the time when relatively fewer women had the necessary skills than was later the case, such women may have come disproportionately from economically better-off homes and have been uninterested in teaching at the wage offered.

TABLE 1.2 Feminization of Teaching, 1829–60, Massachusetts
and New York

	Percentage of Women among Teachers					
	Massachusetts (large towns excluded until 1850)			New York State (excluding New York City)		
Year	All	Winter Session	Summer Session	All	Winter Session	Summer Session
1829	53					
1834	54					
1841	62	30	97			
1842	62	33	95	56	25	85
1844						
1850	71[a]			69[b]		
1860	78[a]					

Source: Annual state school reports. Only public schools included. Figures would differ
slightly if private schools were included.
[a] Includes places > 10,000 pop.
[b] 67 when all cities are excluded.

to that year. In 1829, 53 percent of all rural district teachers were women.
Even if the entire increase in the proportion of woman teachers between
1829 and 1841 had occurred in the winter sessions, the comparison suggests
that in the earlier year 14 percent of winter session teachers must have
been women. And if we assume that only half of the increase in the fraction of women teachers in that period occurred in the winter sessions, then
in the earlier year 23 percent of winter session teachers would have been
women.[21]

21. Let f_t, f_w, f_s = proportion female among teachers in total, winter session, and summer
session, respectively. Let w, s = proportion of all teachers working in winter and summer
sessions, respectively. Let 1, 2 = 1829 and 1841/2, respectively.

1. Calculate the average of the proportions of female teachers by sessions for the years
1841 and 1842 from table 1.2: $f_{t2} = .62$, $f_{w2} = .315$, $f_{s2} = .96$.

2. Calculate the proportion of all teachers working in each session in 1841/2: $f_{t2} = f_{w2} \times w_2 + f_{s2} \times s_2$. And $s_2 = 1 - w_2$. Solving, $w_2 = .527$ and $s_2 = .473$.

3. Assume $w_1 = w_2$ and $s_1 = s_2$. Then $f_{t2} - f_{t1} = w_2(f_{w2} - f_{w1}) + s_2(f_{s2} - f_{s1})$.

4. If all of the rise $f_{t2} - f_{t1}$ occurred in $f_{w2} - f_{w1}$, then $.62 - .53 = .09 = .527(.315 - f_{w1}) + 0$. Solving, $f_{w1} = .14$.

5. If half the rise in $f_{t2} - f_{t1}$ between 1829 and 1841/2 occurred in $f_{w2} - f_{w1}$ and half in $f_{s2} - f_{s1}$, then $.5 \times .09 = .045 = .527(.315 - f_{w1})$ and $.045 = .473(.96 - f_{s1})$. Solving, $f_{w1} = .23$, $f_{s1} = .86$.

Maris A. Vinovskis, "Trends in Massachusetts Education, 1826–1860," History of Education
Quarterly 12 (winter 1972): 501–29, compared the Massachusetts towns that reported in 1829
and those that did not. Vinovskis believed the underreporting was not a crucial bias, at least
for the study of enrollment rates (p. 505). The fit with the figures of 1834 suggests the same
may be true for studying the gender of the teacher.

THE IDEOLOGY OF DOMESTICITY AND
EARLY INDUSTRIALIZATION

Consequently, it would appear that the first steps toward hiring women for the winter season were being taken before the reforms of the common school era. With the gender differential in wages, and the availability of many women who had mastered the advanced English curriculum, such an evolution is hardly surprising. This perspective encourages us to see the New England arrangements described by Carter in the mid-1820s as part of an evolving institutional reality rather than as an established situation. The women taught virtually all the summer schools before Horace Mann reached office; that teaching alone would have made them more of a presence in teaching than their sisters were in the South. But in New England women had also begun to teach in the winter sessions in notable proportions before Mann took office. This increasing role for women in the winter sessions presumably would have continued even without the reformers' efforts; or, to put the matter in a less ahistorical way, the forces that led to increasing utilization of female teachers before 1837 very likely continued to operate after 1837. In the 1830s, 1840s, and 1850s, Mann's reports and travels as well as the work of reformers such as Catherine Beecher and Henry Barnard added new pressure to this trend.

Women, these reformers claimed, were more nurturing, and therefore their services should be used more widely. Young, unmarried women who had completed their own schooling could fulfill their natures best while occupied as teachers. Women could handle the disciplining of the older boys, and indeed might do so better than men could, because they offered not the discipline of brute force but discipline based on their gentler natures. And then, too, often women could be hired at half to one-third the wages of men. Women should teach only until marriage, when new responsibilities required their attention and their husbands would provide for their support.[22] In gross, the basic ideas were continuous with those of the late

---

22. See, e.g., Horace Mann's *First–Twelfth Annual Reports of the Secretary of the Board of Education* (Massachusetts, 1837–48). Especially interesting are the discussions in these *Annual Reports:* first (supplement "On the Subject of School Houses"), 28–33; fourth, 24–28 and 45–48; sixth, 27–35; eighth, 60–62; eleventh, 24–31; and twelfth, 21–22. For examples of formulations by others, see Catherine Beecher, "Remedy for the Wrongs to Women: Address" in Nancy Hoffman, ed., *Woman's True Profession: Voices from the History of Teaching* (New York, 1981), 36–56; Tyack and Hansot, *Learning Together,* chap. 2; Deborah Fitts, "Una and the Lion: The Feminization of District School-Teaching and Its Effects on the Roles of Students and Teachers in Nineteenth-Century Massachusetts," in B. Finkelstein, ed., *Regulated Children/Liberated Children: Education in Psychohistorical Perspective* (New York, 1979),

eighteenth century and early nineteenth century, namely that a republic needed educated women to bring up educated citizens. Both arguments, the earlier and the later, were grounded in the belief that women would be raising young children. The early argument stressed that women had better be discerning themselves; the later argument stressed that, *since* women were the natural child raisers, they should be teachers where possible.

The social role of these intellectual formulations, this "ideology of domesticity," should be reconsidered in the light of the institutional evolution just described. By 1840, the role of women teachers had been quietly evolving in the New England countryside for well over 150 years. Just what, then, is the role of the ideology of domesticity in the process after 1840? The arguments of Beecher and the other reform writers helped make intellectual sense of, and may have accelerated, a trend of hiring women for the winter sessions that was already underway. Moreover, the ideology of domesticity gave special force to certain behaviors rather than others. The requirement that the teacher be unmarried may be a case in point. The dame school mistress was often a married woman; so too, apparently, were many of the women who taught in the outlying district schools of the towns in the late seventeenth and early eighteenth centuries. Yet by the time James Carter and Warren Burton wrote about the district school, the teacher was apparently much more likely to be an unmarried woman, and usually young. Possibly, as the job was taken out of the home and demanded fairly long-term commitments, it became less attractive for married women. We have no systematic evidence on this point or on how many women teachers were unmarried in 1840. The reform writers' arguments, however, may have provided the articulation to solidify the tendency to hire the unmarried woman.

Note too that there were two parts to the argument: that female teachers were better suited by character and that female teachers were cheaper and capable of doing as good a job (conveying the material, keeping order, etc.). The reformers' influence might well have been larger in drawing attention to the option of a cheaper solution rather than in stressing the character of women in child raising. First, the school boards of New England had long utilized women overwhelmingly for the summer sessions, for teaching the younger pupils. The more novel element in the 1840s involved women working with the *older* children, those for whom analogies to maternal nur-

---

140–57. For examples of county superintendents' comments, see, e.g., the annual school reports of Pennsylvania after 1852.

turing were probably less obvious; surely this domestic ideology did not imply that fathers were irrelevant to raising young adolescents, for example.

On the other hand, when reformers urged that with a little ingenuity far more schools could be organized in a graded fashion, and that women could handle more of the curriculum than might be realized in a local area, this argument may have been new and therefore relevant.

The long evolution of New England teaching also leads us to reconsider the importance of social and economic transformations, transformations that help us understand why the ideology of domesticity was important at this historical juncture. Historians have claimed that that ideology crystallized in the period between 1780 and 1830, when the economy transformed the nature of men's work outside the home and of women's work in the home (especially toward the end of the period). Concomitant transformations in production, such as the replacement of homespun cloth by cloth produced for mass purchase, meant that unmarried young women were freed to leave the home much more often than they had been earlier—to teach in winter sessions or labor in factories.[23]

No doubt this decline of "homespun" did operate to free women's time and could have facilitated the entry of women into the winter teaching force. And, indeed, social historians have documented how some women, at least in the early stages of industrialization, alternated between factory work and teaching.[24] Moreover, the period of early industrialization corresponds rather well with the period—roughly 1820–60—in which the teaching force of the winter session in New England and New York evolved from predominantly male to predominantly female.

However, women had worked for pay outside the house (and not infrequently boarding in another village than their own) as summer session teachers for at least several decades before 1820. Consequently, had towns wanted to hire women for the (equally short) winter sessions back in 1800

23. Nancy Cott, *The Bonds of Womanhood: "Woman's Sphere" in New England, 1780–1835* (New Haven, Conn., 1977); Christopher Clark, *The Roots of Rural Capitalism: Western Massachusetts, 1780–1860* (Ithaca, N.Y., 1990); Thomas Dublin, *Women at Work: The Transformation of Work and Community in Lowell, Massachusetts, 1826–60* (New York, 1979); Myra Strober and David Tyack, "Why Do Women Teach and Men Manage? A Report on Research on Schools," *Signs: Journal of Women in Culture and Society* 5, no. 3 (spring 1980): 494–503.

24. Thomas Dublin, *Women at Work*; Nancy Cott, *Bonds of Womanhood*; Richard M. Bernard and Maris A. Vinovskis, "The Female Schoolteacher in Antebellum Massachusetts," *Journal of Social History* 10 (1977): 332–45.

or 1810, it seems unlikely that the needs of the household economy would have been a barrier.[25] Perhaps for some reason families did find it much harder to spare young women from household production in winter; even so, families could probably have hired domestics to replace the labor of the young women leaving the household to teach. True: the wages offered to women teachers may not have been much higher than those of female domestics. However, the wages offered to female teachers were only half to a third the wages of male teachers. Towns should have been able to offer female teachers a wage that, while well below male teachers' wages, was still sufficiently high for their families to easily replace them with domestic help.

The most likely reasons that this result did not often occur have to do not with the supply of young women workers but with the nature of the demand for teachers. The nature of winter session teaching differed from summer session teaching; the children were older, the curriculum more advanced. The townspeople who hired teachers early in the century judged few women able to handle the discipline challenge and to have adequate mastery of the cognitive tasks. And, indeed, whatever biases contemporaries may have brought to these judgments, it is also quite possible that the average level of women's education was in fact rising in this period; in 1800, relatively few women in fact had received enough schooling to teach in the winter session, although they did have enough knowledge of reading, and even rudimentary writing, to handle the summer sessions. Not merely a supply of women workers, then, but a supply of adequately educated women workers was needed, and that may have been the stumbling block to feminizing the New England winter sessions in 1800 or 1810; alternatively, townspeople may have been slow to respond to an already adequate supply of educated women.

Finally, there may have been a norm concerning the appropriate wage for a woman teacher that restricted contemporaries from raising the wage of women relative to men; thus it may not have been worthwhile for families to send girls to teach in the winter and replace them with female domestics. Some evidence, consistent with this suggestion, suggests that when

25. We do not have systematic evidence on the gender breakdown of the summer sessions at the turn of the century. But memoirs and anecdotal evidence are entirely consistent on this point, and the systematic evidence from Massachusetts and New York, from the late 1820s and 1830s, discussed earlier in this chapter, shows over four-fifths of summer school teachers were women by then in both states.

women did begin to teach in the winter sessions, they were not paid much more, relative to men, than was the case in the summer sessions. In New York state, in the mid-1840s, women's wages averaged $5.55 in the summer session and $6.98 in the winter session, while men received $13.61 and $14.06 respectively, producing female-to-male wage ratios of 0.425 for the summer and 0.496 for the winter session; obviously most of the gender gap was not erased when women entered winter session teaching.[26]

The socioeconomic changes around 1820, then, like the related ideological transformations, probably did facilitate the movement of women into the new role of teaching both winter and summer. But the constantly evolving female role in New England teaching, and the transformations in female education by 1820, had very likely generated considerable development in this direction on their own.

26. Averages across forty-six counties for the winter sessions of 1844 and the summer sessions of 1845; counties with large cities excluded. The data are found in the *New York State School Reports* for the relevant years. The level of wages for women may have improved relative to wages in other occupations during the feminization of the winter session. The wages of men may have improved too, but there were fewer and fewer of them, and the men were increasingly restricted to special roles, so that comparison is not very meaningful. See Bernard and Vinovskis, "Female School Teacher," graphs 4 and 5.

T W O   *South versus North*

INSTITUTIONS

Introduction

The southern educational system reflected the nature of southern society, with an elite committed to supporting secondary and collegiate institutions, but leaving the diffusion of popular primary schooling less well supported than in the North. Nevertheless, as economic historian Albert Fishlow cautioned long ago, "Lack of . . . sympathy with the educational philosophy should not obscure an ongoing process of instruction in the Southern states."[1] Southern primary schooling in some form seems to have reached high proportions of white children, and, by the 1840s, adult literacy was at 80 percent of the level reached in the North.[2] The involvement of women in schoolteaching was much less prevalent in the South than in the North not because arrangements for schooling in the South were scant but because arrangements differed from those in the North. Teachers were not as common in the South as in the North, but southern teachers were not rarities. In 1860, some 2.2 million children (ages five to nineteen) lived in New England and New York, whereas some 2.7 million white children lived in the South; yet despite the greater population to teach, there were fewer teachers in the South than in New England and

1. Albert Fishlow, "The American Common School Revival: Fact or Fancy?" in Henry Rosovsky, ed., *Industrialization in Two Systems: Essays in Honor of Alexander Gerschenkron* (New York, 1966), 47.

2. Fishlow, "American Common School Revival"; Lee Soltow and Edward Stevens, *The Rise of Literacy and the Common School in the United States: A Socioeconomic Analysis to 1870* (Chicago, 1981), 117.

New York. Thus our 1860 sample of teachers includes 794 in the South but 1,272 in New England and New York; the South supported only about half (0.51) as many teachers per 100 children as New England and New York did. Nevertheless, in the same year the rest of the settled northern states (Pennsylvania, New Jersey, and the midwestern states), with nearly 4.5 million children, also supported far fewer teachers per 100 children than New England and New York—0.59 as many—in fact only slightly more than the South provided. The unique dearth of southern female teachers cannot be traced to a dearth of southern teachers generally.

The most common form of schooling in the South, especially before the early reforms of the 1840s, were the "old field schools" (schools kept on land that had been depleted of its agricultural productivity). These institutions, and not the charity schools or endowed free schools or tutorial arrangements (which historians have tended to describe in greater detail), demand our attention if we are to understand the education of most antebellum white Southerners. A schoolmaster would contract with local families to operate a school in their vicinity. Each family paid a tuition to the teacher. State support for the education of the poor often took the form of paying a voucher of sorts to the schoolmaster for seats in an old field school.[3]

Absence of a Two-Tier System

New England's two-tier pattern of schooling, with its association of gender of the teacher, season of the year, and age and sex of the pupil, did not develop in the South. It is difficult to prove the *absence* of a pattern, except from the dubious evidence of the silence of contemporaries; still, it cannot be ignored that many descriptions of antebellum southern schools exist, and they fail to describe the two-tier pattern whose New England history we narrated in the preceding chapter. Furthermore, there is, after all, direct evidence of a sort in the 1860 figures with which we began our study (table 1.1): the low proportion of female teachers in the South on the eve of the Civil War must be understood to mean that at least one crucial constituent element of the two-tier pattern of schoolteaching, namely the association of the summer school with the female teacher, simply could not have been widespread in the South.

Other statistical evidence is also highly suggestive of the fact that the two-tier system so common in New England was uncommon or absent in

3. See, for example, Carl F. Kaestle, *Pillars of the Republic: Common Schools and American Society, 1780–1860* (New York, 1983), 193–94.

TABLE 2.1 School Attendance at Different Ages by Region, 1850 (native-born white children only)

A. Percent in Each Age Range at School

| | Northeast | | | | | |
Age	New England + New York (a)	Entire Northeast (b)	North-Central (c)	South (d)	Odds Ratio: Attendance Cols. a:d	Difference in Percent: Cols. a–d
4–7	67	58	39	18	13.4	49
8–11	89	85	70	50	8.09	39
12–14	85	81	69	51	5.44	34
15–19	51	46	44	30	2.42	21

B. Percent School Attendance at Specific Young Ages

| | Northeast | | | |
Age	New England + New York	Entire Northeast	North-Central	South
3	8	6	2	1
4	36	28	13	3
5	67	55	33	12
6	80	71	48	21
7	87	82	63	37
8	88	83	66	45
9	88	85	71	30
10	90	84	71	50
11	91	87	75	54

the South. Not only were fewer southern teachers female; fewer southern schoolchildren were to be found at the tender ages that populated the New England summer schools. In 1850 and 1860, we can trace the proportion of children of each age found in school. We already know that the proportion was lower in the South; this was the case at every age. We can now add that in the South a child's schooling typically started at an older age than in the North, and, consequently, the proportion of very young children among all young people in school was especially small (table 2.1). Moreover, there is evidence that, in the middle third of the nineteenth century, school reformers fought against the New England habit of sending children as young as three or four years old into the schools; the evidence from the 1850 and 1860 censuses, then, is evidence that comes well into the period in which the presence of the very youngest had already declined in New England.[4] Nevertheless, in 1850 the proportion of schoolchildren who were

    4. Maris Vinovskis, "Trends in Massachusetts Education, 1826–1860," *History of Education Quarterly* 12 (winter 1972): 501–29.

TABLE 2.2 Teachers' Ages and Gender, across Regions, in Places of Less Than 4,000 Inhabitants (1860 national teacher sample)

A. Proportions Male and Female for Specific Age Groups

Age	Northeast % Each Sex This Age Range M	F	N	North-Central % Each Sex This Age Range M	F	N	South % Each Sex This Age Range M	F	N
<20	10	90	326	12	88	281	30	70	84
20–24	23	77	522	33	67	384	62	38	233
25–29	31	69	191	50	50	161	73	27	157
30–39	40	60	123	62	38	95	73	27	142
40+	63	37	81	85	15	61	73	27	96
All	25	75	1,243	36	64	982	64	36	712

B. Age Distribution of All Teachers, and of Male and Female Teachers, within Each Region

Ages	Northeast All	M	F	North-Central All	M	F	South All	M	F
<20	26	11	31	29	9	39	12	5	23
20–24	42	38	43	39	36	41	33	32	35
25–29	15	19	14	16	23	13	22	25	17
30–39	10	16	8	10	17	6	20	23	15
40–49	7	16	3	6	15	1	13	15	10
All teachers	100	100	100	100	100	100	100	100	100

Note: Adjusting southern to northeastern age distribution. If the age distribution of the southern teachers had been the same as the age distribution of the teachers in the Northeast—while the gender distribution of southern teachers within each age range remained as shown in the table—the proportion of female teachers in the South (in the last row of the table) would have been 7 percentage points higher than shown.

Adjusting southern to northeastern age-specific sex distribution. If the gender distribution of the southern teachers at each age had been the same as the gender distribution of the teachers in the Northeast in that age range (but the age distribution of southern teachers remained as shown in the table), the proportion of female teachers in the South in the last row of the table would have been 32 percentage points higher than shown.

in the four- to seven-year-old range was highest in New England and New York and lowest in the South, a stunning 67 percent versus 18 percent respectively.

We also have some consistent evidence in the ages of men and women teachers, North and South, in 1860 (table 2.2). Everywhere, the youngest teachers were the ones most likely to have been women, probably because these teachers were assigned to the very youngest scholars; even in the

South, for example, 70 percent of teachers under twenty years of age were women. However, in the South, teachers under age twenty comprised 12 percent of all teachers; in the Northeast, 26 percent; similarly, teachers aged twenty to twenty-four comprised 33 percent of all southern teachers and 42 percent of all teachers in the Northeast. It is likely, then, that one important reason there were fewer young teachers in the South is that there were fewer younger children in school in the South, and to some extent this factor explains why there were fewer female teachers as well. Nevertheless, as the note to table 2.2 indicates, the larger part of difference in the gender of the teacher is not explained by the distribution of ages, but by the age-specific sex distribution among them in each region; even if the teachers in the South had had the same age distribution as the teachers in the Northeast, the age-specific sex differences would have guaranteed that most of the regional gender difference in teaching would have remained. Our point here is not to fully resolve the puzzle of North-South difference in the gender of teachers but to argue that the prevailing age distribution of teachers, and the prevalence of young women in particular among the teachers of each region, is consistent with the argument that the two-tier system, which encouraged young female teachers, had not developed in the South.

Still, did no contemporaries discuss what we suspect was a major difference in educational arrangements, at least during much of the first half of the nineteenth century? At least one observer did in fact discuss these differences in print. In 1828, at almost the same moment that James Carter published his description of the New England two-tier system (discussed earlier), the governor of North Carolina included in his message to the legislature a "Plan of Public Schools" for the state drafted by one Charles R. Kinney. Kinney had grown up in New England and settled in North Carolina. Part of Kinney's comments concern the utility of hiring women teachers:

> You will observe that I have spoken of a female teacher. This is a custom common in the New England States, where I have witnessed its great utility. I myself received the first rudiments of education from a country girl, and during the summer never went to any but a female teacher. They never teach but in the summer, and are employed for the young misses, and those boys that are too small to be serviceable on the farms.[5]

5. Charles R. Kinney, "Plan of Public Schools," in Charles L. Coon, ed., *The Beginnings of Public Education in North Carolina: A Documentary History, 1790–1840* (Raleigh, 1908), 1:440–44, esp. 442–43; see also Coon, ed., *Public Education*, 1:436–39, for related material.

The particular context of Kinney's remarks, with the governor's message, lends weight to his observation, because it suggests review by the state authorities before the statement was circulated; were Kinney mistaken in his obvious assumption that the association of season, gender of the teacher, and age and sex of the pupils was uncommon in the South, the error would probably have been corrected before the governor circulated Kinney's plan.

We have not been able to find other direct comments on the absence of the two-tier system and its implications for women teachers. It appears to have been reasonably common knowledge that fewer women taught in the antebellum South than North. However, we have found little reflection on how this difference came about. Rather, contemporary friends of education in the South tended simply to stress the reduced expense and the nurturing of young children that would accompany a greater reliance on women teachers.

Several factors could explain why more speculation on the regional sources of the difference in the gender patterns did not occur. First, the gender difference in teaching was not the most glaring difference between schooling in North and South; differences in finance, teacher preparation, length of term, and other such factors received more attention. Second, reformers were not speculative social historians; they were agitating for reform in education (including the hiring of more women)—rather than explaining *why* fewer women taught in the South. Third, the difference in women's educational roles may have seemed bound up with distinctly southern norms of womanhood; challenging these norms was not the way to win support for school reform in the South. We will return to this issue later. Fourth, after 1850 there was increasing sensitivity about copying northern norms and institutions; belaboring the North-South comparisons on any issue would not help the cause of southern school reform.

Whatever the reasons for the absence of more direct discussions of why women taught less in southern schools, Kinney's "Plan" and the numbers of female teachers, as well as the riskier argument *ex silencio*, leave us confident in concluding that the two-tier system was not commonplace in the South. And the question, then, is why the system had not developed there. Several aspects of the history of educational institutions in the South provide a tentative answer.

The Social Bases of Southern Institutional Developments

In the first place, the South apparently did not develop the dame schools of the seventeenth century, the institution that served as the basis for later increase of female employment in the New England teaching force. Histories of southern education typically include no mention of the dame school; the only author we have found who commented on the point directly (C. J. Heatwole, in a 1916 history of Virginia education) describes the occasional use of female governesses on colonial Virginia plantations and notes in passing, "This kind of school is probably the nearest approach in Virginia to the dame school of New England."[6]

Because of differences in land cultivation, from the beginning southern communities were dispersed over larger areas than the New England townships. The dame schools may have been a particular casualty of distance; they may have seemed inefficient to maintain when it was necessary to transport young children a long way.[7] The advent of slavery at the end of the seventeenth century accentuated the dispersed settlement pattern, since much of the laboring population was removed from consideration for schooling.

Thus, assuming we are right that the two-tier system so common in New England was not widespread in the South, the reason may have something to do with the still more distant history of the dame school, from which the two-tier system developed in New England; by contrast, in southern educational history, there appears to have been no such preparation for the two-tier system. Whatever the connection to the long evolution of the dame school, the dispersed settlement patterns of the South would also have discouraged two sessions of schooling, with somewhat different functions and clienteles; specialization requires a sufficient number of pupils per local area. So too, late in the nineteenth century, when a new generation of the "friends of education" agitated for graded schools, with women teaching all but the upper grades, dispersion may have slowed the reforms.

The absence of the two-tier system in the South may also have to do with its much longer agricultural seasons; it was harder there to find two "seasons," in one of which many children could be spared and teachers lured from agriculture. Another aspect of climate may have played a role too: the need to avoid exposing young children to the winter was obviously much weaker than in New England.

Finally, recall that the two-tier system required coordination of at least two and often more instructors in a local area, one a young woman and the other a man (also young, but typically older than the woman). As such,

6. Cornelius J. Heatwole, *A History of Education in Virginia* (New York, 1916), 56.

7. Edgar G. Knight, *Public Education in the South* (Boston, 1922); on dispersion, cf. Kaestle, *Pillars,* esp. chapter 8.

the system may well have developed more easily in a region where hiring and school organization were in the hands of a centralized authority rather than in the hands of independent entrepreneurs. At first sight it may seem bizarre to speak of the loosely organized and local district school boards of New England as centralized authorities, yet they were so by comparison to arrangements in the South, where the initiative of educational entrepreneurs—independent schoolmasters negotiating with local parents—was the pattern by which teachers were chosen.

In addition, quite apart from these suggestions as to why the two-tier system did not develop, other factors may have made it harder to hire women teachers for southern schools, regardless of the structure of those schools. For example, if southern women were less likely to have received the requisite schooling than southern men (compared to northern women versus northern men), it would have been harder to find women to teach in that region. So too, if southern women had been much more in demand in southern than in northern agriculture (because of the tasks required for southern crops), the competition for their work time would have been keener in the South.

In upcoming sections, we will consider the evidence to support these and other hypotheses—hypotheses that seek factors to explain why there would have been fewer female teachers in the antebellum South even if arrangements for the support and operation of schools would have been identical in the two regions, even if the school itself is treated as a black box. We undertake this analysis for the period 1850–60, the earliest for which we have decent data. Finally, in the last sections of this chapter, we will speculate about how these factors might have operated during the two centuries prior to our evidence, when antebellum educational institutions were taking their characteristic forms. In this manner, we will add more considerations to our effort to understand why the two-tier system did not develop. In sum, here we have presented some aspects of institutional evolution, but other relevant considerations, concerning the difficulty of hiring women, will supplement these historical speculations at the end of the chapter.

First, however, we consider another dimension of institutional growth.

INEVITABLE RESULTS OF RAPID GROWTH? FEMALE TEACHING IN THE CONTEXT OF THE SCHOOL REFORM ERA

If there is one generalization in the historical writing on schools in the middle third of the nineteenth century, it is that a "common school reform era" that occurred in New England, New York, and parts of the Midwest was much less successful in the South.[8] In many places a direct attention to the nurturing and financial advantages of female schoolteaching was a central concomitant of the school reform era. And there is no doubt that feminization of schoolteaching did enter a new phase in New England and New York in the decades between 1840 and 1860; nevertheless, it is just as clear that stark differences in the use of women teachers preceded that period. So a vague explanatory appeal to the reform era will tell us very little indeed. And we have tried at the end of chapter 1 to deal more carefully with the relation between reform ideology and the extension of female teaching to the winter sessions ca. 1840–60 in New England and New York.

On the other hand, in some states rapid increases in the size of the schoolgoing population accompanied the school reform movement. The connection between the school reform era and the rapid rise of school enrollments is far from straightforward; in many states (perhaps most) the impact of the reform agitation on increasing actual enrollment levels was not great. Still, in some places there was a connection. In any case, the deeper issue for us here is the connection between increases in enrollment (whether or not related to the common school reform movement) and the implications for female teaching. Rapid expansions of a public school enrollment were (and are) likely to put budgetary and personnel strains directly on the system and indirectly on those who bear the costs of the system, ultimately the taxpayers in education's public sector. Under such conditions, the temptation to broaden the pool of potential teachers would be great, especially if doing so meant bringing in applicants who might well be hired at a lower wage than the traditional applicants.

Can such a process explain why teaching became more feminized in the North but not in the South in this period? We think not. Not only can we point to the long evolution of institutions operating in the North and not in the South on which we have concentrated thus far, we can also now show that rapid growth could occur throughout a state without changing the gender mix of teachers much at all—in both North and South. Consider developments in Pennsylvania and North Carolina, two states in which the common school reform era brought dramatic changes in school arrangements (table 2.3).

In both states, new tax arrangements increased public funding and school administrators actively pressed for changes in the way schools were run.

8. For the most thoughtful treatment, see Kaestle, *Pillars*.

TABLE 2.3 Feminization of Teaching in Two States

A. Pennsylvania				
Measure of Schooling	1837	1840	1850	1852	1860
---	---	---	---	---	---
Pupils enrolled (thousands)	182			481	
Pupils/all children, 5–19 (%)		31	56		59[a]
Number of teachers	4,841			11,713	13,003
Women among teachers (%)	31			33	37

B. North Carolina			
Measure of Schooling	1840	1850	1858	1860
---	---	---	---	---
Pupils enrolled (thousands)			102	
Pupils/all children, 5–19 (%)	11	52		50
Number of teachers			2,199	
Women among teachers (%)			9	

Sources: Pupils/all 5–19 from census reports. Other rows from annual state school reports. Only public schools included. Figures would differ slightly if private schools were included.
[a] Philadelphia included here only.

In Pennsylvania, the number of children in the publicly supported schools rose dramatically between 1838 and 1852 (and not because of any shift from private to public schools, but rather because more children were attending school). The number of teachers also rose very quickly. Nevertheless, neither the changes in school arrangements nor the need for many new teachers forced the state to hire more women teachers. Between 1838 and 1852, the percentage of women among teachers hardly changed, climbing only from 31 percent to 33 percent, and it only rose to 37 percent in the eight years thereafter.

In North Carolina too, there was a dramatic rise in the percentage of pupils enrolled in the 1840s, when the funding arrangements changed. But neither those changes nor the presence of articulate, reform-minded Superintendent Calvin Wiley in the next decade meant that many women teachers would necessarily be hired. Women comprised a mere 9 percent of the state's teachers on the eve of the Civil War.[9] Thus the greater prevalence of women teachers in New England compared to the South predates common school reform, and in any case the impact of those reforms—whether

9. The 1840 census reports on pupils may well be especially flawed for the South, as argued in Fishlow, "American Common School Revival," 67. However, the rapid rise in North Carolina enrollments during the 1840s fits with the timing of changes in taxation arrangements and with school reports. Note also that the percentages of female teachers based on school reports in many states differ from those based on census reports—but trends in the two series are parallel and trends within each series seem consistent.

policy choices about the teaching force or rapid expansion of enrollment (in some states) that sharply raised the demand for teachers—did not necessarily bring many women to a state's teaching posts.

South versus North: The Broader Social Context

Thus far we have explored how the evolution of schools over decades and even centuries encouraged the prevalence of female teaching in New England more than in the South. In the next five sections of this chapter, we ask how the broader social context might have directly encouraged women to teach in New England, and the Northeast generally, and how, by contrast, the broader social context of the South might have inhibited female teaching. We have mentioned the broader context only insofar as it might have produced differing educational institutions across regions. Here we ask how the context might have directly affected the behavior of individuals even if the educational institutions themselves had not differed from North to South. Social arrangements, economic structure, and demographic characteristics of the two regions were radically different: are these differences enough in themselves to explain why the South hired so many fewer women for its teachers than the North did? We have reasonable data with which to answer this question for the mid-nineteenth century.

Wherever possible, we limit our analysis to rural areas (where the great majority of southern teachers lived in any case). The regional difference in the prevalence of female teachers in urban areas did not vary nearly as much as it did in rural areas, a point we have already noted in passing and to which we return in the last chapter. Consequently, the explanatory task before us concerns especially the rural areas.

We begin with the social class structure. First, most women teachers were recruited from the middling orders of the society. Was that "middle" smaller in the South than elsewhere? Second, recent histories often stress the distinctive nature of woman's place in southern culture; a patriarchal slaveholding society drew rigid defensive lines around white womanhood, and one result was less tolerance of female employment in the South than in the North. Was the lower participation of women in the teaching force simply a reflection of their lower labor force participation generally in the South, or perhaps in the middling orders of southern vs. northern society (since teachers came primarily from those middling orders)? Third, the age of marriage might have been lower in the South than in the North, reinforcing and being reinforced by a relatively lower southern female labor force participation rate. Fourth, higher fertility rates might have led to a greater demand for child care in the South.

Fifth, another reason for regional differences in the demand on women's time (in addition to child-care demand) might well have emerged from the distinctive nature of southern agriculture, since the southern crop mix was more conducive to women's work (as we will explain). Greater demand for women's time would have bid up the cost of hiring women, relative to hiring men—making it less likely that women would be hired in the South than in the North. And, sixth, there is a particular prerequisite for teachers, namely education; if a gender difference in schooling favored southern boys over southern girls more than it favored northern boys over northern girls, that factor too could account for the regional differences in the proportion of female teachers.

Wherever possible we assess these arguments here by comparing characteristics of three regions: the Northeast, the South, and the Midwest. Did the prevalence of female teachers across regions support the arguments just listed? For example, were fertility rates high in the South and low in the other two regions, consistent with a prediction that high fertility rates reduced the likelihood that women would be free to teach? In order to assess some other arguments, more refined comparisons—of subregions, or states—are required. Appendix 2 reports research that explored these issues across hundreds of counties, alluding to the results in the text.

REGIONAL DIFFERENCES IN THE SOCIAL CLASS STRUCTURE

Obviously the social structure of the South, with large plantations and slave labor, differed in crucial ways from the social structure of New England and the North generally; but it is harder to grasp just how this difference might have affected the likelihood that women would become teachers. The great plantation owners may have held more wealth and more political power than the northern elite, but it is well to recall that these plantation owners constituted only a tiny percentage of all southern white families. Moreover, neither elite, northern or southern, probably sent many of its daughters into teaching, and even if the northern and southern elites differed in the treatment of their daughters, the direct impact of such a difference on the regional prevalence of women teachers would have been trivial.

The important question here is whether other differences in class structure might have influenced who would teach. One possibility is that the southern elite did indeed treat its daughters differently and that the southern yeomanry followed that lead. Another possibility is that other differences in social class structure (indirectly related to slavery of course) also distinguished South from North. We suspect that in any region the poorest families did not often have the means to prepare girls for work as teachers; such families in particular were less likely to have given their girls an extended education (extended in relative terms: through age fourteen, e.g.). At the other end of the social order, the very wealthy probably only rarely sent girls into work, especially relatively unremunerative work. And so teachers generally, and perhaps especially female teachers, were likely to have been drawn from the middling orders. Perhaps the southern social structure could support only a smaller cadre of female teachers, especially if the teachers were drawn principally from nonfarm households.

The 1860 census gathered information on the value of property (real and personal) held by individuals. We treat the sum of the values of real and personal property as a measure of wealth, focusing on the wealth of the teacher's father (or mother if the father were absent). There may indeed have been a tendency for young female teachers to hail from the middling orders, but it was not a terribly strong tendency; and, in any case, the size of the middling orders in the South, while perhaps somewhat smaller than elsewhere, was not much smaller. Thus, for example, while half of all northern girls aged sixteen to twenty-five were growing up in households in which the head held $1,000–$7,000 of property, the comparable proportion in the South was only three-eighths. By contrast, both those with more and those with less wealth were more prevalent in the South. Such a difference in proportions could have an effect, of course, but these proportions hardly suggest an absent middling order; at most, we might say that a giant fraction of society was rather smaller in the South, but still three-fourths as large as in the North. Yet the number of southern female teachers makes it exceedingly unlikely that the group produced anything like the same proportion of female teachers as the corresponding group did in New England.

Women's Occupations

Most teachers were young, and most teachers in New England and New York were women, so that seven-tenths of all teachers there were women under twenty-five. Historians have stressed how the cultural norms of the plantation elite eschewed women working outside the household; in a slave society based on race, it is argued, the "need" to protect white women was a first line of defense against interracial mixing and resulted in rigid limits on white female activity, including distinctively firm strictures against white women working for pay. We need not study the cultural configurations prominent among the plantation elite in any detail here; we have neither the sources nor the need to do so. The pressing question here is whether these ideals of southern womanhood permeated down from the tiny plantation elite to the social groups in the middle ranks of the agricultural order, that is, to the farm families that in other regions would have supplied so many of the young women teachers. Put more precisely, did elite ideals permeate society in such a way as to limit work outside the home by women from these farm families? Whatever the ideals, in other words, did they actually determine behavior? A simple test of this question leads to a negative answer. The 1860 census provides information on the proportion of women in gainful occupations across the country. In addition to the results published in the census reports of the time, we are fortunate that only a few months before our analysis a national sample of households drawn from the 1860 census was made available to historians. While the sample includes only the first wave of a larger effort, it is still nationally representative and immense by the standards of most social science work. The huge advantage of this sample is that we can not only address the question of whether women worked for pay less often in the South than elsewhere but also study female employment rates among the unmarried daughters of the middling orders in particular.

Table 2.4 shows that in fact the proportion of women in the labor force (among those for whom an occupation was listed in the census) was about the same (outside the larger cities) in Northeast, the Midwest, and the South. It was somewhat higher in the Northeast, probably because of the greater prevalence of small- and middle-sized towns, the prevalence of manufacturing, and the (related) lower economic potential of family farms there. But in the South and the Midwest—one slave, the other nearly all free—women were equally prevalent in the labor force.

However, was the recruitment of these women workers in the South as likely to be from the middling orders as it was in other regions? Or were southern women workers drawn overwhelmingly from the social groups at the bottom, those who told the 1860 census takers that they owned no property or very little property? The answer is that the middling orders sent roughly comparable proportions of their daughters to work in the South as they did in other regions (table 2.4). We again focus on households which included an unmarried daughter between sixteen and twenty-five years of age, and we classify these households into three broad levels of wealth:

TABLE 2.4 Comparisons of Northeast, Midwest, and South in 1860
(native-born whites living outside the 98 largest cities)

Regional Patterns	All	0	1–1,000	1,001–7,000	7,001–15,000	15,001–50,000	>50,000	N
			Percentage by Household Wealth Levels ($)					
Northeast								
1. % female teachers	75							1,243
2. % female labor	33							5,885
3. Wealth among parents of females 16–25		7	22	52	13	5	0	738
4. Wealth of parents of female teachers		6	19	63	10	2	0	633
5. Females 16–25: % empl.		38 (220)		37 (383)	39 (135)[a]			
6. Females 16–25 (excl. teachers): % empl.		32 (202)		26 (327)	34 (125)[a]			
North-Central								
1. % female teachers	64							982
2. % female labor	30							4,702
3. Wealth among parents of females 16–25		5	29	53	10	3	0	620
4. Wealth of parents of female teachers		6	21	60	11	2	0	412
5. Females 16–25: % empl.		34 (208)		30 (330)	23 (82)[a]			
6. Females 16–25 (excl. teachers): % empl.		30 (195)		22 (296)	20 (79)[a]			
South								
1. % female teachers	36							712
2. % female labor	29							4,603
3. Wealth among parents of females 16–25		4	37	37	9	10	4	653
4. Wealth of parents of female teachers		3	18	45	13	18	2	174
5. Females 16–25: % empl.		26 (266)		22 (242)	22 (145)[a]			
6. Females 16–25 (excl. teachers): % empl.		25 (264)		19 (235)	19 (140)[a]			

Note: Full titles for rows 1–6: (1) Percentage of females among teachers; (2) Percentage of females among all gainfully employed; (3) Wealth distribution among heads of families with a girl 16–25 (unmarried); (4) Wealth distribution among heads of families of female teachers 16–25 living with parent; (5) Percentage of all females 16–25 gainfully employed, by head's wealth; (6) Same as row 5, but excluding females listed as "teacher." Rows 1 and 4 are based on the 1860 teacher sample; other rows are based on the 1860 IPUMS.

[a] 7,001 or greater.

$1,000 or less, $1,001 to $7,000, and over $7,000. We are most interested in the middle category, although the highest is interesting as well. The proportion working in these social groups was again somewhat higher in the Northeast than in the other two regions. It was also somewhat higher in the Midwest than in the South: 30 percent and 23 percent versus 22 percent and 22 percent in the two higher wealth categories of the Midwest and South respectively. However, the Midwest also had more opportunities for women in teaching than the South did. Our question is whether women's participation in the teaching force reflected women's participation in the labor force generally; so we should also consider separately women's participation in the *rest* of the labor force. These proportions for the two wealth groups are 22 percent and 20 percent versus 19 percent and 19 percent in the Midwest and South respectively—virtually equivalent and well within the range of expected sampling variability.

In a word then, there is no quantitative evidence that young women, in general, did not work for pay in the South, nor that women from the middling ranks worked less for pay in the South compared with the Midwest before the Civil War. We do not imply that a distinctively southern ideal of female domesticity held no sway below the levels of the southern elite, but we do insist that the issue needs close scrutiny and that its behavioral outcomes ought to be considered explicitly. To say that some members of these middling orders were compelled by economic pressures into violating norms they held dear could explain why some daughters from these homes worked, but not why as many did so as daughters of the Midwest's middling orders. Recall too that the age range involved in our inquiry is broad, sixteen to twenty-five. So it is likely that the proportion that worked for wages *at some point* between the time they were sixteen and the time they were twenty-five was much greater than the fifth of all women in that age range who happened to be working at the time the census enumerated them. What sort of work were these young women doing? The answer is that in every region the work (exclusive of teaching and a very small percentage running stores or farms) was in a very few occupations: dressmaking and related garment production, domestic work, and some farm labor. In the Northeast, another fifth were working in other blue-collar (virtually all low skill) occupations, many probably as operatives in manufacturing (table 2.5). In any event, for our purpose it is clear that the lower participation of young women in teaching in the South is not simply a reflection of very low participation of women in general, or even of young daughters from middling orders, in the paid labor force there.

AGE OF MARRIAGE

We had originally speculated that the age of marriage might be lower in the South than elsewhere, and that lower marriage age might reinforce a lower likelihood of female participation in the paid labor force. We now know that female participation in the labor force was not in fact notably lower in the South than elsewhere, but it is still possible that age of marriage was lower in the region. This factor might have reduced

TABLE 2.5 Occupations of Gainfully Employed Daughters, 16–25
(in families in which the head's wealth exceeded $1,000)
(native-born whites living outside the 98 largest cities)

A. All Such Daughters

	Percent of All at Work, by Region		
Occupation	Northeast	North-Central	South
Teacher	36	31	15
Other white-collar	5	11	4
Dressmaker, etc.[a]	23	17	28
Domestic	20	40	38
Farm labor	3	1	9
Other blue-collar	12	1	6
Total (100%) N	182	119	79

B. All Such Daughters Who Were Not Teachers

	Percent of All at Work (except teaching), by Region		
Occupation	Northeast	North-Central	South
Other white-collar	9	16	4
Dressmaker, etc.[a]	35	24	33
Domestic	32	57	45
Farm labor	5	1	10
Other blue-collar	19	1	8
Total (100%) N	116	82	67

[a] Includes dressmaker, tailor, milliner.

the likelihood that young women would take up teaching for a spell, either because they were less likely to leave home (for only a short time before marriage) or because teaching seemed to require more of an investment of time and money in terms of training than other work did, and that investment seemed pointless for a duration soon to be ended by marriage.

But was the marriage age in fact lower in the South? For this analysis we rely on the national sample of households drawn from the 1850 census; this sample is many times larger than the one currently available for 1860, and so patterns should show up more reliably in it. We look at the marital status of women, ages sixteen to twenty-nine, in each of the three large regions (outside the larger cities) (table 2.6). The age at which half the young women had married appears to have been over a year lower in the South than in the Northeast, twenty-one years five months rather than twenty-two years eight months. However, in the Midwest half the girls appear to have married by twenty years and five months—a year younger

TABLE 2.6 Women Married at Each Age, 16–29, by Region (native-born whites, living outside the 98 largest cities)

Age	Percentage of Women Married		
	Northeast	Midwest	South
16	3	5	8
17	7	15	19
18	11	22	21
19	21	32	35
20	28	47	42
21	35	56	47
22	43	62	55
23	53	67	61
24	63	76	63
25	62	78	66
26	70	80	75
27	70	85	75
28	73	85	75
29	72	83	78

Note: Estimated age at which half the young women had married: Northeast, 22 yrs. 8 mos.; Midwest, 20 yrs. 4 mos.; South, 21 yrs. 5 mos.

Cell sizes on which the percentages are based vary between 223 and 670; cell sizes for the two ages just above and below 50% married vary between 369 and 587.

than was the case in the South. These marital ages may reflect above all the ability to set up a farm of one's own where the population was less dense. In any event, while the girls in the Northeast may have married at somewhat later ages than in the South, they did not do so in the Midwest; yet the proportion of female teachers in the Midwest was nearly as large as in the Northeast, and far higher than in the South (64 percent female vs. 36 percent). Thus age of marriage, like the likelihood of employment, does not appear able to explain much about the low prevalence of female teachers in the South.

COMPETING DEMANDS FOR WOMEN'S TIME: CHILD CARE

Did the care of younger siblings restrict southern women from seeking employment as teachers more than it restricted women in the northern regions? Throughout the antebellum era, southern families had more children, on average, than families in the Northeast. Table 2.7 offers a crude but simple summary. The ratio of children under age ten to women age twenty-six to forty-five is used as a rough measure of the number of young children for whom a mother had to care in New England and in the South Atlantic region (Virginia, Maryland, North Carolina, and South

TABLE 2.7 Regional Fertility Differences and the Availability of Young Women for Teaching, 1800–1850 (white population only)

		Ratios: Children (ages 1–10)/ Women (ages 26–45)		% Southern Women Ages 16–25 Required to Make the Ratios in Cols. 1 and 2 Equal in Both Regions	
Year	Region	Simple (1)	Allowing for Slave Help (2)	Simple (3)	Allowing for Slave Help (4)
1800	New England	3.07			
	South Atlantic	3.79	3.16–3.37	22	3–10
1820	New England	2.72			
	South Atlantic	3.63	3.03–3.23	30	12–19
1850	New England	1.66			
	South Atlantic	2.41	2.01–2.14	55	31–40

Source: Calculated from the census year for the appropriate year (1800, 1820, 1850), using the Inter-university Consortium for Political and Social Research (ICPSR) state and county data sets for those years.

Explanation of calculations: South Atlantic includes Virginia, Maryland, North Carolina, and South Carolina. Col. (1) = (children 1–10)/(women 26–45). For col. (2), assume that 1/8–1/5 of Southern women 26–45 received a slave's help with child care; col. (2) denominators for South Atlantic = (number of women 26–45 multiplied by 1.125–1.2). For cols. (3) and (4), first calculate the number of additional child-care workers needed to make the ratio of children to child-care workers in the South Atlantic equal to the ratio in New England in cols. (1) and (2), respectively. Then divide the number of additional child-care workers needed by the number of Southern women 16–25.

Carolina).[10] This estimated ratio of children to mothers falls in both regions during the first half of the nineteenth century, but it is considerably higher in the four old southern states than it is in New England. Southern mothers might therefore have turned to their eldest unmarried daughters for help with the younger children; how much help from these southern daughters would have been required in order to bring the southern child-woman ratio down to the New England ratio? The results are striking: very substantial fractions of the young women would have had to provide child care to meet that goal, 22 percent in 1800, 30 percent in 1820, and 55 percent in 1850.

One source of child care in the South, of course, was slave women. However, devoting enough female slaves to child care to reduce the child-woman ratio of the South to New England's level would have involved considerable expenses, since slave time spent in child care was not free of costs to the

10. Because fertility was higher in more recently settled areas, we limit the comparison to these older southern states. On early American fertility, east and west, see, e.g., Yasukichi Yasuba, *Birth Rates of the White Population in the United States, 1800–1860: An Economic Study* (Baltimore, 1961).

owner. In any case, only about a quarter of southern households held slaves, and surely not all devoted slaves to the tasks of child care. If we assume that one household in five to eight devoted a female slave's time partly to child care, and if the cost of a slave's time is ignored completely,[11] the estimated percentage of young white southern women required to reduce child-care burdens to the New England level is considerably lessened; nevertheless, even given this use of slaves, the percentages of white women required to equalize the mother/child ratios of the South and New England would have been far from trivial, especially in 1820 and 1850 (table 2.7, col. 4).

Despite this seemingly compelling contrast, there is good reason to reject the suggestion that young unmarried women were less prevalent in southern teaching because they cared for siblings. The most important reason for skepticism is the same we have seen before: when the South and Midwest are compared, there is no regional difference in child-care needs and yet the difference in the prevalence of female teachers is very large. The point is especially striking if we compare the South Atlantic to the northern midwestern region, for example in the states of Michigan and Wisconsin, where settlers from New England and New York established school arrangements like the ones in their states of origin. Fertility rates in these new northern farming areas were as high as or higher than those in the South Atlantic region; yet these fertility rates coexisted with high proportions of female teachers and did so despite the absence of slaves that might have reduced the burden of child care in the South.[12] Also, while New England curtailed fertility much before the South did, that process may not have been far along in either region before the close of the eighteenth century, so that the fertility rates in New England may not have been much lower than those in the South in the mid-to-late eighteenth century, particularly

11. The slave was not a source of child support without cost. From the point of view of a family economy, material costs and benefits were involved whether a young woman's time was used as a paid teacher or in caring for her younger siblings, and whether to buy and maintain a slave for this purpose or for fieldwork. Perhaps, however, the slave's time could be used for child care while she did other work as well, thereby greatly reducing the expenditure exclusively for child care. In that event, it may make sense to think of some of the slave's time as an advantage without cost, and at the extreme to think of her entire contribution in that way. Column 4 of table 2.7 reflects that line of reasoning.

12. In 1850, the ratio of children under age ten to women age twenty-six to forty-four stood at 2.55 in Michigan and 2.52 in Wisconsin; as the text table shows, the ratio was then 2.41 in the Chesapeake. In 1840, the first census after Michigan became a state (and before Wisconsin became a state), the ratio in Michigan was 2.84; in the four states of the Chesapeake the 1840 ratios were 2.78 in Virginia, 2.87 in North Carolina, 2.96 in South Carolina, and 2.26 in Maryland.

outside the larger urban areas in each region. Yet the pattern of hiring women teachers in some capacities in New England began early in the region's history. Perhaps, then, where fertility was high and female teaching prevalent, mothers simply absorbed more child-care burdens without help from elder daughters, at least during the relatively short school terms.

COMPETING DEMANDS FOR WOMEN'S TIME: WORK IN THE RURAL ECONOMY

The Relative Value of Women's Time in Agriculture and Manufacturing

In the past as in the present, whether an individual chose an activity depended on the competing demands on his or her time. Such demands include other paid work, unpaid work such as raising a family, unpaid work such as participating in the chores of a family farm, and leisure activities. Of course, some of these demands would have been quite similar across regions, but important regional differences existed too. We have just explored one way in which regional differences in the demands on women's time might have been relevant to the prevalence of female teaching in terms of child care. In this section we focus on ways in which differences in demands for women's time in the regional economies may have influenced the prevalence of women teachers in those regions.

Nearly all Americans lived within the agricultural economy in the early nineteenth century, and nearly all Southerners still did in 1860; even in New England and New York, notwithstanding the transformations of the early industrial revolution, a majority of the rural population also made their livelihoods in agriculture on the eve of the Civil War.[13] Most American women did not work for wages in the agricultural economy (partly because many of the women who did do agricultural work full time were enslaved). However, the fact that a free woman on a farm did not work for wages does not mean that her time was not valuable for agricultural production, quite apart from her contributions to household maintenance through child care, preparation of meals, and other tasks. After all, most men on farms were also not working for wages; they worked their own or their fathers' farms. Free women may not have worked as regularly as free men in fieldwork, but many did work in the fields on occasion, such as during the harvest; also

13. An occupational profile of rural heads of household in the two regions appears in table 2.4.

TABLE 2.8 Estimates of Wages of Females Relative to Males in the United States, 1815–68

Year	Mid-Atlantic	New England	South[a]
1815		.29 (.15)[b]	
1820	.30	.37	
1832	.42	.43	
1850	.52	.45	.57–.76[b]
1860			.58
1868			.57
1885	.58		

Note: This table is a simplification of data reported by Claudia Goldin and Kenneth Sokoloff (see text), esp. "Women, Children, and Industrialization," 758–61, and "Relative Productivity," 472. Our simplification includes (1) averaging two close estimates for 1832 and 1850, and (2) reporting only the midpoint and not the range for the two northern regions, 1820–50. The early data for the northern regions are based on wages of domestics and day laborers, principally in agriculture; the later data are based on wages in manufacturing. Elizabeth B. Field-Hendrey and Lee A. Craig report consistent results for agriculture and manufacturing separately (see notes to text).

[a] Old South (chiefly Maryland, Virginia, and the Carolinas) for 1850, all South for later years.

[b] Net of the value of board.

some other farming tasks were typed as female work.[14] Historian Stephanie McCurry recently documented in detail the extensive fieldwork carried out by women in southern yeoman households.[15]

Moreover, the nature of female work in agriculture probably differed between New England and the South as a result of the crops distinctive to each region. Economic historians Claudia Goldin and Kenneth Sokoloff argued that southern crops—and especially cotton—were easier for women and children to care for and harvest than was the case with most northern crops, because physical strength was less important in growing those southern crops. As a result, in the early nineteenth century, the relative value of a woman's time—the value of her time relative to the value of a man's time—was greater in the southern than in the northern agricultural economy. The magnitude of the difference may be appreciated from the summary of Goldin and Sokoloff's findings on relative wages, seen in table 2.8,

14. See, e.g., Percy Wells Bidwell and John I. Falconer, *History of Agriculture in the Northern United States: 1620–1860* (New York, 1941), passim; and Elizabeth Fox-Genovese, "Women in Agriculture in the Nineteenth Century," in Lou Ferleger, *Agriculture and National Development: Views on the Nineteenth Century* (Ames, Iowa, 1990), 267–302.

15. Stephanie McCurry, *Masters of Small Worlds: Yeoman Households, Gender Relations and the Political Culture of the Antebellum South Carolina Low Country* (New York, 1995), chap. 2.

and in particular by comparing the earliest figure available for New England, which is from 1815 (prior to the onset of much industrialization), to the figure for the South. The southern figure is for a later year, but since there occurred comparatively little movement out of agriculture in the South, the comparison is meaningful. In the New England of 1815, the ratio of female-to-male wages (net of board) stood at a mere 0.15; the lowest estimate for the South is about four times as high (0.57–0.76). And estimates for the immediate post–Civil War era show that the southern estimates do not result merely from the use of female slaves.

Implications for the Employment of Teachers

Goldin and Sokoloff argue that during the first half of the nineteenth century, manufacturers were successful in sparking an industrial revolution in the Northeast partly because they were able to rely on the low relative wages of women and child workers—lower than the wages manufacturers would have had to pay New England men, and lower too than the relative wages that would have been required to recruit women and children in the South.[16] For our purposes, the crucial point is that the higher relative value of a woman's time in the early nineteenth-century South would have made it less of a savings in that region to lure women rather than men from agricultural work than was the case in New England or New York.

The point here does not concern only (or even principally) women who were employed for wages in either region's agricultural economy; the argument holds with equal force whether the women (and men) were paid wages or whether they were contributing to the productivity of their family farms. Our measure, the ratio of the female and male wages prevailing in each region, would have been influenced by both the paid and unpaid demands for women's agricultural work.

The difference in the value of women, relative to men, in producing northeastern and southern crops early in the nineteenth century could also have influenced the prevalence of female teaching indirectly, by influencing

16. Claudia Goldin and Kenneth Sokoloff, "Women, Children, and Industrialization in the Early Republic: Evidence from the Manufacturing Censuses," *Journal of Economic History* 42, no. 4 (December 1982): 741–74, and "The Relative Productivity Hypothesis of Industrialization: The American Case, 1820–1850," *Quarterly Journal of Economics* 99, no. 3 (August 1984): 461–87. See also Elizabeth B. Field-Hendrey and Lee A. Craig, "Industrialization and the Earnings Gap," *Explorations in Economic History* 30 (January 1993): 60–80.

educational patterns. Specifically, regional differences in the relative value of female time in agriculture could have created regional differences in the chances that a girl, compared to a boy, would be kept in school into adolescence, into the period in which she might be expected to acquire the skills needed to be a teacher. One outcome could have been higher differences between female and male literacy in the South than in New England; and indeed we will later explore the importance of just such differences. This educational advantage of New England girls might not have amounted to much at the time when town schools did not admit girls (described in chap. 1); but it may still have meant something, and it would have meant more as increasing numbers of New England town schools began to admit girls in the late eighteenth century.

As the early industrial revolution progressed, especially after 1820, the demand for female labor by manufacturers raised the value of women's time compared to men's time in the Northeast. Thus, over the four decades between 1820 and 1860, wages paid to women in that region rose relative to wages paid to men (even in the agricultural sector, which now had to compete with the manufacturing sector for the use of women's time). Table 2.8 presents a summary of the changes Goldin and Sokoloff found in the female-to-male wage ratio over the four decades. The rising trend in the female-to-male wage ratio reported by the economic historians was also noted by observers at the time. Thus Henry C. Carey, author of an 1835 *Essay on Wage Rates,* compared their levels in different countries and commented, "Agricultural labor has not varied materially in these forty years [1793–1833] in its money price . . . the wages of men having been very steadily about nine dollars per month [with board]. . . . [But] the wages of females have greatly advanced being nearly double what they were forty years since."[17]

This rising trend in the female-to-male wage ratio in New England was occurring across the very same decades during which that region substituted female teachers for male teachers in the winter sessions. The bargain for the region, in other words, was not as good as it would have been earlier in the century, but it was still a bargain. In terms of the comparison across regions, the relative value of women's time was increasing in the North and stable in the South. Consequently, as the regional difference in the prevalence of female teachers was *rising* across these decades, the regional

17. Cited in Goldin and Sokoloff, "Women, Children, and Industrialization," 761.

difference in the relative value of women's time was *declining*. Obviously, therefore, the demands for women's time in the broader agricultural and manufacturing economies of North and South cannot alone provide a full explanation for the regional differences in the prevalence of female teachers.

Nevertheless, regional differences in the value of female-to-male time in the agricultural economy had by no means disappeared entirely by 1860. The regional differences still show up clearly in census publications based on wage data from that year (table 2.9). The female-to-male wage ratios were indeed generally low in New England and highest in the South. And unlike the comparisons shown earlier, for female labor force participation, age of marriage, and child-woman ratios, in this comparison the Midwest and the Northeast appear reasonably similar, while the South remains the outlier—as we would require for any straightforward explanation of why the South differed from these other regions in the prevalence of female teachers.

Evidence from Teachers' Wages

A further dimension to this argument about the value of women's time also seems consistent, at least at first sight, with the evidence about teachers; the female-to-male wage ratio in teaching should have been higher in the South than in the North (bid up by the higher female-to-male wage ratio in agriculture in the South). And this is a point on which we have some evidence in southern school reports. Unfortunately, most southern school systems were only beginning to organize at the state level before the Civil War and did not publish the sort of detailed school reports that were common in some northern states. We have in fact systematic and detailed reports over a period of years only for North Carolina; however, we may substitute these with figures from other states for the first decades after the Civil War, when the United States commissioner of education began soliciting information and regularly publishing the details about each state. Since the pattern of hiring male teachers in the South declined slowly in the late nineteenth century, these postwar reports are of some use, and they are consistent with what little evidence we have from before the Civil War. This evidence shows that the wages of southern women teachers do in fact appear to have been much higher relative to male teachers' wages than was the case in the North; in fact, in the South, so far as we can tell from the scanty reports, women's wages were typically 85–100 percent of those of men.

TABLE 2.9 Female-to-Male Wage Ratios by State, 1860

State	Day Labor Ratio	Farm Labor Ratio
New England	.287	.432
New Hampshire	.343	.492
Massachusetts	.292	.446
Connecticut	.284	.430
Vermont	.276	.401
Rhode Island	.274	.405
Maine	.258	.398
Middle Atlantic	.286	.422
Pennsylvania	.299	.431
New York	.281	.410
New Jersey	.262	.447
South	.395	.552
Louisiana	.577	.856
South Carolina	.514	.693
Florida	.508	.703
Alabama	.495	.726
Texas	.462	.676
Georgia	.441	.605
Mississippi	.441	.585
Arkansas	.408	.580
Tennessee	.361	.464
Kentucky	.345	.469
Maryland	.336	.522
North Carolina	.333	.451
Virginia	.311	.432
Delaware	.251	.373
West	.317	.449
California	.653	.970
Oregon	.538	.696
Kansas	.369	.489
Missouri	.345	.467
Nebraska	.341	.427
Illinois	.311	.461
Michigan	.307	.397
Minnesota	.306	.485
Indiana	.292	.404
Iowa	.289	.417
Ohio	.286	.403
Wisconsin	.277	.403

Note: Day Labor Ratio: The ratio of a female domestic's weekly wages to six times the value of a male day laborer's wages (both with board).

Farm Labor Ratio: The ratio of a female domestic's weekly wages (multiplied by 52/12) to a male farmhand's monthly wages (both with board).

Ratios shown for each region were calculated as the weighted mean of the state ratios, using the total state population as the weight.

Reasons for Skepticism about the Influence of the Female-to-Male Wage Ratio in Agriculture

Despite this seemingly compelling argument that explains both the prevalence of female teachers and the levels of the female wages in the South, we must unfortunately report strong reasons to doubt that the wages of women in southern agriculture in 1860, relative to those of men, can account for the teaching patterns. Most important, this argument about the value of female time for working southern crops needs to be refined in terms of geographic areas and particular crops. In particular, it seems to hold best for cotton-intensive areas, but not for tobacco-intensive areas; and consequently the female-to-male wage ratio actually varied dramatically across the states of the South. Where cotton production was extensive, the female-to-male wage ratio was high (those cited here are for the series "day labor ratio" in table 2.9): South Carolina 0.51, Georgia 0.44, Arkansas 0.41, Louisiana 0.58, Alabama 0.50, Florida 0.51, and Texas 0.46. However in states in which cotton production was minimal and tobacco production was prominent, the ratio was much lower: Virginia 0.31, Kentucky 0.35, Maryland 0.34, North Carolina 0.33, and Tennessee 0.36. Moreover, the ratios in these tobacco states were in fact notably closer to the female-to-male wage ratios in the states of the Northeast, where the ratio averaged 0.29, than to the ratios in the southern cotton states. And even if the Northeast ratio had been far lower (as in 1815) the crucial point is that the tobacco states of the South showed a notably lower female-to-male wage ratio than did the cotton states of the South, and almost certainly would have shown the same pattern in 1815. Yet there is no comparable difference in the prevalence of female teachers in the two subregions of the South: 32 percent in the tobacco states, 30 percent in the cotton states.[18]

Similarly, there is no evidence that teachers' wages differed across the cotton/noncotton divide. We may take as an illustration North Carolina, which produced little cotton and much tobacco, and South Carolina, where the situation was reversed. The wage ratio in agriculture follows the expected pattern: 0.33 in North Carolina, 0.51 in South Carolina; but the wage ratio in North Carolina teaching throughout the 1850s was virtually 1.0, when the agricultural situation would predict a wage ratio like that of the Northeast. And after the Civil War, when both states reported wages of male and female teachers, they were identically high for decades. Thus, like

---

18. Indeed when the area of the future state of West Virginia is excluded from the comparison, the difference is smaller still.

the proportion of female teachers, the wage ratios of teachers simply do not suggest any internal divisions in the region, divisions that the hypothesis of a demand for women's time based on agricultural work would have required. We return, later in the chapter, to an effort to explain why wage ratios in the South were in fact higher than elsewhere; but whatever the reason, it seems clear that the ratios in teaching were not simply responding to the prevalent ratios in agriculture. Appendix 2 presents more detailed evidence on teachers' wages deriving from all southern states after the Civil War, evidence consistent with that from the Carolinas. The appendix also presents evidence based on county-level data on the connection, or rather the absence of a connection, between the gender of the teacher and the wage ratio in agriculture prevalent in the teacher's county across the South (evidence which we gathered from manuscript records for hundreds of counties).

EDUCATIONAL LEVELS

Both men and women in the South received, on average, less education than their counterparts in New England and New York. If the gap in educational levels between southern women and southern men was also greater than the comparable gender gap in the northern region, then the supply of women who were educated enough to teach may have been greater in New England and New York in than it was in the South.

Our earliest data are from the census of 1850, which collected evidence on both literacy of adults and school attendance of children (see tables 2.10, 2.11). Moreover, the large national sample drawn from this census allows us to study the literacy levels of older age cohorts; the literacy levels of

TABLE 2.10 Percent Literate among the Northeast-Born and Southern-Born by Age in 1850

Age Cohort in 1850	Age 20–29 in	Northeast		South		Percent Women among Southern Literates
		Men	Women	Men	Women	
20–29	1850	98	98	86	79	48
30–39	1840	98	96	87	73	46
40–49	1830	98	96	85	73	46
50–59	1820	98	96	84	73	46
60–69	1810	97	95	79	69	47
70–79	1800	97	96	79	67	46

Note: Cell sizes exceed 1,000 in all but the oldest cohort in the Northeast, and in the two oldest cohorts in the South, which exceed 300.

TABLE 2.11 School Attendance of Youth, 15–19 Years of Age, 1850 and 1860: By Region (native-born whites, living outside the 98 largest cities)

| | Pupils Age 15–19 at School (%) | | | | | |
| | Northeast | | Midwest | | South | |
Sex	1850	1860	1850	1860	1850	1860
Male	52	54	51	58	37	41
Female	40	39	38	46	22	28
Percent female of all at school, 15–19	43	42	42	45	38	44

Note: All cell Ns exceed 2,300 in 1850 and 225 in 1860.

those people sixty to seventy years of age in 1850 tell us a good deal about the literacy levels of the cohort twenty to thirty years of age in 1810. Of course, we cannot say just how much literacy the older adults acquired in later adulthood (after 1840, e.g.). And there was very likely also some differential mortality by literacy, the illiterate being more likely to die at younger ages. Nevertheless neither of these tendencies (the adult acquisition of literacy or the differential mortality) are likely to have been so strong as to invalidate the use of the 1850 census to study the general patterns of literacy in the first half of the nineteenth century.

The results show clearly the impact of the southern school arrangements on both men and women: literacy was less prevalent in the white South than in the Northeast. Reasons why southern literacy lagged well behind the Northeast, and especially behind New England, have often been noted, and we find these explanations convincing: one source lay in the legacy of Puritanism's emphasis on the ability of each individual to read the Bible. Eventually, too, an economy more oriented to the market and a social life developing in the context of nearby towns probably encouraged a greater concern for the education of girls relative to boys than the southern reality would have done. In addition, social conditions that inhibited development of basic schooling in the colonial South (dispersion of population and the power of an elite) would have retarded the development of literacy for both men and women. And lower levels of literacy, in turn, might well have hindered the spread of ideas that encouraged a more favorable evaluation of female education.

Women had comprised just about half of the Northeast's literate population in every decade since at least the end of the eighteenth century. In the first half of the nineteenth century literacy was climbing gradually among southern whites, but there was a gap between male and female literacy; how are we to interpret that gap? If we consider the proportion of illiterates among men and women, we might say the gap was very large. For example, among those twenty to twenty-nine years of age, 14 percent of the men were illiterate, as were 21 percent of the women; among those seventy to seventy-nine years of age the comparable percentages of illiterates would be 21 percent male, 33 percent female. In each case, then, we may say that illiteracy was about one and a half times as prevalent among women as among men.

However, this would not be the right way to approach the question. The issue for us is what proportion of those who were sufficiently educated to teach were women, and here we are taking literacy as a crude measure of that educational requirement. Looked at in this way, the gender gap in literacy is of much less consequence. Whereas women in the Northeast comprised about 49 percent of the literates, women in the South comprised between 46 percent and 48 percent of the literates in different cohorts.

We can bring this same perspective to bear on the percentages of young people attending school in 1850. Here we can exploit a somewhat more refined measure of the educational requirement for teaching and ask how great were the gender gaps in the proportion of women among those who had received sufficient education to teach. We do not know much about the average levels of schooling obtained by early or mid-nineteenth-century teachers; in the countryside we suspect that the typical requirement was to have persisted in the local schools and shown mastery of the curriculum offered there. Further attendance at academies would have been an advantage, of course, but there is no systematic evidence on how many women had such additional schooling—in any region. We can however observe who remained in school until a fairly advanced age by the standards of 1850; probably these would have been good candidates for teaching. Specifically, we look at young people fifteen to nineteen years of age who were in school, North and South, and ask what proportion of these older pupils was female (table 2.12). The regional disparities were minor. In 1850, girls comprised 42–43 percent of these students in the northern regions and 38 percent in the South. By 1860, even this modest difference had disappeared.

We also wondered whether the picture might look very different if we took into account the social class origins of the young people receiving an education. After all, if the educated young southern women came from especially well-to-do families (from the top quarter of the wealth distribution, e.g.) relative to the educated young southern men and relative to youth in the other regions, then they might not have been likely recruits

TABLE 2.12 Determinants of Schooling for Girls Age 15–19, 1850–60 (native-born whites, living outside the 98 largest cities)

	Northeast		North-Central		South	
	1850	1860	1850	1860	1850	1860
Percent child of household head	70	74	72	69	73	72
Percent at school: by living arrangement						
Child of head	48	48	47	57	26	34
Other	20	15	15	21	11	15
Wealth of head:[a] percent at each level						
0–$1,000	56	36	63	34	71	41
$1,001–$7,000	39	49	34	52	25	36
$7,001–15,000	4	11	2	11	3	8
>$15,000	1	4	1	3	1	15
Percent at school: children of head by wealth of head						
0–$1,000	44	44	41	54	24	24
$1,001–$7,000	56	51	55	56	30	39
>$7,000	43	49	65	69	29	44
Percent children of heads						
Head is a farmer	60	54	78	78	79	78
Percent at school by father's occupation[b]						
Head is a farmer	55	53	49	58	29	35
Head is other	43	44	44	57	19	31

[a] Real property, 1850; real and personal, 1860. In 1860, 55% of these southern heads of household had real property valued at up to $1,000; 31% had $1,001–$7,000; 8% had $7,001–$15,000; and 6% had over $15,000.

[b] Limited to children of household heads.

for schoolteaching. But such was not the case. As table 2.13 shows, the proportion of girls among adolescents at school was about even across three broad levels of well-being in the South (as well as in the Northeast).

SOUTH VERSUS NORTH: THE BROADER SOCIAL CONTEXT PRIOR TO 1850

We began with institutional developments in historical context and then turned to the social factors that might have impinged on individuals in such a way as to make women less likely to teach in the South compared to the North: class structure and the size of its middling order, female labor force participation, age of marriage, fertility rates, educational levels, and demands for women's time in the wider agricultural economy. In connection with each of these issues, we asked whether the earliest systematic evidence (from 1850–60) supports the connections hypothesized between these factors and the prevalence of women teachers in 1860. The answer in a word is no. We found quite strong evidence for rejecting these connections. The straightforward notion, that something about the wider

TABLE 2.13 Adolescents in School in Each Region, 1860: Decomposition
(native-born whites, living outside the 98 largest cities)

A. Wealth Levels among Household Heads with a School-Attending Child, 15–19

| Region | Percentage of Heads in Each Wealth Group | | |
	$1,000 or Less	$1,001–$7,000	$7,001 and Over
Northeast	31	55	15
North-central	29	53	17
South	30	40	30

B. Percentage of Girls among School Attenders (15–19) in Each Wealth Group

| Region | Wealth Groups | | |
	$1,000 or Less	$1,001–$7,000	$7,001 and Over
Northeast	45	41	45
North-central	47	43	43
South	42	44	44

Note: Both panels restricted to those households in which an adolescent school attender lived with a parent who was the household head.

economic or demographic context of the South was keeping the women of 1860 out of teaching, cannot be sustained.

We must turn to other sorts of explanations to understand the patterns. One central explanation we have already offered: women did not get hired because the structure of the system that demanded them in other parts of the country—the two-tier system—did not develop in the South.

Other factors were probably at work as well, however. First of all, consider the six aspects of the social context that we just explored, not merely as they operated from 1850 to 1860 but as they operated earlier, helping to shape the educational patterns that developed over the long term. With regard to most of these factors, we do not suspect that they would have distinguished South from North more strongly in 1790 or in 1820 than they did in 1860. However, two deserve more consideration: the educational disadvantage of girls relative to boys in the South, and especially the wage disadvantage of women relative to men in the South. It is conceivable that during much of the century before 1850, the female-male gap in levels of schooling was greater than it was in that year, and as such the historical patterns of educational difference could have created regional differences in the nature of teaching by 1850, even as the hypothesized source of those regional differences in teaching (the gender gap in educational attainments, 1750–1850) was declining. But the best evidence we have on the point, while imperfect, emphatically works against this hypothesis. This evidence is the literacy levels of older adults in 1850; admittedly, the evidence does not cover advanced schooling, but it should be recalled that teaching the New England summer sessions of 1820 did not require educational adornments much loftier than literacy. In any case, this single window on the schooling of the earlier period suggests that the gap in male and female literacy rates in the South differed but little across the century, and that the supply of women among the southern literate population was relatively stable across the first half of the nineteenth century.[19]

On the other hand, the relative demand for the use of women's time in agriculture North and South, which we have tried to capture in the female-to-male wage ratio, probably did change during the half century before the 1850s. The reason was not developments in the South but those in the North. In 1815, the female-to-male wage ratio in New England had probably been much lower than in any part of the South (since the New England ratio rose over the decades because of manufacturing but changed little in the South). And so the regional differences in the value of women's and men's time might have mattered early in the history of American schooling, from as early as the seventeenth century until roughly the 1830s. These earlier regional differences in the wage ratio may have encouraged New Englanders more than Southerners to introduce particular educational arrangements involving women (as teachers in the lower tier of schools) just as they encouraged New Englanders more than Southerners to introduce particular manufacturing arrangements involving women. Later, the economic advantage of turning to women teachers in New England was no longer so much greater than the economic advantage of turning to women teachers in the South. However, by then, the institutional differences in educational arrangements were considerable, and women already had an important place in the institutions. It was, moreover, always a bargain to replace men with women in New England, even if it was not necessarily as much of a bargain as it had been in earlier decades, or as much of a *greater* bargain in New England than in the South. Following this logic returns us to the possibility that the demands of the wider agricultural economy may

---

19. Data presented here differ modestly from some presented in Joel Perlmann and Dennis Shirley, "When Did New England Women Acquire Literacy? New Evidence and a Reconsideration of Late-Eighteenth-Century Patterns," *William and Mary Quarterly* 48 (January 1991): 50–67—especially for Southerners in 1870. Perlmann and Shirley relied on a small sample they had collected as a check on their New England data; the quality of that small sample cannot be compared to the huge 1850 IPUMS data set from which the figures presented in this chapter are drawn.

have mattered to the development of the relevant institutions, notwith-standing the fact that by 1860 we were forced to conclude that the wage ratio could not account for the relative dearth of women teachers in the region. We cannot test such a suggestion with the evidence currently avail-able; we only suggest that it is consistent with the outcome and with expec-tations about the nature of the economic demands on the actors.

And what, then, are we to make of the southern female-to-male wage ratio within teaching, which was nearly equal to 1.0? We cannot explain the difference away by saying that probably teaching by women more often was the same as teaching by men in the South than in the North (due to the absence of the two-tier system in the former region). After all, we have already remarked that in our earliest teacher wage data from the 1840s in New England and New York, most of the gender inequality in wages is found within each session and not merely between sessions. Nevertheless, since southern women were not teaching in a split system, in which one tier had often been called the women's school, the absence of this institu-tional form may have retarded the establishment of a distinctive woman's rate. Most women hired may have been doing the same work as men and have been nearly as old on average as the men teachers in one region; most women hired may have been doing work different from that of men and have been notably younger in the other region. Of course these consider-ations are no guarantee that there would be nearly equal pay for equal work; but the absence of equal pay for equal work is a sociocultural imposition on gender-blind hiring arrangements; here we are dealing with the context that would help explain why that imposition might have occurred in one circumstance much more fully than in another. Another factor may have been southern pride, at least by the 1850s, when comparisons with the North may have emphasized the possibility of reducing wages. Calvin Wi-ley of North Carolina, for example, was gratified that he could contrast the salaries paid to his female teachers with those paid to female teachers in six northern states.[20]

The gratification, of course, cost him little if he could not in fact do much to increase the handful of women teachers in his system. And perhaps women would not work for less—not because of the female-to-male wage ratio in agriculture but for other reasons, notably a hesitation on the part of the women, and perhaps among those hiring, over violating accepted norms about teaching.

20. See Calvin H. Wiley's *Seventh Annual Report of the Superintendent of Common Schools of North Carolina for the Year 1859* (Raleigh, 1860), 11–12.

Norms, Legacies, Traditions: Other
Constraints on Midcentury Behavior

By 1840 New England and the South had been developing their distinctive institutions for over two centuries. As we have suggested repeatedly, an institutional legacy was itself a constraint of great importance; if the two-tier system encouraged women teachers and if that system was rare or absent in the South, then it was harder for women to get teaching positions there by 1860, even if no identifiable factor except the institutional arrangement itself operated to distinguish the regional hiring patterns.

But other factors that are not so readily measured may also have played a role in the process of hiring. Patterns of behavior developing differently over a long period are likely to have taken on normative force, difficult to oppose. We have already expressed skepticism about one commonly mentioned norm: that women were enjoined from work outside the home. As we have seen, southern women worked in the same proportions as they did in other regions in 1860, and even those from the middling orders did so. Whatever the discourse, women were working in some occupations; why not more often in teaching?

Some relevant considerations apply to the young woman seeking income, and some apply to the employer seeking to hire a teacher. Insofar as school boards were choosing teachers, it may well have appeared unseemly to violate the ideal that women should not work, especially women who were not desperately poor. It would have been one thing for women to violate this ideal individually, another for representatives of the public (especially those supposedly raising the level of public morals through schooling) to do so as a matter of policy. We get an inkling of such a stance in Charles Kinney's 1828 "Plan" for North Carolina's schools. In speaking of the advantages of hiring women teachers, he adds, "I ought perhaps here to remark that delicacy would forbid, and necessity not require that she [a potential woman teacher] pass an examination before the [local school] committee."[21]

Like Kinney, other "friends of education" in the South may have found it harder to make arguments about female teachers than did reformers in the North, to find the rhetoric that would argue it was not only necessary for the poor woman to work but a positive good to have young women

---

21. Kinney, "Plan," 443.

working—even as teachers, with that occupation's overtones of mother-hood.

Yet to a greater extent than in the North, southern schools were *not* run by representatives of the public; and southern educational institutions received less support from the colonial and later state governments. Southern local arrangements for schooling may very often have involved a greater private initiative from the teacher and the parents than the public arrangement of a representative board hiring a teacher. We have already noted that this regional difference made the local district school board of New England a kind of centralized authority in hiring that facilitated the creation of two tiers of schools. Here we add that the absence of that centralized authority in the southern context meant that getting work as a teacher had more the flavor of entrepreneurial self-employment, while the parallel northern context offered the more straightforward hiring of a young person by a local board. Women may have had an easier time breaking into the latter, given gendered norms of behavior. A male schoolmaster did not have an incentive to offer cheaper arrangements for schooling the younger children (a lower tier of schools), particularly if many children only received brief schooling. Female teachers might have competed with the masters for the work of instructing the young pupils, but such competition would have required a direct, new intervention into the labor market, establishing contracts with parents, and probably an itinerant life for many as well. Schoolmasters could have teamed up with women assistants, but such an arrangement involved disincentives for the schoolmasters and logistic complexities concerning facilities, and, for itinerants, difficulties of travel with a female assistant. If competition among schoolmasters had been intense, perhaps some of these difficulties would have been surmounted by innovators. But such competition hardly seems to describe the picture of the schoolmaster striking a deal with a rural community.

By midcentury, local villagers and farmers, whether negotiating with a entrepreneur who established a school or hiring a schoolteacher for a community, may have developed strong expectations about the appropriateness of male teachers. Perhaps these expectations were based on precisely the same factors that operated in the calculations of school boards in the North: that the female teacher could not control the older boys, and that the female teacher lacked the education or intellectual ability for the more advanced instruction. But whatever the explicit rationale, the inappropriateness of the female teacher within southern school arrangements and possibly within southern cultural norms had a history of its own, even if it was *not* a pattern related to the demography, social structure, and prevailing wages that we have studied for midcentury southern life. These diverging regional contexts of school arrangements and perhaps of cultural norms were carried with the settlers as they moved west.[22]

22. Readers with a background in economics may find it useful to translate the narrative to this point into the language of "relative" supply and demand. By relative we mean "female-to-male."

The relative demand for female teachers can be characterized in terms of a "substitution" and a "scale" effect. The substitution effect measures the responsiveness of the school board (or whomever hires teachers) to changes in the relative wages of female teachers. The presumption of the economist is that a reduction in the relative wages of female teachers would encourage the school board to increase the ratio of females to males in the classroom. The scale effect measures differences across school boards in their willingness to hire women relative to men at a given relative wage; that is, even if they faced the same relative wage, some school boards may have been more willing to hire female teachers, relative to men, given the particular institutional setting and historical context.

The relative supply of female teachers is also characterized by substitution and scale effects. The presumption of the economist is that, on the supply side, the substitution effect is positive: an increase in the relative wage of female teachers in a given location (e.g., New England) will induce more women, relative to men, to seek teaching positions. The scale effect in supply measures differences across locations—for example, the South versus New England—in the relative propensity of women to become teachers, at a given relative wage.

In economic terms, our argument is that differences in the degree of feminization between North and South prior to the Civil War cannot be explained by regional differences in readily measurable factors that might have influenced the size of the scale effect in the relative supply of female teachers. If this were the case, we would have been able to attribute the regional differences in feminization to such variables as the relative wage of women outside of teaching, demographic factors, and so on. While differences between the South and New England in these factors appear to be "in the right direction," the same comparisons between the South and the Midwest, or perhaps more tellingly, within the South, do not bear fruit. We are thus led to a narrative that focuses primarily on differences across regions that were embedded in institutions (e.g., the use of winter and summer sessions) and norms derived from historical experience (the dame schools of New England)—while acknowledging the likelihood of subtler, perhaps unmeasurable differences in relative supply. Such differences in supply could help explain why female teachers in the South commanded wages close to parity with men although, as we noted in the chapter, greater gender similarity in wages could reflect greater similarity in tasks performed, or skills, or even an arbitrary pay policy. Further and better evidence than the scanty wage data we have collected would be needed to advance our understanding of this issue.

THREE *Migrations*

Thus far we have only concerned ourselves with the origin and evolution of the differences in the propensity to hire female teachers in two of the oldest regions, the South and the Northeast, and particularly New England within the Northeast. We paid no special attention to the Middle Atlantic region. And we glanced at the Midwest only in order to show that characteristic features of midcentury southern life—especially high fertility and low age of marriage—were only associated with low proportions of women teachers in the South.

We turn now to other regions of the country, in order to show that patterns established in New England and in the southeastern states migrated with the settlers to other parts of the continent. First we broadly delineate the teaching patterns in the Middle Atlantic region and in the Midwest, and then we focus intensively on a case study of the Illinois teaching patterns.

THE MIDDLE ATLANTIC

In the third major region of original settlement, the Middle Atlantic, women teachers were neither as prevalent as in New England nor as rare as in the South. We concentrate on New York and Pennsylvania. The migration of New Englanders was a noteworthy factor in the history of both states, but especially in New York, from the last decades of the colonial era until well into the nineteenth century. In the national sample drawn from the 1850 census, high proportions of older New Yorkers had been born in New England—35 to 40 percent of those who had come of age between 1790 and 1820, and quite possibly more in earlier years (table 3.1). Among the other large group, those born in New York state itself, there would have been many individuals of New England ancestry. The

TABLE 3.1 Place of Birth of Rural New Yorkers in 1850, by Age

Age in 1850	Age 20–29 in	Percentage Born				N
		New York	New England	Other States	Abroad	
20–29	1850	73	5	3	20	4,132
30–39	1840	67	8	3	22	2,738
40–49	1830	65	14	5	16	1,947
50–59	1820	57	23	6	15	1,326
60–69	1810	45	36	6	12	729
70–79	1800	44	39	7	10	315
80+	−1790	43	41	7	9	125

Source: IPUMS 1850. Rural places were unincorporated or with populations of under 2,500. This definition is more restrictive than the one used to exclude the 98 largest cities in earlier tables, which often compared New England patterns (or patterns in New England and the Middle Atlantic) to those elsewhere. In New England, "towns" included countryside and urban areas, and eliminating people who lived in New England "towns" with populations over 2,500 would remove many residents of rural areas. The rural restriction has little effect; for all New Yorkers, the percentages born in New England in the four oldest cohorts were respectively 21, 33, 35, 38.

very similar teaching patterns that we observed in New York and New England (tables 1.1 and 1.2), then, may well have had their source in the migration of New Englanders.

We can say little of the patterns of teaching among the early New Yorkers who did not come from New England, and little about the extent to which women were used as teachers before 1840. The Dutch may have supported the dame school much as New Englanders had done and thereby encouraged the use of women as teachers for the young. Dame schools "were common in Holland at the time of American colonization," according to the most careful student of the Dutch schools of New Netherland. However, there is no direct evidence that such schools existed in the colony itself; "a confession of discreet ignorance seems the wisest course."[1] And so we must suggest an equally discreet silence concerning dame schools as well as other sources for female schoolteaching among the early English settlers in New York.

The migration of New Englanders, in any case, is a parsimonious explanation for the similarity of schooling patterns related to the prevalence of female teachers in the countryside of 1840. On the other hand, the nature of public support for schools differed in New York and New England before the Civil War. New Yorkers supplemented public monies with parental con-

1. William Heard Kilpatrick, *The Dutch Schools of New Netherlands and Colonial New York* (Washington, D.C., 1912 [New York, 1969]), 110–11, 173, 189.

TABLE 3.2 Women Teachers in Selected Pennsylvania Counties

Year	Percentage of Women among Teachers	
	Northernmost Counties	Southernmost Counties
1837	55	14
1861	68	26

Source: Annual state school reports; included are the 9 counties bordering on New York and the 10 counties bordering on Maryland.

Note: N of teachers in first row cells > 900; all other cells N > 2,000.

tributions (rate bills) that provided half of the total expenditures in 1840 and a third of the total in the 1850s. There was also no energetic state superintendent's office in New York quite comparable to the one in Massachusetts. Similarities between New England and New York throughout the antebellum years, then, did not result from school financing arrangements or from reforming state administrators like Horace Mann. Only a few intermittent and halfhearted experiments had been made with centralized educational administrators in New York state (a superintendent of common schools in the late 1810s, an official responsible for the school reports in the secretary of state's office thereafter, and county superintendents of schools for a few years in the 1840s).[2]

In Pennsylvania, the northeastern counties known as the Wyoming Valley were settled by migrants from Connecticut. From these counties, and presumably from across the border in New York state, migrants moved into the northern tier of counties in western Pennsylvania as well. This migration history is important because the state's northernmost tier of counties was notably different from the rest of the state in hiring teachers (as well as in other matters of schooling).[3] In 1837, when systematic data begin, the percentage of female teachers in the northernmost tier of Pennsylvania counties was 55 percent (table 3.2). For the remainder of the state, the percentage was 24 percent. In the tier of nine southernmost counties, women comprised only 14 percent of the common schoolteachers.

2. Samuel S. Randall, *A Digest of the Common School System of the State of New York* (Albany, 1844), 83; and Thomas E. Finegan, *Free Schools: A Documentary History of the Free School Movement in New York State* (New York, 1921 [1971]).

3. See, e.g., Lois Kimball Mathews, *The Expansion of New England: The Spread of New England Settlement and Institutions to the Mississippi River, 1620–1865* (Boston, 1909), 120–25, 145–69; J. P. Wickersham, *A History of Education in Pennsylvania* (Lancaster, Pa., 1886 [New York, 1969]).

Some aspects of Pennsylvania's experience with schoolteaching, then, reflect migration from New England and perhaps later from New York. It is difficult to find direct evidence of female teachers among the many other cultural groups in the state. One partial exception is the Quakers, who may also have utilized many women teachers at a relatively early date. As Joan Jensen has argued, the Quakers stressed that the inner light was no less available to women than to men, and the tradition of permitting women to preach probably led directly to the use of women teachers. Slight evidence also suggests that in the seventeenth and early eighteenth centuries, the dame school was prevalent among this group.[4] On the other hand, areas of principal Quaker settlement do not show as high a fraction of women teachers as the northern tier of the state's counties. In 1837, in the three counties with the largest concentration of Quakers—Delaware, Chester, and Bucks—female teachers comprised 20 percent, 20 percent, and 22 percent respectively of the common schoolteachers, not quite equal to the prevalence of women teachers in all counties below the northern tier described above (24 percent), and well below the percentage within that northern tier (55 percent). The showing for the Quaker counties was more impressive in 1861, with 44 percent, 58 percent, and 38 percent respectively; whereas 34 percent of all teachers in counties below the northern tier were women in that year. However, within the northern tier itself, 68 percent of teachers were then women. Possibly the pattern of hiring women as teachers was not as developed among the Quakers as in New England; possibly the prevalence of other groups within the same counties as the Quakers masks the Quaker pattern.[5]

THE MIDWEST

We observed at the outset (table 1.1) that in parts of the Midwest the prevalence of female teachers was already very great by 1860; in the most northerly states of Michigan, Wisconsin, and Minnesota, 86

4. Wickersham, *Education in Pennsylvania;* Thomas Woody, *Early Education in Pennsylvania* (New York, 1920 [1969]); Joan M. Jensen, *Loosening the Bonds: Mid-Atlantic Farm Women, 1750–1850* (New Haven, Conn., 1986), chap. 10.

5. Wickersham, *Education in Pennsylvania;* Woody, *Early Education in Pennsylvania;* Jensen, *Loosening the Bonds,* chap. 10. Counties with the largest density of Quakers can be determined from the 1850 census survey of churches and their accommodations. The prevalence of female teachers in the Quaker counties may have been exceptionally low in the state school reports of 1837 because the denomination maintained its own schools. However, by 1860 the teachers would probably have entered the common school system (see Jensen).

TABLE 3.3 Settlers in the Midwestern States, 1860

	Birthplace of State's Residents	
State	New England and New York (thousands)	The South (thousands)
Michigan	229	6
Wisconsin	175	6
Minnesota	40	3
Iowa	71	49
Ohio	129	133
Indiana	44	152
Illinois	188	166
Missouri	23	271

Source: 1860 census.

percent of the sampled rural teachers were women. Further south, the percentage of women teachers was lower, 58 percent for the region's seven other states. The lowest percentage in the region was found in rural Missouri.[6]

As table 3.3 shows, this pattern follows the pattern of migration of settlers from different parts of the country. The northern tier of midwestern states, settled especially by New Englanders and New Yorkers and almost not at all by Southerners, had the highest fraction of female teachers. Missouri, settled principally by Southerners, had the lowest fraction of female teachers. And the states in the middle zone of the Midwest, with many settlers from both regions, fell between these two extremes in the prevalence of female teachers.

Moreover, within the middle zone of midwestern states, we know that Southerners predominated in the southern parts of the states, Northerners in the northern parts. A wealth of local histories describe these patterns, and U.S. census reports confirm them (table 3.4).[7] These patterns of settlement are crucial to any explanation of the geographical variations in the pattern of female teachers in the Midwest. Where migrants from New England and New York settled, the teachers were principally women; where

6. Our sample of Missouri teachers is quite small (sixty-seven in rural areas), but the finding is supported by U.S. Office of the Census, *Ninth Census*, table XVII A and B.

7. R. Jensen, *Illinois*; Richard Lyle Power, *Planting Corn Belt Culture: The Impress of the Upland Southerner and Yankee in the Old Northwest* (Indianapolis, 1953). Unfortunately, the data are not available in published reports on the county level before 1870, and then only for selected states.

TABLE 3.4 Teaching and Social Origins of Settlers in Selected Counties of Ohio, Indiana, and Illinois

A. Birthplaces of Inhabitants, by County of Residence (1870)

	States of Birth	
State and Counties of Residence	New York (thousands)	Selected Southern States (thousands)
Ohio		
Northernmost	44	7
Southernmost	8	54
Indiana		
Northernmost	10	2
Southernmost	2	24
Illinois		
Northernmost	65	2
Southernmost	3	17

B. Women Teachers by County Groups

		Percentage of Women among Teachers	
State	Year	Northernmost Counties	Southernmost Counties
Ohio	1838	59	39
	1860	61	42
Indiana	1859	42	14
Illinois	1858	55	24

Source: Panel A: U.S. Census reports for 1870. County-level data on state of birth were first published in 1870, but only for selected states of birth. The number of northern and southern counties respectively are as follows: Ohio, 1838, 8 and 10; Ohio, 1860, 22 and 18; Indiana, 7 and 12; Illinois, 22 and 24.

Panel B: Annual state school reports.

Note: N of teachers in cells > 600 in Ohio, 1838, and southern Indiana; all other cells N > 1,500.

migrants from the South settled, far fewer teachers were women. Table 3.4 shows the remarkable consistency of this pattern across the northernmost and southernmost tier of counties in Ohio, Indiana, and Illinois. In Illinois, for example, 55 percent of the teachers in the northern tier of counties (excluding Chicago's Cook County) were women; in the southern tier of counties, 23 percent were women.

We have tried to explain the differing histories of New England and the South in their use of the female teacher, and we have now noted the migration of regionally distinct patterns into the Midwest. The next section continues the story of regional differences by exploring much more closely the sources of the regional differences within one state of the Midwest.

SOCIAL STRUCTURE, SETTLERS' ORIGINS, AND THE
PREVALENCE OF FEMALE TEACHERS: ILLINOIS, 1860

Illinois has often been noted as the example par excellence of a midwestern state in which settlers of diverse regional origins settled, creating differences in local social conditions. For example, in *Battle Cry of Freedom*, James McPherson describes Ohio, Indiana, and Illinois in 1850:

> Most of the initial settlers there had come from the upper South and Penn-sylvania. They populated the southern part of the region and evolved a corn-hog-whiskey economy, selling their small surplus in markets accessible by the Ohio-Mississippi river network. . . . They remained rural, south-ern, and localist in orientation, hostile to the "Yankees" who settled the northern portions of these states made accessible by the Erie Canal after 1825. These Yankees established a wheat-cattle-sheep-dairy economy linked to eastern markets by a burgeoning rail network after 1850. The railroads and the rapidly multiplying banks, industries, towns and cities . . . caused these parts of the states to grow faster. [I]n 1850 . . . the Yankee areas [of Illinois] positively correlated with the production of wheat, cheese and wool, with farm value per acre and the percentage of improved land, the value of farm machinery, banks, and pro-bank sentiment, urbaniza-tion, population growth, schools, literacy, Congregational and Presbyte-rian churches, and temperance and anti-slavery societies . . . Yankee coun-ties voted Whig, and after 1854 Republican.[8]

The mix of cultural and structural factors that McPherson mentions cre-ated the great split between parts of the state in the critical presidential election of 1860, with 68 percent of voters in the northern tier of counties, 60 percent in the central tier, and 24 percent in the southern tier supporting Lincoln. And this sectional divide again showed up a very different cultural domain when it came to deciding whether to hire women teachers: 55 per-cent of the teachers in the northern tier were women, whereas 41 percent in the central tier and only 24 percent in the southern tier were women.

Our goal here is to go beyond the observation that local conditions varied across the state and to try to understand which of the myriad of local charac-teristics really mattered most in creating and sustaining the dramatic differ-ences in the percentage of female teachers. The percentage of the presiden-tial vote cast for Lincoln, for example, is significantly correlated with the percentage of teachers who were women across the hundred counties of

---

8. James McPherson, *Battle Cry of Freedom: The Civil War Era* (New York, 1988), 31.

the state ($r = .26$; $p > .01$). However, the association exists because voting for Lincoln and hiring female teachers were related to the same cluster of outlooks and social conditions, not because one of these patterns directly influenced the other. Once we take into account several powerful determinants of the prevalence of female teachers across Illinois (discussed later in this chapter), the association observed between the Lincoln vote and the prevalence of female teachers drops to trivial levels.

On the basis of our preceding analysis, we are especially interested in the possibility that settlers' origins, as Yankees or Southerners, helped determine the gender of the teacher in an area; as we shall see, that issue is central to understanding the social reality of Illinois. As such, we will be asking whether or not the observed relationship between states of origin and the percentage of female teachers remains important even after we take into account as many other factors as we possibly can.

Published state school reports from 1858 provide us with the number of male and female teachers hired in each of Illinois's ninety-nine counties, as well as the wages of the teachers of each sex. The unpublished census reports for 1860 give us the female-to-male wage ratio in the agricultural economy (the same source used in chap. 2 for this ratio); and published census reports give us information on the child-woman ratio and some (if imperfect) data on educational levels. Specifically, the educational information (from the 1850 census) includes the proportion of women among adult illiterates and the proportion of girls among all schoolchildren. Because this last proportion includes all school attenders from the youngest ages as well as those in their late teens, it understates the gender gap at the later levels, but it is all we have at the county level.

The major difference between this analytic strategy and that used in the preceding chapter is that we have also gathered information on many other social characteristics of each county from mid-nineteenth-century census reports, and we control for these additional social characteristics as well— over a score of them (table 3.5). These social characteristics include measures of agricultural crops, livestock, and other farming practices (e.g., percentage of farmland placed under cultivation or otherwise "improved") and the degree of industrialization and urbanization as well as county population density and rapidity of population growth over the preceding decade in each region.

Concentrations of population may have influenced schooling in these areas in ways that affected the prevalence of female teachers. The most straightforward possibility—that towns permitted graded schools, in which

TABLE 3.5 Explaining the Percentages of Women among Teachers across Illinois Counties, 1858

A. Percentage of Women among Teachers	
Northern tier of counties	54.9
Southern tier of counties	23.7
Observed difference in percentage points	31.2

B. Results of the Multiple Regression Analysis (from appendix)

Predictors of the Difference in Percentage Points	Percentage Point Difference Accounted for by These Factors
1. All measures taken together (15 measures in the model)	29.4
2. County economic characteristics (6 measures)	5.9
3. Population concentration (4 measures)	8.0
4. Both kinds of measures together (rows 2, 3; 10 measures)	13.9
5. Fertility rate and education, esp. women's prevalence among the literate (3 measures)	3.4
6. Economy, population, fertility, and education (rows 2, 3, 5; 13 measures)	17.2
7. Settlers' origins (2 measures)	12.1

women were assigned to the lower grades—was probably of minimal importance in the Illinois of 1860 (judging, e.g., from the figures on graded schools listed in school reports later in the century). However, it is possible that the hiring of teachers was done on a more systematic basis here than in the rural areas because an administrative unit was hiring teachers in quantity and as such was more sensitive to arguments about systematic savings that could be incurred by hiring women. Also, it is possible that the demand for relatively educated male labor was greater in the villages and towns than in the countryside; and possibly, too, more of these relatively educated male workers in the villages and towns could work year-round and did not seek a fill-in occupation in a down season, as in the countryside. It is also possible that simply more "enlightened" opinion obtained in the villages and towns than in the open country, because the former were more in touch with views gaining favor in urban areas, such as the view that hiring female teachers was wise. All these considerations lead to the expectation of a positive association between population concentration and the prevalence of female teachers.

Most or all of the social characteristics on which we have gathered information might have influenced the value of female time compared to male time; if our measure of wages, the female-to-male wage ratio in agriculture, reflected those relative values perfectly, we would not need the other controls in order to measure the relative value of female time. However, in fact, that measure is an astonishingly poor predictor of the prevalence of female teachers. We cannot tease out why the measure works so poorly in this analysis. This puzzle is the more glaring since the female-to-male wage ratio in teaching was clearly related to the proportion of female teachers across the Illinois counties. And, as one would expect, that female-to-male wage ratio in teaching was in turn related to variations in the crop mix, urbanization, and other county-level characteristics—but the gender ratio of wages in teaching is unrelated to the gender ratio of wages in agriculture in Illinois.

Why the female-to-male wage ratio in agriculture, by contrast, is so poorly related on the one hand to the county-level structural characteristics and, on the other, to the proportion of female teachers and to the female-to-male wage ratio in teaching is the puzzle. Perhaps for some reason the quality of the data is poorer in Illinois (although the one test we could make of data quality did not indicate such a problem). In any case, given the uselessness of the female-to-male wage ratio in agriculture, we are well advised not to ignore a range of socioeconomic characteristics in the state. Also, some of these controls, such as the degree of urbanization, may have influenced the nature of hiring in other ways, such as by affecting the organization of schools.

For information on the origins of settlers we are unfortunately obliged to rely on published county-level data from 1870. Moreover, even in 1870, the Census Office only published partial county-level information on settlers, listing only the number of settlers from selected states of origin. Nevertheless, this information made it possible to construct an estimate of all settlers' origins or, more precisely, to estimate for each county the proportion of American-born migrants from other states that had come from New England or New York, and the proportion that had come from the South. Appendix 3 describes the estimation process.

What is important to stress here is that the measure of settlers' origins is crude, but not so much because it involves estimation nor because the data pertain to 1870 and not to 1860. Rather there is a certain conceptual limitation to the measure. The residents of Illinois in 1860 included many early settlers who arrived between 1820 and 1850, but they included many others as well, including the children of these early settlers. By 1860, whatever outlooks the settlers from the Northeast and Southeast had brought into Illinois had been interacting for decades with local structural conditions to create new social amalgams—especially in the southern part of the state, which was settled earlier than most others.[9]

We have divided the state, for analytical purposes, into a northern tier of twenty-four counties, a southern tier of twenty-four counties, and a central tier of fifty-one counties; we omit Chicago's Cook County from the northern tier, since we are not concerned with large cities. The settlers' origins differed dramatically across these tiers: by our estimates, 2.1 percent of the American-born migrants to Illinois in the northernmost tier of counties had come from the South, compared to 57.9 percent in the southernmost tier. Similarly, 47.1 percent of the American-born migrants in the northernmost tier had come from New England or New York, but only 9.1 percent in the southernmost tier.

In the northern tier, the average county had 225 teachers; in the central tier, 176 teachers; and in the southern tier, only 78 teachers. In the northern tier (as we noted earlier), 55 percent of the teachers were women; in the central tier, 41 percent; and in the southern tier, 24 percent. The consistency of the gender pattern is striking. If we divide the ninety-nine counties into quartiles according to the prevalence of female teachers in each, only two counties in the top quartile are found in the southern two-thirds of the state, and only four counties in the bottom quartile are found in the northern two-thirds of the state.[10]

How much of this stark contrast in the prevalence of women teachers across the state could we explain? Since the structural characteristics of the state are highly associated with the origins of the settlers, with Southerners concentrated in the southernmost tier and Yankees in the northernmost tier, we find that both measures of structural characteristics and of settlers' origin explain much of the variation in the prevalence of female teachers across the counties of the state. Eventually (as described in app. 3) we narrowed down our multivariate work to a small number of powerful measures of social structure—powerful in the sense that they were highly correlated with the prevalence of female teachers. These include economic factors, the concentration of population, the child-woman ratio, the relative prevalence

9. The state had been settled first in the south, with settlers moving west from the upper South, and then from the North, with settlers moving southward from the counties bordering Lake Michigan.

10. Moreover, all six of these exceptional counties are found in the middle third of the state, not in the northern- or southernmost sections.

of female-to-male education, and settlers' origins. Nevertheless, when these are all taken into account simultaneously, settlers' origins continued to exert an important independent impact on the gender pattern in teaching across the state's counties, indeed with as large a share of the entire difference as all the other explanatory factors together.

More specifically, the proportions of women teachers in the northernmost and southernmost tiers of counties were separated by a gap of 31.2 percentage points (54.9 percent vs. 23.7). The values produced in our fullest model would yield an estimated gap of 28.7 percentage points, the remaining 2.6 percentage points of the actual gap remaining unexplained. Of this "explained" gap of 28.7 percentage points, 5.3 percentage points were associated with the economic factors, 6.8 points with the differences in the concentration of population, 2.4 with fertility differences and the differences in women's education—and 14.2 percentage points with settlers' origins.

Does this analysis untangle a complex of socioeconomic and cultural factors that in fact developed closely together? We are far from satisfied that it does so adequately. On the one hand, both structural measures and measures of settlers' origins themselves are poor. And the interpretation of these results is ambiguous. The differences across the state that are "associated" with settlers' origins, even after the other factors have been taken into account, could simply reflect the inadequacy of our measures of structural differences between the northern and southern tiers of Illinois counties.

On the other hand, the association between economic variables and the prevalence of female teachers is open to a similar line of critique. Consider, for example, the strong connection between counties that produced cheese and butter and counties with high proportions of female teachers. The relative demand for women's time was probably higher where dairy farming was important: "the making of butter and cheese . . . was the duty of the women on the farm."[11] The most straightforward prediction based on a theory of the relative value of women's time therefore would be that the prevalence of female teachers was lower where dairy farming was developed. However, the mean production of dairy products by tier serves as a warning that the reality may well have been far more complex. Cheese production was in fact much more common in the northern tier of counties, just where schoolteachers were most likely to be women, than in the other

---

11. Bidwell and Falconer, *History of Agriculture*, 424. These authors also noted, "Milking by women was, however, becoming less customary." Also Goldin and Sokoloff mention dairy products as less open to women's work than cotton.

two tiers, and butter production weakly reflected the same northern dominance.

Perhaps, then, the demand for women, relative to men, was high on dairy farms but seasonal—in a way that did not much interfere with the relatively short schoolteaching terms. Or perhaps these activities could be restricted to times of the day in ways that might allow a teacher to contribute to cheese production when she returned home from schoolteaching. But it would still be necessary to understand not merely why dairy production was not a hindrance to women's teaching but why the correlation between dairy production and the prevalence of women teaching was strongly positive.

The dairy farming example underscores the point that knowing the demand for women's time relative to men's in certain farm activities (including its reflection in the relative wage of women in certain farm areas compared to others) may contribute but little to understanding patterns of schoolteaching—either because any number of other factors were more important or because the competing demands for women's time, while the most important consideration, operated in a manner too subtle for us to fully capture with the available measures.

In a similar way, our educational measures may also not reflect differences in the supply of teachers so much as more subtle complexes of cultural affinities. The supply hypothesis is that the proportion of women among the educated was lower in the southern tier of the state and therefore the supply of women for teaching, relative to men, was also lower in the southern tier. Unfortunately the measure of the supply of educated women that we used in the preceding chapter (the proportion of girls among those in school at ages sixteen through twenty) is not available to us at the county level, so we are forced to use two poorer measures, the proportion of girls among all schoolchildren and the proportion of women among the adult illiterates (which, respectively, we expect to be positively and negatively correlated with the proportion of women among teachers). The proportion of girls among schoolchildren, however, proves to be a useless measure (no doubt because most schoolchildren were younger than sixteen and, at most of the younger ages, boys and girls attended in about equal numbers across the state). However, the proportion of women among illiterates proves to be quite strongly correlated (negatively, as predicted) with the proportion of female teachers; and this conclusion is consistent with the supply hypothesis.

However, it also turns out, first, that women were a larger fraction of the illiterates in areas where illiteracy was high and a lower fraction of the illiterates in areas where illiteracy was low, and, second, that high illiteracy was associated with male teachers in the area (see the regression models presented in app. 3). And, finally, when the overall illiteracy rate is included in the regression analysis, this rate is much more strongly associated with the proportion of women among teachers than is the proportion of women among illiterates. Yet the overall illiteracy rate does not measure the supply of women relative to men who could teach. The overall illiteracy rate may be related to a complex of attitudes (and those attitudes were quite possibly in turn related to southern birth), rather than to the supply and demand factors that would determine the gender composition of the teacher workforce.

In sum, if we take the regression analysis at face value, there is a strong independent relationship between southern origins and the gender of the teacher that is consistent with this formulation: quite apart from any reasons related to the local economy, the nature of urbanization, or the relative levels of male and female education, areas in which southern settlers predominated were far less likely to have hired women for their teaching force than were areas in which Yankees settlers predominated. If, by contrast, we are skeptical of the measures in the regression analysis, the skepticism should extend not only to the way we have captured the independent power of settlers' origins on local decisions about hiring women teachers but also to some of the economic and demographic factors most relevant to the competing explanation for the pattern of local decisions.

██

At the end of the preceding chapter, we concluded that the large differences in the prevalence of female teachers observed between New England and the South in 1860 could not be explained by differences in the social structure, demography, or gender wage ratios in the two regions. We suggested that, at least by 1860, differences in the internal institutional development of schools and probably in long-established norms (about schools and perhaps about women's work generally) must be called on if we are to explain the regional difference in the prevalence of female teachers. The analysis of the midwestern states supports this latter interpretation. Across the Midwest, the prevalence of female teachers was associated with the prevalence of Yankee rather than southern settlers, and the same seems to have been true in the middle band of eastern states, especially Pennsylvania. Could the broader social-structural, demographic, and wage-ratio factors where Yankees settled have been the same as those in New England and New York? Could those factors have been the same as in Virginia or Alabama, where Southerners settled? And could those factors then be the reason we see the migration of hiring patterns in schooling? This suggestion hardly seems likely on commonsense grounds and is in fact contradicted by our intensive analysis of the Illinois experience.

Note, finally, that this conclusion also reinforces our previous analysis of the early and midcentury patterns back East, in the regions from which Yankee and southern settlers eventually migrated. If the social-structural, demographic, and wage ratio characteristics of the new areas cannot explain the hiring patterns there, that finding adds weight to our earlier suggestion that the same was true in New England and the South. To put the matter positively, if settlers had left the Northeast with different views about school arrangements and female teachers than those with which settlers left the South, and those differing views shaped midwestern schools, that is all the more reason to think that those differing views had also helped to shape the schools in the eastern regions from which the settlers had come.

F O U R   *Explaining Feminization*

Regional legacies can explain why teaching became feminized more rapidly in some places than others. However, regional legacies cannot explain why feminization was occurring in every region of the United States during the last half of the nineteenth century. In this chapter we turn from regional differences to patterns common across the country, to factors that led to feminization in every region. The first section of this chapter considers the unique impact of the Civil War on the course of feminization. The second surveys the evolution of feminization during the half century between the Civil War and First World War.

The later sections of this chapter are concerned with explanations for feminization, focusing especially on the Midwest and South in the second half of the nineteenth century; however, much of the discussion is also relevant to the Northeast, several decades earlier, when that region underwent the crucial steps in the feminization of schoolteaching. The third section concerns the impact of population concentration in urban areas—particularly the crucial role of graded schools. Where graded schools could be established, in the towns and cities of every region, feminization triumphed early and completely. However, as shown in the fourth section, much of the feminization of schoolteaching after 1860 occurred in the rural areas of the United States, in ungraded schools. The fifth section assesses a more subtle theory (which we call the Tyack-Strober thesis) concerning the sources of rural feminization: that certain changes in rural school organization made teaching less attractive to young men than to young women. We are skeptical of this thesis, and we then offer our own effort to explain rural feminization across the country; in the Northeast this pattern occurred in an accelerated way on the basis of the earlier two-tier system, but everywhere it occurred sooner or later.

THE IMPACT OF THE CIVIL WAR

The Civil War created unprecedented opportunities for women in teaching. Whether male teachers left to fight, or whether they left to take the jobs of men who were fighting, the departure of males from teaching during the Civil War meant that many school boards that had not hired women (or not hired them for the winter session schools) were now obliged to do so, at least for a time. Typically, the effect of the war was therefore to create a sharp surge in the percentage of female teachers between 1861 and 1865. Then, in some states, part of this gain for feminization was lost between 1865 and 1870. Nevertheless, all these states sustained some gain from the war years. Other states did not show any regression from the 1865 high or, in any case, made it up again by 1870.

We have good evidence of the war's effect from about a dozen states, states that reported the gender composition of their teaching forces for some years before the Civil War and then during or after the war as well. This evidence is presented in appendix table A4.5; for comparison, the table also presents the percentage of women teachers in these states at five-year intervals during the period 1870–1915. These percentages are drawn from the U.S. commissioner of education reports that began to provide such information in 1870. Since the early data come from state reports, and the later data from the national reports, there are no doubt inconsistencies in the way the percentages of female teachers were calculated (e.g., does a particular percentage include all who filled teaching slots in the summer and winter sessions, or does it include the much lower number of different individuals who taught during the school year?). Nevertheless, the state and federal time series are in fact quite consistent, as can be seen by comparing the percentage of female teachers for 1870 that is reported for both series.

In twelve of the thirteen northern states for which we have evidence, the percentage of female teachers rose by at least 10 percentage points during the decade 1860–70. At the same time, only in six of the thirteen states—Maine, New Hampshire, Pennsylvania, Indiana, Michigan, and Iowa—was the rise during the war years so large that it was never equaled during any other five-year interval. In Indiana, for example, the percentage of female teachers rose from 20 percent to 47 percent in the five years of the war and then dropped back only to 40 percent by 1870; in Pennsylvania, the percentage of women among teachers rose from 37 percent to 61 percent during the war and had dropped back only to 54 percent in 1870. In the eight states in which the effect of the war was large but not unique, gains in feminization of teaching between 1860 and 1870 were certainly impressive; however it is hard to say just how much of the gain was due to the war, since there were gains of roughly comparable magnitude in the preceding years as well. Thus in Connecticut, the percentage of female teachers rose sharply from 52 percent to 68 percent in 1852–56; then during the war, it rose from 69 percent to 82 percent. Perhaps evidence that much more than the war was involved is the fact that in 1870 the state had not dropped back at all from the 1865 level of 82 percent. Similarly, in Massachusetts, the percentage of female teachers rose from 66 percent in 1847 to 72 percent in 1850, and to 78 percent in 1855; by 1865 it had climbed only another 8 percent, and by 1870, instead of slipping back, the percentage of female teachers had risen slightly to 88 percent. The Massachusetts pattern might suggest that as the percentage of female teachers rose to very high levels, the difference that the Civil War could make was necessarily smaller. This suggestion seems especially true for the dramatic spurts we noted in connection with Pennsylvania and Indiana. Such spurts were unknown in wartime New England.

On the whole, however, it seems best to say that the effect of the war was notable everywhere, and that it had a uniquely great effect in some states, in which the percentage of female teachers rose by 20 percentage points or more. In most states, the effect was to raise the percentage of female teachers by a smaller but still significant amount. In many of these states, especially where Yankees comprised a large fraction of the population, the effect of the war was felt in the context of a longer term shift toward feminization, and the changes in the war decade are therefore noticeable but not dramatically discontinuous with the long-term shifts.

Nevertheless, the magnitude of a 10 percentage-point shift, even if not unique, should be appreciated in the context of school arrangements in which the summer session was already typically reserved for women teachers. For example, we noted that in Connecticut the war increased the percentage of female teachers from 69 percent to 82 percent. However, in Connecticut, well over nine in ten summer session teachers were women before the war. Fortunately, the Connecticut state school reports allow us to distinguish the impact of the war on the summer and winter sessions separately. In 1860, 91 percent of the summer session teachers were women; in 1865, 95 percent. However, in the winter session, women were 48 percent of the teachers in 1860 and 69 percent of the teachers in 1865. Thus even where the effect of the war was not unique, and even where its effect was limited to a change of some 10 percentage points in the total teaching force, the effect of such a shift could easily mean a substantial gain—a shift in one of five or six teachers—within the winter session, where resistance to feminization had been greatest. The importance of such a change in stimulating the diffusion of a new norm, a perception that the female teacher was an acceptable teacher, must have been great. Even if the effect of the war was not unique within particular states, its overall effect—bringing so much sustained change to so many places in the same short period of time—certainly was unique.

At the same time, the fact that the shift could be so great and that so much of the effect was sustained rather than erased after 1865 also suggests that there was a certain fit between the effect of the wartime shock to the system and the social and cultural conditions on the eve of the war. Large gains for female machinists during World War II, after all, were not sustained after 1945.

The effect of the war in the absence of a welcoming cultural and socioeconomic context can be seen in the case of the one southern state for which we have systematic data prior to 1870, North Carolina. We noted in chapter 2 that North Carolina had accepted substantial public support for schools in the 1840s and a secretary of education in the 1850s; its school system had grown rapidly by 1860. Yet on the eve of the war only 9 percent of its teaching force was female. During the war years, the North Carolina schools had been obliged to accept female teachers to remain open at all; by 1865 those schools that still did remain open (about half the prewar number, it appears) were taught in almost equal numbers by male and female teachers. But a large part of this gain was erased in the years after the war: by 1870, the percentage of women among public schoolteachers in the state had dropped back to 27 percent. There was less of a tradition of women teachers and less of a male-female salary differential for teachers in the South; these factors help to explain why the impact of the war changes were not sustained more fully in North Carolina.[1]

---

1. In proportional terms, the slippage in the percentage of female teachers in North Carolina between 1865 and 1870 amounted to 56 percent of the gain: from 9 percent in 1860 to some 50 percent in 1865 to 27 percent in 1870 ($50 - 9 = 41$ points gained by 1865, $50 - 27 = 23$ points lost by 1870; $23/41 = 56$ percent). Only in Ohio among the northern states was there any comparable pattern (see table A4.5). In the twelve other northern states for which we have relevant data, the extent of the slippage in proportional terms was much lower.

THE COURSE OF FEMINIZATION IN SCHOOLTEACHING: 1870–1915

In the half century after the Civil War, the female teacher came to predominate in the elementary schooling of the nation. The clearest measures of this trend are found in the annual reports of the United States commissioner of education, which began to note the gender of teachers in each state in 1870. We have analyzed these reports for five-year intervals between 1870 and 1915, by which point feminization of elementary school-teaching had all but reached its all-time high (and after which time the relevant reports are less useful). Table 4.1 shows how each region evolved toward this norm of nearly universal female teaching. The regional differences discussed in the two preceding chapters continued to shape the feminization of schoolteaching until well into the twentieth century.

Relatively little change occurred in the prevalence of female teachers in New England after 1870, because the prevalence achieved by that date had already been so great. In 1870, 82 percent of New England's public school teachers were women; forty-five years later the figure had risen by only 9 percentage points. The extent of feminization in New York state was almost as high as in New England, with 77 percent female teachers in 1870 and 89 percent in 1915.

In the other Middle Atlantic states, however, the pattern of change was more dramatic. Female teachers had been less prevalent, and their numbers now rose more rapidly than in the states further north. In Pennsylvania, for example, only 57 percent of the teachers had been women in 1870; by 1915, the figure had risen to 78 percent. By 1915, then, while some evi-

TABLE 4.1 Percentage of Female Teachers in the United States, by Region: 1870–1915

| Year | Percent of Female Teachers in Each Region | | | | |
	New England	Mid-Atlantic	Midwest	South	West
1870	82	69	57	33	60
1875	81	68	48	29	55
1880	81	66	58	35	60
1885	84	73	60	36	66
1890	88	76	68	46	69
1895	88	78	70	50	70
1900	89	78	72	55	75
1905	91	83	78	63	80
1910	91	84	81	69	82
1915	91	84	82	73	82

dence of the historical legacy of difference between Pennsylvania and New England–New York could still be found, the differences were much more muted than they had been earlier.

The same points may be made about the Midwest. The region continued to be characterized by much the same divisions as earlier in the century, with Michigan and Wisconsin hiring women for over 70 percent of their teachers as early as 1870, and Missouri reaching that level only in 1905. But overall, the percentage of female teachers in the Midwest rose by 25 percentage points during the years 1870–1915, whereas the comparable figure in New England was 9 percentage points and in New York state 12 percentage points, so that by the end of the era, the differences between the regions were less than half of what they had been in 1870.

The West emerged as a major region in its own right in these years, with a substantial population. The prevalence of women among teachers in the western states typically began at lower levels than in many other places, reflecting in all likelihood the prevalence of frontier conditions, including unequal sex ratios. However, virtually every western state rapidly reached high levels of feminization in teaching: four states reached the level of 75 percent women teachers by 1890, one more state in 1895, and three more states in 1905.[2] Throughout the period, the percentage of female teachers in the West was actually slightly higher than in the Midwest.

All in all, women accounted for four out of five public school teachers in every region of the country except the South by 1910, and for nine out of ten public school teachers in New England. The starkest regional contrast during the years 1870–1915 remained as before the contrast between the South and the rest of the country. As late as 1885, no more than 36 percent of the southern public school teachers were women. Thereafter, the prevalence of women among schoolteachers rose steadily, to 55 percent in 1900 and to 73 percent in 1915. By World War I, then, the predominance of the female teacher was clearly a fact of life in the South too. And yet even as late as 1915, the southern pattern still lagged somewhat behind that of the rest of the nation; the level of teacher feminization in the South in 1915 was below that which New England experienced in 1870. Nor was the difference due simply to the greater degree of urbanization in one region, as a glance at the largely rural area of northern New England shows: the level

2. One other reached that level by 1910. Only New Mexico, with a distinct Spanish subculture, and Utah, with a distinct Mormon subculture, did not reach that level of feminization by 1915.

of teacher feminization in Maine in 1870 was 76 percent, in Vermont 84 percent, and in New Hampshire 85 percent—in each case above the level the South reached only in 1915.

Much of the change in the South appears to have come as part of the agitation for progressive reform of the southern educational system, especially in the quarter century after 1890. But these efforts, in the assessment of Lawrence Cremin, "remained sporadic and fluctuant until the late 1890s."[3] And, indeed, the extent of feminization in southern teaching shifted markedly in the years after 1895, and especially between 1900 and 1905. For example, at some time during the years 1870–1915, ten of the fourteen southern states experienced a single, rapid increase in the prevalence of female teachers—a rise of at least 10 percentage points within a five-year interval. In some states the magnitude of the rise was much higher still: from 37 percent to 70 percent in Alabama, from 52 percent to 79 percent in Louisiana, and from 57 percent to 77 percent in South Carolina. Of these ten large, rapid increases in the percentage of female teachers (each in a different state), one occurred between 1895 and 1900, six between 1900 and 1905, and one between 1905 and 1910.[4]

At the same time, the movement toward feminization of the teaching force in the South does appear to have been well underway, albeit on a more modest scale, well before the progressive reform movement of the century's end. In all the southern states except possibly Alabama and Louisiana, a never-reversed trend toward feminization is noticeable well before the late nineties—in fact in the early 1880s.

The late nineteenth-century history of southern public education and, in particular, of the changing role of southern women as teachers during that period surely needs more scholarly attention. Nevertheless, the early rise in the percentage of female teachers, well before the reform movements of the late nineties, seems comprehensible as part of a wider pattern of diffusion: even before the later waves of southern reform, changes in attitudes at the state and local levels were important.

In the preceding discussion, we have described the southern public school teachers as though there were one system of southern public schools, when in fact there were two: one white, one black. During the years immediately

---

3. Cremin, *American Education: The Metropolitan Experience,* 217.
4. Oklahoma began reporting data on the percentage of female teachers only late in the nineteenth century; the state has been excluded from the counts relating to individual states in this and the next paragraph, although not from the regional totals.

after 1870, the schools for black children came to be taught overwhelmingly by black teachers. Given the sharp differences rooted in custom, law, and funding arrangements between these school systems, it is striking just how similar levels of feminization of black and white teachers came to be. While the United States commissioner of education annual reports do not distinguish between white and black teachers, our sample data, drawn from the manuscript schedules of the U.S. censuses for 1860, 1880, and 1910, do allow us to observe the prevalence of women among white teachers and black teachers separately.

In 1860, the proportion of blacks among teachers had been trivial. In the South as well as in the North, they comprised perhaps 1 in 100 teachers.[5] Outside the South, this situation hardly changed during the half century after the war. In the North and West, blacks remained tiny fractions of the teaching force, reflecting both their small representation in the northern population and their social position; in 1910, for example, two nonwhites were found among 720 teachers in the northeastern states. However, within the South, the number of black teachers had risen to notable levels by 1880.[6] In both 1880 and in 1910, blacks comprised roughly a fifth of the teaching force of the South (20 percent in 1880, 17 percent in 1910). In both years they were also somewhat better represented among the urban teaching force (small as that sector was), perhaps because the black institutions in the towns and cities were more fully developed: in the South, 27 percent of urban teachers and 19 percent of rural teachers were black in 1880, 27 percent and 14 percent respectively in 1910.[7]

In terms of our interest, the most striking point about these black teachers of the South is that the percentage of women among them was almost identical to what it was among the southern white teachers: 52 percent for black teachers and 56 percent for white teachers in 1880, and 77 percent and 76 percent respectively in 1910—differences well within the range of sampling error.[8] At the same time, it is not difficult, even within the narrow

5. Based on the 1860 teacher sample.

6. One hundred twenty blacks were included in the 1880 teacher sample, and only slightly less (105) in the 1910 sample, numbers large enough to study in some detail.

7. These black teachers are found throughout the South, although in 1880 they seem to be more concentrated in a few states (Alabama, Georgia, and Mississippi) than the black population as a whole was, a pattern of concentration that reflected, perhaps, the uneven development of black education in the first decades after the Civil War.

8. Since the percentage of black teachers in urban areas was somewhat greater than for white teachers, and since urban teachers were more likely to be women than rural teachers, we might have expected, other things being equal, to find slightly more women among black

range of information available in the census, to find racial differences between the white and black teachers related to gender. Among southern
white women teachers, only 4 percent were married in 1880 and only
5 percent as late as 1910. Among southern black teachers, 13 percent were
married in 1880 and fully 22 percent in 1910—reflecting the general tendency of married black women to enter the paid labor force much more
often than white women did.[9]

SCHOOL ORGANIZATION: GRADED SCHOOLS

Schools that could be graded by pupil age were especially
likely to have women teachers. This connection between graded schools and
female teachers is the crucial link between school organization and feminization. Graded schools provided an organizational solution to the challenge
of disciplining the older boys at school: in a graded system, a very few male
teachers could work with the oldest classes, which included the difficult
older boys. Also, graded schools might solve a related curricular issue too.
If male teachers were, or were perceived to be, better trained academically
to handle the highest levels of the curriculum, graded schools could resolve
that issue too. Indeed, even a relatively small town might have an official
designated as the schools' administrator, and a violent youth could be re-
ferred to him. Finally, graded schools were most feasible in towns and cities,
and in towns and cities rebellious boys were less likely to remain in school
until late ages; they were at work (whereas there was less such work available during the rural winter). As a result, nearly all teachers in graded primary schools and high proportions of teachers in graded grammar schools
could be women.

Graded schools became universal in larger towns and cities. But even
in small towns and villages, and even in the countryside, in certain rural
townships, assigning pupils to different teachers according to academic level
could be arranged. Just how large, then, did a place have to be before it
could have graded schools? Annual state school reports reflect this fact; by
1880, fairly small places had graded schools of some sort. In both Illinois
and Iowa, for example, there is evidence that places of under 1,000 residents,

---

teachers than among white teachers. On the other hand, the percentage of urban teachers was
not so high within either group for the difference to affect the totals by much—by enough,
indeed, to expect the sample-size numbers to show the differences clearly.

9. These race differences in the percentage of married women teachers are not due to any
peculiarities of the samples, as they may be observed also in the published aggregate figures
of United States Bureau of the Census, *Twelfth Census of the United States.*

and many places of 1,000 to 4,000 residents, had graded schools. Indeed, in Illinois, it appears possible that some 26 percent to 40 percent of teachers in graded schools were actually in places of fewer than 1,000 residents (app. table A4.7). In Iowa, the most detailed report indicates that 30 percent of the teachers in graded schools were in such places (app. table A4.8), and that report (which lists graded teachers by community) may have been incomplete for the smallest communities.[10]

Graded schools depended on there being a large enough number of children in a small enough area to justify dividing the pupils among two or more teachers. In such a circumstance one teacher could concentrate on the higher grades, one on the lower. As population rose, even finer gradations by academic level (and hence by age) could be introduced. But how large a number of children was too much for one teacher? The number depended on the perceptions of contemporaries, and was probably fairly high—probably somewhere between 50 and 100 in most places. And the willingness to tolerate the larger numbers depended in part on how the community's decision makers viewed the future: did they think that the number of children needing schooling would be declining within a short time (e.g., as the local farm families grew a few years older), or did they think that the numbers would at least hold steady and perhaps increase (as more residents came into a village, town, or farming area). Moreover, another consideration figured as well: on the eve of a decision about graded schools, most places probably had school buildings meant to serve one teacher only. Such places faced the need to have a new building as well as an additional teacher. In such a situation, villages and farmers might elect to have all grades served in all

---

10. These numbers are in fact so large that they lead one to suspect a misunderstanding. It is possible that some communities were reporting as graded schools those in which a single teacher worked—but arranged her pupils' studies according to the gradations of work (a development described by historian Wayne Fuller). In any case, it also seems clear from the Iowa data that the graded schools in smaller communities often had relatively few teachers per school (see below). Perhaps for this reason, the largest communities in both states had somewhat more female teachers than the others. The crucial reason that graded schools could employ more women was that school boards believed that women could be assigned the lower grades, and a single male could be assigned the teaching and disciplining of the older grades. However, the percentages of women teachers that such a policy would produce depend on the number of women teachers in a school. If one male was to be hired to handle the older boys, a school with two teachers could have only 50 percent female teachers, a school with three teachers could have two-thirds female teachers—and a school with eight teachers could have 88 percent female teachers. In smaller communities, the total number of teachers per school may have been lower. A complicating trend was that high school teachers were more likely to have been male than teachers in the elementary grades.

parts of their community rather than face having their young children make a long trip to school. Alternatively, the population might be concentrated enough to accept the prospect that older children would have to travel across town, while several corners of the town (or rural township) offered instruction in the younger grades. In short, the nature of the area (the size and the quality of the roads in particular), the size of the local population, and the sensitivity to ideas of educational reform would all help to determine when a place would shift to graded schools.

The greater degree of feminization in graded compared to ungraded schools can be seen everywhere after the 1820s. Graded schools help explain the national trends in feminization because, as the country urbanized, more schools came to be graded schools and more teachers came to be women simply as a result of this shift.

THE EVIDENCE FOR RURAL FEMINIZATION

While urbanization unquestionably contributed to the feminization of schoolteaching, a great deal of the feminization process was simply not occurring in urban schools, or in any graded schools. A good example is Michigan, for which we have annual data for the later nineteenth century on the distribution of male and female teachers in graded and ungraded schools (see table 4.2). Between 1880 and 1910 the female share of teachers in the state increased from 71 percent to 86 percent—while the proportion of teachers in graded schools rose from 19 percent to 53 percent. It is true that the percent of women among teachers was greater in Michigan's graded schools than in its ungraded schools; however, the rise in the percentage of female teachers in the state came mainly from the increase of female teachers *within the ungraded schools;* three-fifths of the change was due to the increased hiring of women teachers in that sector, while less than a quarter of the total change was due to the large increase in the number of graded schools during the course of these three decades.

We can make the same point in a more systematic way with the help of our national samples of teachers drawn from the U.S. census manuscript schedules of 1860, 1880, and 1910. We should appreciate first of all the simple point that the majority of the American teaching force, like the majority of the population, was found in the rural areas. Our sample data allow us to distinguish those living in places with under 4,000 residents from the rest—and 83 percent of teachers in 1860, 76 percent in 1880, and 59 percent even in 1910 lived in such places. How much of the national changes in feminization was the result of developments in the rural areas (places of

TABLE 4.2 Feminization of Michigan's Ungraded and Graded Schools, 1880–1910

Type of School, Teachers	1880		1910	
	N	Percent Female	N	Percent Female
Ungraded				
Female	7,776	68.8	7,102	83.6
Male	3,526		1,395	
Total	11,302		8,497	
Graded				
Female	2,101	79.4	8,377	88.3
Male	546		1,113	
Total	2,647		9,490	
Total	13,949	70.8	17,987	86.1
Percent of teachers in ungraded schools	81.0		47.2	
Percent of teachers in graded schools	19.0		52.8	

Percent Female Teachers Expected in 1910 under Various Assumptions	
Shift to 1910 % of teachers in graded schools, 1880 % female in ungraded and in graded schools	74.4; rise of 3.6 (23.5% of actual rise)[a]
No shift from ungraded to graded, 1880 % female in ungraded, 1910 % female in graded	72.5; rise of 1.7 (11.1% of actual rise)[a]
No shift from ungraded to graded, 1910 % female in ungraded, 1880 % female in graded	80.2; rise of 9.4 (61.4% of actual rise)[a]

[a] Under these assumptions, the total rise in the percentage of female teachers in the Michigan public schools between 1880 and 1910 would have amounted to this much of the rise actually observed, namely the rise from 70.8% to 86.1%. Thus, the actual rise in the percentage of female teachers amounted to 15.3 percentage points (86.1 − 70.8 = 15.3) and, e.g., under the first assumption, the rise would have amounted to 3.6 percentage points, or 23.5% of the actual rise (3.6/15.3 = 23.5%).

under 4,000 in population)? We answer the question by decomposing the change in feminization into its rural and urban components. We can do this by calculating what the percentage of women teachers would have been in the United States as a whole in 1880, or 1910, had the percentage of women teachers increased from 1860 only in the urban areas. Between 1860 and 1910, the percentage of female teachers in our national samples increased from 64 percent to 81 percent. Yet had the percentage of female teachers in the rural areas remained unchanged, the increase would have been well below half as great, bringing the percentage of women teachers for the entire United States in 1910 to 71 percent.[11] Yet these results actually greatly

11. We reach this result by computing the percentage of female teachers in rural areas in 1860 multiplied by the number of teachers in rural areas in 1910, adding the percentage of

understate the degree of change in rural feminization and its impact on the national outcomes, because the results ignore huge regional population movements within rural America. The regions increasing their share of the rural American teacher population were the regions in which feminization had been lowest in 1860 (in particular the western regions).[12]

Thus suppose the percentage of women among rural teachers had remained the same in 1910 as it had been in 1860—within each region—and the relative size of each region had changed in the manner that it actually did change. Then the proportion of women among all rural teachers would actually have *declined* during the half century (from 61 percent to 55 percent) and the proportion of female teachers in the entire United States—rural and urban—would have increased only from 64 percent to 68 percent, instead of to 81 percent.[13]

The unmistakable conclusions, then, are that graded schools in urban areas stimulated feminization, but that considerable feminization was occurring in the rural areas as well. Our national sample does not tell us whether those rural teachers worked in the ungraded sector or not, of

---

female teachers in urban areas in 1910 multiplied by the number of teachers in urban areas in 1910, and dividing by the total number of teachers in 1910:

$$[(0.61 \times 1,441) + (0.86 \times 1,013)]/(1,441 + 1,013).$$

For the two decades 1860–80, a comparable calculation shows that the impact of change in the rural area is half the total change observed. But, as the text proceeds to argue, this measure actually understates the importance of rural change.

12. During the fifty years between 1860 and 1910, the fraction of the rural population within each major region of the country changed greatly. In 1860, 42 percent of the rural teacher population had been in the North, 24 percent in the South, and 34 percent in the West (including the Far West). By 1880 the North's share of the rural teachers had dropped sharply, and the West's share had risen sharply: 26 percent North, 23 percent South, 51 percent West. This pattern still held in 1910, although because the South was so much less urbanized than the other two regions, a higher fraction of the rural American teachers were found there by 1910: 20 percent in the North, 30 percent in the South, and 42 percent in the West.

13. Calculated as follows:

$$(\text{North } 0.75 \times 0.20) + (\text{South } 0.36 \times 0.30)$$
$$+ (\text{West } 0.65 \times 0.42) + (\text{Far West } 0.26 \times 0.07) = 0.55,$$

the expected proportion of female teachers in the rural U.S. in 1910, and

$$(0.55 \times 1,441) + (0.86 \times 1,013)/(1,441 + 1,013) = 0.68,$$

the expected proportion of female teachers in the entire U.S. in 1910.

Note also that for the sake of simplicity, in the text we speak of three regions only, including Far West in West; we also produced another estimate in which these calculations were performed within eight subregions of the United States, the seven subregions the Census Bureau designates for North, South, and Midwest, plus the small Far West region. The results of this refinement simply sharpened the point: the expected proportion female in rural America would fall from 0.55 to 0.53, and the expected proportion female for the entire United States would fall from 0.68 to 0.67.

course. But on this point the Michigan data are invaluable. In some places, the shift from ungraded schools to graded schools may have accounted for more of the feminization than it did in Michigan. But the Michigan data show us that there is no reason to assume that feminization was mainly a result of the shift from ungraded to graded. It was occurring in the truly rural, ungraded schools as well.

DIFFUSION OF BELIEFS: WOMEN'S ABILITIES AND WOMEN'S PAY

Throughout the nineteenth century, women almost everywhere received lower wages than men in teaching. Almost everywhere: everywhere in the urban graded systems, and apparently everywhere outside the South in the rural areas. The South, as we have seen, presents a more complicated exception. The early history of very low female-to-male wage ratios in rural teaching that characterized the rest of the country until at least the Civil War, and often very much later, did not extend to the South, where antebellum wage ratios, from the little evidence available (mostly from North Carolina), were about equal. Later, the wage ratios in other regions typically become somewhat less unequal, and wage ratios in the South seem to have drifted downward toward modestly more inequality than had existed before. We return to the case of the South at the end of this section; for now, we focus on other rural areas between roughly the 1850s and 1910, wherein women were paid less than men but were recruited for rural teaching less in the early years of this period than they would be by its end.

Described in this way, the puzzle concerning these areas can be restated: if employing women saved money, why did school boards persist in hiring relatively many men for decades? Or, where the sessions remained divided into the two tiers of winter and summer, why did the school boards persist in hiring men as a rule for the winter sessions? The most straightforward explanation is that school boards did so because they thought that men had something to offer that women did not. In the early nineteenth century, when it was common for girls to have studied less writing and arithmetic than boys, it is quite possible that school boards typically found (and still more typically assumed) that women applicants were unsuited for instructing the older pupils. By later in the century, however, girls' learning in the district school differed far less from boys' learning than it had earlier. Of course, we can still point to starkly sexist statements in most any school report indicating that boys and girls should be educated differently for their different life roles; but the point here is that both boys and girls were now learning the same basic curriculum that typified the upper tier of the district schools in late eighteenth- and early nineteenth-century New England: the same writing skills, elementary mathematics, and so on. We therefore suspect that the objection to female mastery of the curriculum became harder to sustain except by long-ingrained prejudice. Another argument, however, was surely sustained for many decades, namely that women would have more trouble maintaining discipline in the schools. As historian Deborah Fitts has documented, the mid-nineteenth-century reformers came to stress ways in which woman's unique nature would provide a different basis for school discipline—charming and shaming the rebellious boy rather than overpowering him physically. But this argument may have left skeptical farmers less than ready to abandon the disciplinary tactics that had worked in the past with these boys.

When school boards did come to view women as able to master both the curriculum and the discipline needed for the full range of common school assignments, they could comfortably do the financially attractive thing—hire women to do the same work as men for less. The process of rural feminization can be seen as a diffusion of ideas across the countryside. These ideas made it possible to think of women's teaching skills as equal to men's and, at least outside the South, of women's wages as legitimately lower than men's. Feminization made economic sense because women were paid less than men for the same work: the school boards' increasing enlightenment about the abilities of women rested on their discriminatory views about women's wages. But another explanation is probably relevant too: that women worked better with children and were particularly suited for nurturing the young. There is no reason to treat this argument only as a rationalization for doing the inexpensive thing.

In the South, too, both of these arguments were probably relevant, but the relative importance of each may have differed from elsewhere. Southern female-to-male wage ratios seem to have declined modestly over the decades after 1870, and so one can probably speak of at least a modest financial incentive for hiring women even in the rural areas of the South, but at a smaller gain than would have been usual elsewhere. At the same time, the argument about employing women and exploiting their natural qualities for teaching would also have mattered in this region. It might have been especially important to those Southerners who led the struggles for southern school reform after 1880, because bringing in the women teachers seemed to be part of the package of cultural changes that would separate the South from its failed past and bring the region more fully into modern American life.[14]

An Alternative Explanation

Before proceeding, we need to distinguish our argument about the diffusion of this "more efficient division of labor" (based heavily on a context of gender discrimination in wages) from a somewhat similar explanation proposed by David Tyack and his collaborators, Myra Strober and Elizabeth Hansot.[15]

That related argument rests not on a choice by school boards for a "more efficient division of labor" but rather on a choice by school boards to improve the quality of schooling by making greater demands on teachers generally—most notably, demands for more training and for longer school terms. And the crucial point of this alternative formulation is that these additional demands were made without, so the argument goes, commensurate increments in teacher salaries. In such circumstances men voted with their feet to leave teaching, and women, with far fewer occupational choices, came to dominate the teaching force.

Thus, "In rural areas a short stint of teaching in a winter school might be attractive to young men seeking to supplement meager cash income during the slack season. . . . The job required almost no preparation, took only a few weeks out of the year [i.e., for a single term] when other work was dormant, and thus had low opportunity costs."[16] However,

> When rural school terms lengthened and were combined into a continuous year, and when the standards for certification rose, women began to replace men as teachers. Rural wages in teaching did not rise substantially. . . . The pay was still attractive to a woman . . . but for a man, the long school term and the higher entry costs (new laws required certification or atten-

14. William A. Link, *A Hard Country and a Lonely Place: Schooling, Society, and Reform in Rural Virginia, 1870–1920* (Chapel Hill, N.C., 1986); James L. Leloudis, *Schooling in the New South: Pedagogy, Self, and Society in North Carolina, 1880–1920* (Chapel Hill, N.C., 1996).

15. The argument was proposed first in an influential paper (Myra H. Strober and David B. Tyack, "Why Do Women Teach and Men Manage?" *Signs* 5 [spring 1978]) and later in the widely used book, *Learning Together*. The rudiments of the explanation were first suggested by Thomas Morain, "The Departure of Males from the Teaching Profession in Nineteenth Century Iowa," *Civil War History*, vol. 26, no. 2 (1980). Tyack and his collaborators apparently believed that they were resting on Morain's evidence, but in fact they elaborated Morain's argument considerably.

16. Tyack and Hansot, *Learning Together*, 65.

dance at teachers' institutes) were greater barriers. A man was no longer willing to teach a few weeks for cash and then pursue another job as his primary occupation because interrupting other activities to attend a summer teachers' institute or bone up for the county examination seemed not worth the effort if measured against alternative uses of his time and money. . . . In effect the longer terms and increased standards for entry turned teaching into a "para-profession," as Morain (1977) observed. . . . A little "professionalization" of this type drove men out of teaching for it increased the opportunity costs without resulting in commensurate increases in pay.[17]

The theory was no doubt especially appealing because it places feminization at the core of two great problems of modern American society and historiography: the unequal treatment of women's work, and the inability of the teaching profession to undergo the sort of professionalization of "the major professions,"[18] not least because education did not have the status of medicine and law. "By contrast, the more lucrative and prestigious fields, such as medicine or law, which included the upgrading of training programs and licensing requirements, tended to drive women out of these occupations."[19]

This alternative theory stresses not the direct choice of school boards for cheaper, equally talented labor (women's vs. men's) but rather the choice of school boards for other kinds of improvements that drove out the men— indeed, although the theory is not explicit on this point, it suggests that the departure of the men was an unintended result of school board efforts to upgrade. Indeed, without this suggestion, the theory seems to collapse into the simpler point we are making: that school boards chose cheaper, equally talented workers (or, where they chose women as nurturers for the same wage as men had received, they chose more talented workers for wages equivalent to those offered before).

Since there is considerable overlap between these two explanations for the spread of feminization, and only one feature that clearly distinguishes between them (the implication that the departure of the men was unintended), much of the available evidence about feminization will be consistent with either theory. For example, evidence might reveal that those coun-

17. David B. Tyack and Myra H. Strober, "Jobs and Gender: A History of the Structuring of Educational Employment by Sex," in Patricia A. Schmuck, W. W. Charters, Jr., and Richard O. Carlson, eds., *Educational Policy and Management: Sex Differentials* (New York, 1981), 131–52, 140.

18. Nathan Glazer, "The Schools of the Minor Professions," *Minerva* 12 (1974): 346–63.

19. Tyack and Strober, "Jobs and Gender," 140.

ties across the Midwest (or later in the South) with high proportions of female teachers were the same counties that had longer school terms and demanded more training of their teachers. The first theory would explain the result as a decision to hire women rather than men and use the money for improvements such as longer terms as well as women who would be better trained than men who could be lured by the same amount of money. The second theory would explain the result by saying that the school board had extended the term and upgraded the requirements either without realizing that men would leave or—a weaker formulation of the theory—realizing it but not acting for that reason.

The second theory, we think, cannot be sustained. First, it is too restrictive; school boards wanted to save money and provide better education; one way to accomplish these twin goals was a better division of labor: to hire female teachers. The boards could do all manner of good things with the money they saved, and among these good things were longer school years and teachers with stronger credentials to teach. There is no reason to assume that these two reforms were the only possible uses to which financial savings could be put. The stronger version of the thesis argues that boards may not have realized that they were driving out the men, and that they did not realize that they could not have both low teacher wages and male teachers. This consideration also leads to a second objection: why would school boards not be well aware of trade-offs involved in hiring female as opposed to male teachers?

And third, the whole construction of this formulation rests on the assumption that remuneration in fact *did not* grow appreciably as demands on teachers rose. The only evidence that Tyack and his collaborators gave for this conclusion was to be found in a suggestive rather than systematic exploration of trends in Iowa by historian Thomas Morain; that evidence will not support the claims resting on it.[20]

We examined the evidence on two issues. First, we tried to find an association between the organizational features that Tyack and his collaborators cite (length of term and increasing job requirements) and the proportion of female teachers across counties. Finding such an association, it should be appreciated, would not demonstrate the causal connections that led to that association, but at least it would be consistent with the interpretation that a little professionalization drove out the men. Second, we explored the

20. See app. 4.

question of changing remuneration in the midwestern states over the late nineteenth century.

In order to explore the association between school organization (length of term, standards for entry) and feminization of teaching, we studied the counties of Illinois (in 1858 and in 1881) and Iowa (in 1880). We chose Illinois in order to relate school organization to the other factors we have already discussed, particularly the importance of settlers' origins. We chose Iowa partly because the influence of settlers' origins was far less salient there, and also because it is the Iowa experience which Morain had studied and which drew the attention of Tyack and his collaborators to the thesis. We found evidence about entry standards for schoolteaching in the prevalence of teacher institutes and in the length of time an institute lasted in each county. The counties that introduced longer teacher institutes were probably the counties most likely to have been upgrading their academic requirements for entry. And we found direct evidence on the length of the school term in each county.

However, we could find no consistent evidence that such associations did in fact exist in any of our three case studies—in the Illinois of 1858 or in the Illinois or Iowa of 1880. We present the details of these analyses in appendix 4.[21] So we are skeptical for that reason that these school reforms "drove men out."

On the other hand, if school boards were exploiting a "more efficient division of labor" and used the gains for many purposes (including on occasion upgrading requirements for teachers and lengthening the term), sometimes connections will be observed between length of school year or upgraded requirements and the prevalence of female teachers, sometimes not. Some other uses for money include construction of new schoolhouses, other improvement of physical facilities, and books for school libraries. A different category of use was to keep taxes lower than they would otherwise be.

---

21. We had also wondered whether areas in which Yankees settled might well have been the areas that had lengthened the school year and raised entry standards first; areas in which Southerners settled might have experienced these changes later. If so, some of the regional differences in the prevalence of female teachers could have been due to regional differences in the prevalence of longer terms, and in the entry standards for teaching. Had these aspects of school organization, then, led to the patterns we had observed in earlier chapters? But controlling for these organizational differences across counties had an only trivial and statistically insignificant impact on the association between settlers' origins (southern or Yankee) and the prevalence of female teachers in the county.

Thus some connection would be observed between feminization and all sorts of school improvements.

To drive the point home, consider one striking example: a connection between counties that built outhouses for their school sites and counties that had high proportions of female teachers. The Illinois school report for 1886 includes a remarkable survey of school outhouses, reviewing the number of school sites with none, one, two or more, as well as noting the condition of the outhouses—tabulating, for example, the number "in good condition and free from obscene writing and pictures." By 1886, most school sites in fact had outhouses; still 15 percent did not. And we find a positive association between the percentage of county school sites with outhouses and the percentage of female teachers in the county.[22] The association is found with and without controls imposed, and it is statistically significant in both cases. Did the presence of outhouses rather than the absence of outhouses drive men out of teaching? Hardly; but by the same token, whatever weak associations existed between a longer school year and the prevalence of female teachers also need not mean that the longer term drove men out of teaching.[23]

Finally, we turn to the crucial question of whether wages really did not keep up with rising demands on teachers in the late-nineteenth-century Midwest. The only evidence historians had provided for this observation was the trend in Iowa male teacher wages over nine years.[24]

As it happens, in Iowa, the increase in wages over the last three decades of the nineteenth century was lower than the average for the midwestern states. In Iowa, men's wages in teaching simply did not rise at all; women's wages rose by a factor of 1.16. However, for the ten states of the Midwest region, increases between 1870 and 1900 averaged 1.23 for male teachers and 1.36 for female teachers. Even the largest of these increases may not seem so very great for three decades in our inflationary era. But the late

22. Relating the outhouse data from 1886 to our other data on the counties in 1880–81.

23. We obtained similar results when we explored the number of books in the school libraries of counties and the percentage of female teachers in the county. And we obtained similar results too when we explored the connection between the prevalence of female teachers to percentages of school buildings of frame construction in the county (rather than of brick, stone, or logs). It appears that frame buildings were an indication of more recent, and perhaps more expensive, structures, indicating the use of funds for a building program.

24. Specifically, that male teacher wages fell in Iowa 1876–80 and rose 1880–84 while the number of male applicants and teachers fell throughout the period (Morain, "Departure," 167–68).

nineteenth century was not such an era. The cost of living was stable or falling throughout the period, so that these salary increases translated into comparable or greater increases in buying power.[25]

True: we cannot say from such evidence whether or not the increases in teacher wages were an adequate reward for the increased demands placed on teachers in the form of longer terms and upgraded standards for employment. However, we can say that the only evidence that the increases were not adequate was simply atypical. Moreover, it is important to note that the wages of women teachers were typically rising faster than those of men during the period. This was true even in Iowa and was clearer still in the rest of the region. For the ten states of the region the wages for female teachers at five-year intervals averaged (female wages in 1870 = 1.00): 1.11, 1.03, 1.23, 1.23, 1.29, and 1.36 in 1900; while wages for male teachers averaged (male wages in 1870 = 1.00) 1.12, 0.93, 1.09, 1.10, 1.12, and 1.23 in 1900.

Perhaps, therefore, midwestern school boards understood that they could attract more able, better-trained women if they offered a higher wage, and that the wage might still leave a savings over what a (less qualified) male would receive. Working out the precise relation between wages, gender, requirements, and teacher characteristics for rural America is exceedingly difficult given the sparse information.[26] However, since we do know that school boards were raising female wages considerably more than male wages, we would stress the boards' direct role in the process of feminization by favoring women teachers—rather than stress the boards' indirect and supposedly inadvertent role through changes in certain aspects of school organization.

Dynamics of Diffusion

School board attitudes in turn may have been influenced by several changes in social life. The first (and perhaps most widespread

25. Excluded from these averages for the Midwest are North and South Dakota, for which data are unavailable for the earlier years. The averages in the text are unweighted (each state counts as one, regardless of the number of teachers). Several larger states—Illinois and Ohio in particular—had large cities and the unweighted average is a crude way to restrict the effect of urban teachers in the comparisons. In any case, the weighted time series does not differ greatly from the unweighted.

26. The changing structure of local schools (ungraded to graded, the addition of high schools), the changing role of women and men in the schools (women taking over increasingly older grades and advanced curricula, women and especially men taking on supervisory roles), and the changing levels of male and female levels of preparation (in years of schooling completed, e.g.) are all reflected in these wage patterns.

and influential) of these social changes was already described at length, namely the impact of the Civil War. Countless school boards were obliged to conduct social experiments by hiring women when they might have preferred not to do so.

The results were not lost on contemporaries. Connecticut's secretary of education noted in 1864 in connection with district schools that

> The custom in these schools was for a time almost universal to employ male teachers in the winter terms and female teachers in the summer. . . . The practice of employing young women in these schools for the whole year is now becoming common. The change in this respect has been greater for the last three years than ever before, and especially for the last year. . . . It has been clearly demonstrated that well qualified female teachers can control and instruct the ordinary mixed district schools quite as successfully as the young men often employed in these schools in the winter.[27]

Similarly, Wisconsin's state superintendent of public instruction remarked in 1867 that "the number of male teachers may be expected to increase and that of female teachers to diminish relative to the whole number employed." But "no friend of education," he continued, "will regret that the necessities growing out of the war have demonstrated the superior fitness of women as teachers of youth."[28] The immediate effects of the war can be seen in the permanent rise in the prevalence of female teachers that occurred in the years 1860–70. We can assume that there were also long-term attitudinal effects as even school boards that reverted to male teachers still had seen women undertake the work without the school collapsing. The certainty of members of such school boards that they needed males must often have been shaken.

The effect of financial strain in local areas over the course of the nineteenth century must have led to similar decisions to hire women at least for the duration of the crunch. And observation of the results would have chipped away at school board doubts about women. Rising enrollments may have helped impel financially strapped school boards to try cheaper women teachers where they had not been tried before. Yet if so, we would expect population density to correlate with the prevalence of female teachers; in fact, the independent associations between population density and the

---

27. *Report of the Secretary of Education for 1864* (Hartford, Conn., 1864), 6–7.

28. Superintendent of Public Instruction, State of Wisconsin, *Report* (Madison, Wis., 1867), 13. See also Morain, "Departure of Males," for the impact of the war on teaching.

prevalence of female teachers (in the preceding chapter and in this chapter) are not strong, leading us to be cautious about this point.

However, there were other sources of fiscal crisis besides population pressure. In the unstable economic context of nineteenth-century rural America, there were numerous times when a local board might have felt the temptation to hire women as a stopgap measure. And there were other times when their own expenditures may have led a school district to be anxious about money. Historian Wayne Fuller describes such a time—September 7, 1885, in District 5 of Woodstock Township in Lanawee County, Michigan.

> The district had just built a new schoolhouse, and only the year before, after the building had begun, the farmers had authorized their school board to borrow money to construct it. Shortly after this, at a special meeting they had directed the building committee to raise money to erect a fence, and . . . had voted to purchase "the ten dollar bell" for their school.
>
> So when the meeting in the new schoolhouse was called to order that evening and the preliminaries were out of the way, the farmers voted "that the board be authorized to raise as little money as possible" for the ensuing year, and followed this with a motion to have only a six-month school and to employ a female teacher for the year. . . .
>
> In 1886 . . . the farmers voted . . . to return to an eight-month school and to employ a male teacher for the winter term.[29]

A second kind of social change influencing school board attitudes with regard to women has also been mentioned already: women's increasing mastery of the advanced rural school curriculum would have made them more competitive.

A third kind of social change influencing school board attitudes may have involved the nature of school discipline and lack thereof. It is possible that the physical challenge of maintaining a school eased over time, as views about schooling changed in nineteenth-century America. In 1840 school breakups—schools violently disrupted by older boys to such an extent that the school had to be closed—were "not very infrequent," even in Horace Mann's Massachusetts. "The reports of the committees for the last two years [Mann wrote in 1841] have not disclosed a single instance, where the girls belonging to the school have caused its violent termination, or even

29. Wayne E. Fuller, *The Old Country School: The Story of Rural Education in the Middle West* (Chicago, 1982), 56.

participated in fomenting an insurrectionary spirit. Nor among the boys is it the younger who are ungovernable." However, the number of school breakups, about which Horace Mann and others complained, appear to have declined in Massachusetts over time and likewise may have declined elsewhere as well.[30]

Fourth, and finally, as the percentage of women teachers rose higher and higher, the job came to be more fully sex-typed as women's work; the chance that men would apply and be accepted declined. This consideration would help most to explain the very last stages of feminization in any locale; the earlier stages must be explained in other ways, of course.[31]

Whatever the social changes that may have influenced school board attitudes, we should also appreciate that there was a concerted effort to change school board attitudes and to convince boards to try female teachers. One important source of such efforts was each state's superintendent. However, these officials were very far removed from the local district scene. The crucial intermediate bureaucrats apparently were the county superintendents. These superintendencies were introduced in some states before the Civil War, and their influence increased considerably after 1870 (in the South after about 1890).[32] Typically elected, these men—and women—served as the link between the state capital and the rural district school. No doubt their influence, and the extent to which they made feminization a priority, varied with individual personalities as well as with many local circumstances. It is not a process that we can fully capture in generalities. On the contrary: the diversity of county superintendents' powers of persuasion and interest in feminization may help explain some of the otherwise inexplicable local variation that we find in the pace of feminization.[33]

30. *Fourth Annual Report of the Secretary of the Board of Education* (Massachusetts), 1841, 86.

31. It is also not unreasonable to suggest, as Tyack and Strober did, that as school control passed increasingly to bureaucrats, men felt the job involved a subordination more suitable to women. However, whether so much bureaucratic control really typified late nineteenth-century rural—as opposed to urban—schools is far from clear. Tyack's later work (with Hansot) did not repeat this argument.

32. Fuller, *Old Country School;* Link, *A Hard Country;* Wickersham, *History of Education in Pennsylvania.*

33. On the rise of the county superintendents in the Midwest, see Fuller, *Old Country School,* chap. 8. In contrast to our suggestion about the role of the midwestern county superintendents of the late nineteenth century, it should be noted that Pennsylvania during the 1850s introduced county superintendents, but the rise in the percentage of female teachers (as shown in chap. 1) was slight. It is possible that, as in the Midwest later, during their early years of activity the superintendents had less impact than later.

FIVE

Labor Market Outcomes in Urban Schools: The Role of Gender

We have discussed the urban schools only briefly, pointing out in passing how their organization would have facilitated the use of women teachers and (more generally) created distinctive gender differences in teaching. Indeed, in the cities, the regional differences that characterized feminization in rural areas were much less apparent—the predominance of female teachers came into being earlier and more fully in every region. This chapter investigates two related aspects of gender differences among urban teachers: salaries and positions. While women held the overwhelming majority of jobs in large urban school systems by the late nineteenth century, they were paid significantly less than male school employees and they were far less likely than men to become principals or be promoted into other, higher paying administrative positions. We can also determine that, on average, men were likely to have had more extensive education than women and to have had longer experience in teaching than women did. Surely these qualities account for some of the gender gap we observe in salary and promotion into administration? The issue is how much of the observed gender gap can be explained by these and other background characteristics, and how much of the gender gap remains unexplained even after these characteristics have been allowed to explain all they can. The unexplained gender gap can plausibly be attributed to school system arrangements that allocated greater rewards to men over women who were equal in all other relevant respects. This unexplained gender gap is what economists typically refer to as gender discrimination within a firm or bureaucratic system.

Urban school systems were large operations by comparison to an individual rural school district. And these urban systems tended to develop set salary scales as well as set levels of reward for experience and education.

Some economists and historians have argued that, contrary to any expected "rationality" that might be theorized to have accompanied the coming of a systematic bureaucracy, women in fact fared worse under the bureaucratized system than they did in the earlier rural district arrangements. But the two sets of school arrangements were so different that such a comparison cannot be terribly illuminating. What is more important is to understand how each system operated when it came to the utilization of male and female personnel; and so here our focus is on gender in the reward structure of the urban system.

GENDER, INTERNAL LABOR MARKETS, AND SCHOOL ORGANIZATION: URBAN SCHOOL SYSTEMS AT THE TURN OF THE CENTURY

The organization and management of urban schools differed from that of rural schools, most notably in the complexity and hierarchical structure of decision-making control. Each school in the system was managed by a principal and perhaps one or more assistant principals. Large high schools might have department heads. At the top of a typical urban system were the superintendent and staff. The superintendent was beholden directly to an elected school board and indirectly to other elected officials, such as the mayor. There were, to be sure, geographical variations in institutional arrangements, but an elaborated hierarchy was ubiquitous across the country.[1]

In rural areas the dominant organizational form ca. 1860 was the one-room schoolhouse, in which management and teaching functions coexisted in a single person. Over time, as population density and demand for schooling increased, the urban organizational form diffused into rural school districts. By the end of the century, division of labor within rural school districts had increased considerably, although in bureaucratic complexity rural districts still lagged behind urban districts. However, organizational innovation was not neutral with respect to gender within school systems, for men came to fill the vast majority of newly created administrative positions. Feminization did not spread with equal force into the classroom and the principal's office—or, as Myra Strober and David Tyack have put it, "Men manage; women teach."[2]

---

1. David Tyack, *The One Best System: A History of American Urban Education* (Cambridge, Mass., 1974).
2. Strober and Tyack, "Why Do Women Teach and Men Manage?"

The lower relative pay of female teachers long predated the diffusion of new methods of school organization; it was this very difference in pay, we argued in earlier chapters, that provided an economic incentive for feminization. But bureaucratization is alleged to have perpetuated the gender gap in pay in two ways.[3] First, principals and other administrators earned a salary premium over teachers. Even if there were no gender differences in salaries, on average, among teachers or administrators, there would still be an overall gender gap in salaries among school personnel, if men were favored for administrative jobs, because men would be disproportionately represented among higher paying jobs in school systems.

Second, bureaucratization of school systems was accompanied by the adoption of formal personnel policies. Such policies invariably included written salary schedules that tied pay to the position held, teaching experience, and other characteristics of teachers. Given that female teachers had long been paid less than male teachers, it is not surprising that gender entered into the specification of formal salary schedules. For example, the schedule adopted by the Boston school board ca. 1860 stated rates of pay separately for males and females that depended on, among other factors, work experience, the type of teaching certificate held, and the grade level taught. The fact that a salary schedule was gender-specific, however, does not imply that the schedule merely ratified a preexisting gender gap in pay. The adoption of a schedule may have exacerbated such differences by creating new gender-specific opportunities for higher pay, either through promotion into administrative positions, as noted above, or in the manner which teachers were compensated for experience and other characteristics.[4]

Codes regulating appropriate personal behavior in and out of the classroom were also common parts of personnel policies. Perhaps the most infamous codes were "marriage bars"—regulations that required the dismissal of a female teacher on marriage (called a retain bar) or prohibiting the

3. Myra Strober and Laura Best, "The Female/Male Salary Differential in Public Schools: Some Lessons from San Francisco, 1879," *Economic Inquiry* 17 (April 1979): 218–36.

4. As a hypothetical example suppose that, in a district composed of one-room schoolhouses, teachers were not rewarded for experience; they received the same pay (ignoring inflation) year in and year out. Males, however, were paid more than female teachers. Over time, schools are consolidated, principals are appointed, and a formal salary schedule is adopted, linking pay to work experience—perhaps because the district board now wants to retain more experienced teachers. The adoption of the schedule could lower the average female-to-male salary ratio if (1) males are more likely to be made principals; (2) males possess the attributes rewarded by the schedule to a greater extent than females; (3) the schedule rewards male teachers differently for certain attributes (e.g., teaching experience) than female teachers.

employment of a married woman as a teacher (called a hire bar). Originating sometime in the late nineteenth century, marriage bars (either the retain or hire bar, or both) spread throughout school districts in the early 1900s. The earliest national survey, conducted in 1928, revealed that 52 percent of all districts had a retain bar and 61 percent had a hire bar.[5]

A number of cultural outlooks could have led to the marriage bars: biases against a married woman working outside the home (or against such a woman taking a job away from a man who needed to support a family), a view that a married woman would no longer have the advantage of treating her work like surrogate motherhood, especially if she were herself on the way to becoming a mother, and so on. We need not sort all this out here. But was there, behind such cultural outlooks, also an economic logic, whether fully articulated or not? If so, that economic logic behind marriage bars in teaching remains unclear. One possibility is that school boards wished to encourage some turnover in staff. Because salary schedules uniformly rewarded time spent in the classroom, older, more experienced teachers earned more than younger, inexperienced teachers. The return to experience presumably reflected productivity gains; it might also have been a device to keep experienced teachers, but only up to a certain point. If productivity did not increase at the same rate beyond this point, there would be an incentive to terminate the teacher's contract. Most women in the early twentieth century left the labor force at, or soon after, marriage and most women married after a spell of employment while single.[6] The event of marriage, therefore, may have provided a socially acceptable way of firing teachers whom school boards wished to keep for more than a few years but who would have eventually become too expensive to retain.

There are, however, two problems with the turnover explanation. First, the salary schedules were not preordained; if productivity did not keep pace with wages, the schedule could be adjusted to reflect this.[7] Second, the turnover thesis does not explain why single teachers could be kept indefinitely or why married women could not be hired. As was true with marriage bars

5. Valerie E. Oppenheimer, *The Female Labor Force in the United States: Demographic and Economics Factors Governing Its Growth and Changing Composition* (Westport, Conn., 1976), table 4.5.

6. Claudia Goldin, *Understanding the Gender Gap: An Economic History of American Women* (New York, 1990).

7. The schedule could not, however, be altered to fit the personal circumstances of every teacher, otherwise the benefits (e.g., lower management costs because the board did not have to negotiate salary individually with each teacher) of a schedule would be lost.

in other occupations,[8] school boards were concerned about marriage per se in implementing policies. Evidently school boards that adopted marriage bars believed that, for unspecified reasons, married women were less productive teachers, or that married women should not ordinarily work outside the home.

Whatever the explanation for their prevalence, marriage bars altered the incentives for women to acquire characteristics valued by school boards, and thus influenced (indirectly) the gender gap in teachers' pay. In the absence of a retain bar, some female teachers would have remained in the profession after marriage but, since they could not, the average years of experience of female teachers was artificially curtailed. The presence of hire bars lowered the value of investing in education or work experience since a female teacher, on marrying, could not reap the benefits these provided if she were able to return to teaching at a later date (e.g., after childbearing).

When referring generically to business enterprises with structured employment policies pioneered by urban schools in the late nineteenth and early twentieth centuries, economists speak of an "internal labor market." Starting in the 1920s and accelerating in pace during the Great Depression, internal labor markets came to characterize employment relationships between workers and firms in large-scale enterprises throughout the American economy.[9] Recent research suggests that the diffusion of internal labor markets led to an economy-wide increase in gender-based "wage discrimination"—a difference in pay between men and women that cannot be explained by observed productivity differences or differences in characteristics (for example, education) thought to be associated with productivity.[10] In many of the jobs in which female labor predominated at the turn of the century—manufacturing is the primary example—payment was by the piece, and a worker's earnings were directly tied to her productivity. In such occupations the scope for gender-based wage discrimination was relatively small.[11]

In white-collar occupations, such as office work, in which internal labor markets became the norm, pay and occupational status were not so closely

---

8. Goldin, *Understanding the Gender Gap*, 173.

9. Sanford M. Jacoby, *Employing Bureaucracy: Managers, Unions, and the Transformation of Work in American Industry, 1900–1945* (New York, 1985).

10. Goldin, *Understanding the Gender Gap*.

11. Barry Eichengreen, "Experience and the Male-Female Earnings Gap in the 1890s," *Journal of Economic History* 44 (September 1984): 822–34.

tied to current employee performance, and the extent of wage discrimination was much greater than in manufacturing. The gap in pay between male and female office workers was smallest at the point of initial hire, but widened as male workers were promoted internally to higher paying positions. Female office workers were relegated to dead-end jobs that offered little reward to long tenure (experience within a firm), but which did provide a return to education, unlike jobs in manufacturing. Did urban teaching follow this pattern too? Our evidence comes from the urban teacher lists we have collected.

The Urban Teacher Lists

School boards in virtually every American city publish annual reports, some continuously so since the early nineteenth century. In today's litigious climate, school personnel files—revealing, for example, salary histories or supervisor ratings—are kept confidential. But attitudes toward the privacy rights of teachers in the late nineteenth and early twentieth centuries were rather different. Many school boards published the equivalent of personnel files in their annual reports: in effect, the names of teachers, accompanied by information of a personal nature—for example, education, previous teaching experience, marital status, salary, and street address. We can only speculate why this information was made available for public consumption. Perhaps the reason was to reveal to constituents how their tax dollars were being spent or that qualified teachers were being hired—although not all lists reported teachers' salaries or their personal characteristics. A more mundane reason may have been to provide ready access to school personnel, for nearly every list we have discovered includes home addresses.[12] The majority of school boards that published lists did so once or occasionally. For a few cities, however, lists are available on an annual basis, sometimes for many years.[13]

12. The reporting of a street address for the teacher is a ubiquitous characteristic of the teacher lists that we have examined. By contrast, the reporting of salaries, educational backgrounds, and previous teaching experience was less common.

13. We are not the first historians to notice the value of the lists in studying gender differences among urban teachers. Myra Strober and Laura Best ("Female/Male Salary Differential") analyzed a teacher list for San Francisco published in that city's annual report of 1874. Strober and Best found that, controlling for the type of teaching certificate and position held by the teacher, female teachers were paid significantly less than male teachers. Administrators (principals) were paid more than regular teachers; women, however, were less likely to hold such positions, and this, too, contributed to the gender gap in salaries. Strober and Best interpreted their results as evidence of discrimination against female teachers, but acknowledged that the type of teaching certificate held was a less than perfect indicator of the teacher's

Because the lists vary widely in their frequency and in the quantity and quality of information reported, it is not possible to collect a random sample analogous to our national census samples of teachers. We have, instead, collected teacher lists from three cities: Grand Rapids, Michigan; Portland, Oregon; and Paterson, New Jersey. Teachers lists from a fourth city—Houston, Texas—were collected by Margo and Elyce Rotella for an earlier study, and analyses of the Houston data are integrated into the chapter.[14] The choice of cities was not arbitrary. Each city reported an unusually large amount of information about teachers, and each published its lists over a period of years, which greatly increases sample sizes. Table 5.1 shows sample means and the time period covered by the teacher lists.

The teaching force was substantially feminized in all four cities. The Grand Rapids schools had the highest female proportion: on average, fully 95 percent of its public school personnel were women. Consistent with the regional differences documented earlier in the book, the least feminized school system was Houston (85 percent on average). In each city, the pay of female school personnel fell short of that of male school personnel. The lowest ratio of female-to-male salaries occurred in Paterson: there female personnel were paid, on average, 42 cents for every dollar earned by male personnel. The salary ratio was a bit higher in Grand Rapids (0.47) and significantly greater in Portland (0.55) and Houston (0.57). There were, as well, pronounced gender disparities in the assignment of school personnel to administrative positions. On average, about 10 percent of personnel were administrative (the proportion was lower in Paterson, about 7 percent). Yet males were far more likely to hold such positions than females: the proportion of men who were administrators ranged from 36 percent in Grand Rapids to 79 percent in Paterson.

The remainder of the table compares the educational backgrounds and teaching experience of male and female personnel. The educations of male school personnel were generally superior to those of female personnel. The Houston teacher lists—which, as noted earlier, are the most complete in

---

educational background and teaching experience—two variables known to have influenced salary and the likelihood of holding an administrative position. The teacher lists we have collected are generally more informative about the characteristics of teachers than is the San Francisco list; thus, e.g., in our analysis of the gender gap in salaries we can control for the characteristics of teachers to a greater extent than could Strober and Best.

14. Robert Margo and Elyce Rotella, "Sex Differences in the Market for School Personnel: Houston, Texas, 1892–1923," unpublished paper, Department of Economics, University of Pennsylvania, October 1981.

TABLE 5.1 School Personnel in Four Cities: Sample Means

Characteristics of School Personnel	Cities and Years Sampled			
	Portland 1878–1906	Grand Rapids 1880–1903	Paterson 1875–1910	Houston 1892–1923
Percent female	90.6	95.0	92.5	85.7
Female/male salary ratio	.545	.468	.417	.572
In administration				
Percent of all	10.0	10.7	7.4	10.2
Percent of males	73.4	36.1	78.9	47.7
Percent of females	4.3	9.4	1.6	3.9
Degree listed: normal school				
Percent of males	7.8		13.1	30.4
Percent of females	4.5		2.4	19.1
Degree listed: B.A. or higher				
Percent of males	15.8	46.1	38.2	55.0
Percent of females	2.9	2.5	.6	19.3
Years of teaching experience				
Males	17.73	11.21	17.01	22.61
Females	10.26	8.54	8.73	16.60
Years of teaching experience in the city (tenure)				
Males	6.98	4.53	8.03	11.65
Females	5.89	6.06	7.44	11.40
Number of observations	4,262	6,395	2,642	7,581

Sources: See text.

their reporting of education—tell a clear story: men were far more likely to have attended a normal school, college, or university, than women. Fully 55 percent of the men employed in the Houston school system had gone to college, compared with 19 percent of female school personnel. Although the data are not as informative for the other cities, they also point to large gender differences in education. It is also apparent that males had more years of teaching experience, on average, than women, but this difference arose not because men were more likely to persist longer than women in any given system. That is, the average tenures of male and female personnel were about the same. The implication is that the men who ended up in large urban school systems came to their jobs with more prior experience than women, on average. Furthermore, the fact that the difference between years of experience and tenure was generally small for women (for example, 1.3

years in Paterson) implies that many women must have begun their teaching careers in the city system in which they were currently employed. We will now analyze the implications of the gender differences in education and experience for gender difference in salaries and positions.

Because the data cover several years, it is natural to ask whether any of the gender differences observed changed over time. When we explored change over time (app. table A5.1), we found that there was a statistically significant albeit slow shift toward less difference by gender over time (a shift that would have taken numerous decades to equalize rewards). Thus while the gender gaps in labor market outcomes and teacher qualifications were not fixed and unchanging, it does not distort historical reality to focus on their essential stability as the datum to be explained rather than change in the gender gaps over time. And that is the basis on which we conducted the following statistical analysis of salaries and promotions.

Gender and Salaries

By taking advantage of the fact that women were available to staff the schools at lower average wages than men, school boards could realize significant savings; this was so in rural as well as in urban areas. We have yet to examine, however, the extent to which women were able to influence the size of the gender gap in salaries by acquiring skills—education and experience—that were valued by school boards and which, therefore, commanded a salary premium; the urban school lists allow us to examine the issue within the city context. It is true that acquiring these skills was difficult at best for most women at the turn of the century. Women were barred from attending many colleges and universities. Staying in the profession long enough to be promoted to a higher paying administrative position required sacrifices in one's personal life, as noted earlier. Our goal in this section is not to explain the choices made by female teachers but rather the impact of those choices on their pay.

Both men and women benefited from additional years of education and experience (albeit from the latter at a decreasing rate). Except in Houston, the returns to experience were higher for men than for women, and in two cities (Paterson and Grand Rapids) returns for education were greater for men as well. For men employed in the Paterson or Grand Rapids schools, the location of the experience did not matter, whether experience in the same school system (which we call tenure) or experience elsewhere. Holding constant years of experience, tenure per se did not help the men in those two school systems. In the other two school systems, Portland and Houston, however, tenure brought greater rewards at the margin for males than experience elsewhere did.

Surprisingly, in three of the four cities—Portland is the exception—the independent effect of tenure was negative: women gained less, at the margin, from experience in a given system than from years of experience generally (that is, anywhere)—this, despite the fact, noted in the previous section, that the average female teacher in all four systems had acquired relatively more of her experience in the form of tenure than the average male. And since for men the independent effects of tenure were (as expected) positive, men gained more from these effects than women. Even in Portland—the one system where the independent effects of tenure were positive for women—the independent effects were still greater for men.

Were the gender differences in returns to experience, tenure, and education that we found in at least some of the cities due to a greater likelihood that males would eventually hold administrative positions? In part they were, but only in part. Holding constant other characteristics, and regardless of gender, administrators earned significantly more than other school employees, and since men were more likely than women to be administrators, controlling for whether or not an employee was an administrator does reduce the gender gaps in experience and tenure somewhat.

The regressions discussed thus far provide insights into the determinants of salaries, but we have yet to answer the question of how much of the gender gap in salaries is attributable to gender differences in characteristics (that is, experience, tenure, and education). In order to explore this issue we employ a technique familiar in labor economics. Our regression work has produced an estimate of the impact of each characteristic on the wages men received—the impact of education, experience, tenure, and so on. We now use the male regression equation to calculate the average salary a male teacher would earn if he had the same average characteristics as a female teacher. The difference between the average male salary and this hypothetical salary captures the portion of the gender gap in salaries that is due to the gender gap in characteristics. The remainder of the gap is conventionally assigned to wage discrimination.

Gender differences in the characteristics of teachers were important determinants of gender differences in salaries; in each city, if women had had the same experience, tenure, and education as males, their average pay would have been higher. Nevertheless, the bulk of the gender gap in salaries was due to "wage discrimination." The levels of wage discrimination in these four school systems ranged from 63 to 84 percent (table 5.2). These

TABLE 5.2 Gender Gap in Salary and Administrative Position: Percentage of the Gap Due to Discrimination

Gender Gap in:	Percent of Gap Due to Discrimination in Four Cities			
	Portland	Grand Rapids	Paterson	Houston
Salaries	68.1	83.6	70.0	63.2
Promotion to administration	58.2	26.9	–	18.3

Source: This table presents a summary of regression analyses; see text and app. 5.
Note: – = 0 or less.

levels far exceed wage discrimination ca. 1900 in manufacturing, which was a major sector in terms of employment of women. In terms of wage discrimination, in other words, teaching was unusual at the turn of the century. The levels, however, are comparable to those observed among office workers ca. 1940—an occupation, like teaching, in which education was important and in which internal labor markets were common.

GENDER AND PROMOTION TO ADMINISTRATION

Once again we ask how much of the gender imbalance in positions can be attributed to gender per se versus other characteristics of school personnel. For men, the regression analysis of the determinants of promotion broadly support the "internal labor markets" interpretation of urban school systems. The most important factor in raising the chances of holding an administrative position was experience in teaching. The value of an additional year's experience was considerable. In Grand Rapids, for example, the predicted probability that a college-educated man with six years of experience would hold an administrative position was 6 percentage points higher than that of a college-educated man with five years of experience.[15] At the margin, experience in the school system was more valuable in increasing the chances of becoming an administrator than experience elsewhere.[16] This is precisely what one would expect in an internal labor market.

15. The predicted probability, p^*, is computed using the logit coefficients, setting the time trend equal to its sample mean (1893). The value of the logit, L^*, at six years of experience is 0.5163; the predicted value at five years of experience is 0.2635. Using the formula $\ln[p^*/(1 - p^*)] = L^*$, the predicted probability at five years of experience is 0.565 and 0.626 at six years of experience.

16. Continuing the Grand Rapids example in the text, if the additional year of experience (from five years to six years) came in the Grand Rapids system, the chances of holding an administrative position increased by 7.2 percentage points.

Male school personnel who had attended a normal school and, to a lesser extent, college were more likely to be administrators but, in general, experience in the teaching profession was more valuable than higher education for promotion to an administrative position.

The results for women are similar with respect to experience but different with respect to tenure and education. Except in Paterson, the value of tenure in raising the chances of promotion for women was smaller than for men. Except in Paterson, and in Houston where college-educated women had an advantage, higher education did not enhance the likelihood a woman would become a principal. Still, an important point is that women who persisted in the teaching profession enhanced their chances of promotion.

We also calculate the percentage of the gender gap in promotion to administration that can be considered gender discrimination, rather than related to the differing background characteristics of the men and women teachers. This percentage ranges from less than zero in Portland to 58 percent in Grand Rapids (table 5.2).[17] Clearly, while the greater experience and, to a lesser extent, education of male school personnel contributed to their greater likelihood of holding an administrative position, gender per se mattered—there was a bias in favor of males in filling such positions. This bias made the gender gap in salaries larger than it would have been if administrators had been chosen solely on the basis of their qualifications, with sex an irrelevant characteristic.

Discussion

We may now step back from the results of the empirical analysis and offer some discussion. While bureaucratization did not create a gender gap in teachers' pay, it exacerbated the gap. A proximate cause of wage discrimination was the bias in favor of males in filling newly created administrative positions as school organization changed. Yet the outlook for female school personnel under bureaucratization was not entirely negative. Experience and education brought higher pay for women as well as men. Some women managed to become principals or hold other administrative positions—although in achieving this goal they had to persist for many

17. It is unclear why the percent explained is so much higher in Grand Rapids and, to a lesser extent, in Houston. In both cities the percent of males with administrative positions was relatively low to begin with, and it was not uncommon for men to be teachers in high schools. The employment of a man, in other words, was not so clearly tied to the filling of an administrative position, and objective qualifications may have mattered more.

years and, in the process, forgo marriage and a family if their school system had a marriage bar.

Like the gender gap in pay, the preference for males in administrative positions was partly inherited from history and partly from the labor market outside teaching. Men dominated the management of school boards and school committees in the era of one-room schoolhouses. The step into the principal's office was arguably a short one. Outside of teaching, there were few, if any industries, that employed significant numbers of women in managerial capacities—indeed, the opportunities for female advancement in this respect may have been greater in teaching than in other occupations. At the higher echelons of school management—for example, superintendencies— maleness per se would have been an asset. Superintendents had a political role to play in negotiating with school boards and taxpayers, and prevailing social norms made it difficult for women to be effective in such settings.[18]

In one respect the internal labor market model does not well describe gender differences in urban schools. Recall that, in three of the four cities, the coefficients on tenure in the regression of salaries were negative for women. We expected, and found, a gender gap in the returns to tenure in favor of men. But a negative return to tenure is difficult to reconcile with the view that, in an internal labor market, individuals are rewarded for experience specific to the firm.

A plausible explanation of the negative coefficients is that large, urban school districts enjoyed some "monopsony" power over female teachers. Monopsony occurs whenever an employer is large relative to the local labor market and labor is not fully mobile geographically. Under such conditions the employer can effectively influence the level of pay for workers of a given skill. An employer with such power can pay workers less than they are actually worth to the firm. Workers are thus "exploited" in a specific economic sense.

Each of the school systems examined in this chapter—like the majority of large, urban districts of the era—relied heavily on a steady stream of female graduates from local high schools to staff the lower elementary grades. Female high school graduates would enter directly into a city normal school or else take normal courses as part of their high school curriculum. A graduate equipped with such training was qualified for initial employment at the lowest rung—and lowest pay—of the occupational ladder as a student teacher, or "supernumerary" as they were called in Houston. Al-

18. Strober and Best, "The Female/Male Salary Differential."

most by definition, women progressing along such a track were less mobile than women entering a system with experience elsewhere—a fact that school boards were obviously aware of and could easily exploit by paying less for the same total years of experience or, equivalently, a negative return to tenure. It is worth emphasizing that the men employed in the four school systems examined here rarely began their careers as student teachers; most had acquired experience elsewhere. The geographic extent of the market for male school personnel, in other words, was larger than for female school personnel, consistent with the monopsony interpretation.

This method of ensuring a cheap, reliable source of female teachers functioned as intended as long as the range of occupations open to women with a high school education was few in number, few women went on to secure postgraduate degrees, school boards did not desire a higher level of educational preparation, and the market for teachers was geographically constrained. As a factor contributing to a gender gap in teacher salaries, monopsony power declined in importance as the century progressed. The expansion of the clerical sector meant that another occupation—office work—provided competition to school boards for the work of educated women. Over time, women increasingly sought higher levels of educational preparation, partly in response to a growing demand for better-trained teachers. A college or normal degree became a necessary credential, not an unusual one. And over time, urban school boards increasingly recruited from regional and national markets, further eroding the reliance on local sources of supply.

CONCLUSION

Gender has always been among the strongest determinants of who would be most active in the market sphere and who in the domestic sphere; in addition, within the labor market, gender has always been among the strongest determinants of who would be found in specific jobs. Over time, the importance of the gender divide has declined, as more women have entered the paid labor force, and because of broad social, political, and legal changes in American society that have opened up economic opportunities for women in arenas that were previously denied to them. Nevertheless, the preceding generalization is by no means irrelevant even in contemporary American life. A curious feature of the gendered nature of occupations is that, at least in American history, few occupations have undergone a gendered transformation; that is, switched from being male- to female-dominated, or vice versa, while remaining relatively fixed in job content. Such gendered transformations in the labor force may occur because of changes in the supply of workers or changes in the skill levels of men and women (which in turn will need to be explained), or because other opportunities in the labor market make the occupation in question less attractive to men (or women). Alternatively, the changes may occur because the nature of the demand for workers changes: women may come to be seen as more suited for teaching than men, for example; or, finally, the nature of the work, at first glance the same, may change in subtle ways that in turn change who will undertake the work. Because of the range of influences that may be operating to produce the gendered character of an occupation, an adequate understanding of that gendered character of occupations will always require collaboration across disciplinary boundaries. And this need for multiple perspectives is especially obvious when the gendered character of the occupation differs across regions at one moment in time and across time in all regions.

In this book we have sought to explain a prominent historical example of an evolving gendered occupation, that of grade school teachers. We have situated this transformation in what is arguably the central feature of the geography of nineteenth-century America—its distinctive regional character—because even a casual inspection of the historical evidence shows that the relative degree to which female teachers were utilized differed radically across regions. In chapters 1 through 3 we have tried, therefore, to show how and why American regions came to differ in their early hiring of female teachers, and why the schools of the Northeast and parts of the Midwest moved more rapidly to have that hiring pattern dominate than did the schools in the Southeast and other parts of the Midwest. The analytical framework has drawn extensively on the tools of quantitative history— statistical analysis of quantitative historical data in the context of hypotheses informed by social science perspectives—in our case, sociology, demography, and economics. Yet, our efforts along these lines to explain regional differences in the usage of female teachers suggest that the evolving gendered character of teaching in antebellum America cannot be understood merely by differences in social structure, demography, or—the economist's favorite—the ratio of female-to-male wages in other (i.e., nonteaching) sectors of the economy. Rather, in order to explain the phenomenon, we have had to appeal to historically conditioned factors: first, the institutional differences in the schools of the region and, to an extent that we cannot pin down precisely, various sorts of social norms or feminine ideals (the sort of factors economic historians sometimes label "path dependent"). We do not claim that we can make an open-and-shut case for regional differences in norms and ideals, only that some combination of institutions and norms most easily explains the cross-regional patterns.

In chapter 4 we shifted to a discussion of the factors that led to the triumph of feminization in teaching everywhere. For example, we observed that, during the Civil War, women entered teaching to an unprecedented extent, and when the conflict ended men returned to the classroom, but not to the same degree as prior to the war. Thus the Civil War was a "shock" that had permanent consequences for the gender composition of teaching. And then, during the late nineteenth century, a variety of conditions discussed later in chapter 4 led to the more universal diffusion of the desire to capture the benefits of female teachers—that is, lower salary costs and the perceived advantages of women's nature in this sort of work.

The transformation in school organization was (naturally) most complete in urban schools. The availability of detailed personnel lists from several of these cities permitted us, in chapter 5, to study the role of gender in the determination of salaries and administrative positions in the late nineteenth and early twentieth centuries. While women came to dominate teaching per se, gender still functioned as a divide in terms of pay or access to decision-making authority; a portion of the lower salaries of female teachers and their relative underrepresentation in administrative posts cannot be explained by gender differences in experience or training, suggesting that maleness per se was still an attribute valued by school boards, at least in certain settings.

Our conclusions about gendered occupations are important not simply in their own right; they also have implications for further work on this topic and even, we think, for social and economic history more generally. First, with regard to the older history in New England and New York, we have argued that some trends in teaching that have been presumed to be the result of grand trends in American history should not be seen as derivative entirely, or even primarily, from these trends. Rather, the developments in teaching seem to have been rooted in the internal institutional history of the schools. One example of this cautionary point concerns the extension of female schooling, literacy, and eventually teaching ca. 1790 and its putative connection to the American Revolution. Another example concerns the second period of change ca. 1830 and its alleged relation to industrialization and the decline in domestic production with an accompanying release of female labor to the market economy. We do not argue that such trends had *no* effect on the feminization of teaching; on the contrary, the timing of changes (especially in the latter case) leads us to think there was a connection; however a slow evolution of institutions and cultural norms about teaching roles also preceded (and presumably continued during) the years in which those wider social and political changes (stressed so heavily in earlier historical discussions) were occurring.

Second, our explanation of North-South differences in teaching before about 1820 is based, in part, on an argument *ex silencio:* the available sources rarely, if ever, mention the existence of dame schools in the South. If, as the argument suggests, these institutions were not present, the reasons may lie in geographic and political factors: low population density in the South and the apparent absence of well-established procedures to hire teachers thereby left the work to itinerant (hence, mostly male) entrepreneurs. These broader contextual factors would help explain not only the absence of dame schools in the early colonial South but also the dearth of southern female schoolteachers in the later antebellum years; moreover, in those later antebellum years, the absence of the transitional institution of the dame schools would have made it still less likely that institutions that grew out of the dame school in New England would emerge in the South. However, these are mere suppositions on our part and, as such, suggest the need for further local probes into the institutional history of colonial schooling. By contrast, that most respected of colonial historians, Bernard Bailyn, once urged (rightly, we think) that this field of research be left fallow, having been exhausted by too much (and increasingly misguided) cultivation. However, Bailyn urged that strategy fully four decades ago; our work suggests there are now good historical questions to ask about colonial schools.[1]

Third, consider again our analytical strategy in chapter 2 to explain differences in feminization between the Northeast and the South in 1860. Putting aside initially differences in internal institutional structure, we focused on regional differences in social structure, in the labor market for female labor, and in the educational attainment of women relative to men. However, we did not find credible explanations using this strategy. For example, from the view of labor markets, while one part of the South (where cotton cultivation was prevalent) differed from the Northeast in having a higher relative valuation of women's time, another part of the South did not differ in this respect from the North. Yet the relative dearth of female teachers was found across the entire South. Thus we were forced back on an examination of historical developments that created the regional patterns evident in 1860, most especially the institutional history. But, until more work can be done in local sources documenting that history, our explanation should be regarded as exploratory rather than definitive.

Fourth, the quantitative findings have led us to ask whether differing attitudes, norms, and beliefs about women's roles as well as local traditions might have produced the regional differences evident ca. 1860. The logic of chapter 3 is that such factors should be correlated with region of origin and therefore evident in the behavior of migrants. Thus, while some of the differences in feminization across counties in pre–Civil War Illinois can be explained by factors other than settlers' origin, by no means all can—hence our conclusion that norms, beliefs, and local traditions must have mattered.

---

1. Bernard Bailyn, *Education in the Forming of American Society: Needs and Opportunities for Study*, Institute of Early American History and Culture at Williamsburg, Va. (Chapel Hill, N.C.), 1960.

In a related vein, we rejected arguments that the ideology of the domestic sphere was so much more circumscribing in the South that it can readily explain the regional difference in feminization, since census data show that women worked in the rural South in proportions similar to those found in the rural North. And in chapter 5, we noted that a gender gap in salaries and administrative positions remained after we accounted for measures of teachers' more objective credentials (their education and experience). These arguments all depend on the interpretation of a "residual"—an observed association that remains after all other (measurable) factors have been allowed to explain what they can. The disadvantage of residual arguments, as common as they may be in social science, is that they can never prove the case at hand. But the advantages, as far as guiding future research is concerned, are equally obvious. New data, or more complex statistical analysis, for example, might force us to revise our conclusions about the impact of relative (female-to-male) wages on the percent of women in teaching (though, naturally, we are skeptical on this possibility). More to the point, traditional sources such as diaries, travelers' accounts, archival records of school boards, and the like can now be probed anew with the goal of ferreting out qualitative evidence of local attitudes toward female teachers; and, hence, supporting, or perhaps refuting, the emphasis our work places on institutional history and cultural norms.

We have focused in this book on explaining a specific historical phenomenon—the gendered character of grade-school teaching across space and time—but it is reasonable to ask what the ramifications of this phenomenon were for the broader course of American history. In particular, we can comment very briefly on some ways in which the prevalence of female teachers in a region and later throughout all regions may have affected American history generally. The economic historian Susan Carter has noted one important possibility.[2] Although knowledge is to some extent its own reward, it also has economic value. Teachers, in other words, help produce an important intermediate good—"human capital"—that, by raising labor productivity, promotes economic growth in the long run. Because female teachers were cheaper to hire than male teachers were, the economic cost of producing human capital was cheaper than it otherwise would have been, providing a boost to its production and hence to long-term economic growth. Regions that lagged behind in their exploitation of female teachers in this sense,

---

2. Susan Carter, "Occupational Segregation, Teachers' Wages, and American Economic Growth," *Journal of Economic History* 46 (June 1986): 373–83.

such as the South, lagged behind in the production of human capital and, in consequence, in per capita incomes and economic development.

Second, a distinguishing feature of American education has long been the similarity of educational attainments between men and women, despite the fact that, until quite recently, women spent a much smaller fraction of their adult lives in the paid labor force. Indeed, at least a rough similarity must have been a necessary context for the subsequent feminization of schoolteaching (notwithstanding our inability to document much of a statistical association between female schooling and the percentage of women in teaching). Compared with most other occupations, teaching has always required a higher level of educational preparation. As such, once female schoolteaching was an accepted pattern in a region, the level of educational attainment of each successive generation of American women was probably higher than it would have been otherwise, because a notable fraction of the next generation of women would teach at some time in their lives. Furthermore, as educational requirements in teaching rose in the late nineteenth and early twentieth centuries, teachers' colleges proliferated to provide the necessary training. Many of these teachers' colleges, in turn, were transformed into colleges plain and simple as American higher education expanded in the second half of the twentieth century.

Third, while a "glass ceiling" clearly existed in the teaching profession in the early twentieth century (recall the findings of chap. 5), and while, consequently, women may have felt subservient to male educational authorities, it is also true that teaching offered young, educated women a significant degree of autonomy in their work lives that they probably would not have had if the occupation had been closed to them. Also, while women were denied the same opportunities in educational administration as men had, some women did become assistant principals, principals, and even higher-level administrators—in short, they took advantage of opportunities to acquire managerial skills that were scarcely available to women elsewhere in the economy at that time. Then, too, women who had been teachers while younger presumably provided a home environment that valued education highly, thereby laying the groundwork for further social change.

Finally, it is possible that the gender of the teacher influenced the complex process by which children were socialized—or, to put it differently, we may ask whether all those nineteenth-century arguments about the value, especially to younger children, of the tenderness and nurturing nature of the female teacher in fact had some merit. Before we dismiss these arguments as mere rationalizations for keeping teachers' wages low, one might reflect whether they are so very different from the distinctions that Carol Gilligan popularized, between the orientations said to be more typical of women (caring) and those more typical of men (justice). It does not require that any such distinction be innate or even universal, only that the distinctions mattered for what transpired in the classroom in a particular historical period. If so, the existence of regional differences in feminization may have been a causal factor behind regional differences in culture. One might wonder, for example, whether the sort of regional differences stressed by the historian Bertram Wyatt-Brown—the southern emphasis on honor and violence versus a New England culture which internalized the need for good behavior and, in the event of bad behavior, guilt—may have been an outcome related to the earlier feminization of the teaching force in the North than in the South. In raising this possibility we are not of course suggesting that all culture has its roots in formal education; yet the gender of the teacher might have mattered in subtle but important ways in the transmission of social norms.[3]

3. Carol Gilligan, *In a Different Voice: Psychological Theory and Women's Development* (Cambridge, Mass., 1982); Bertram Wyatt-Brown, *Southern Honor: Ethics and Behavior in the Old South* (New York, 1982). We are grateful to historian Mark Lytle for suggesting to us the possible connection between regional differences in the prevalence of women teachers and Wyatt-Brown's distinctions.

APPENDIX 1

Sources

THE IPUMS

As explained in the introduction, we relied heavily on the Integrated Public Use Microdata Samples. These are the result of tremendous work by multiple teams of social scientists and historians over a decade and a half. Census manuscript schedules, which enumerators filled out as they went from household to household, comprise the actual manuscripts of the United States decennial censuses. Since 1850 these have been filled out on all individuals in terms of the households (or group quarters) in which they lived. The original manuscript schedules have been preserved (now on microfilm), with the exception of returns for the 1890 enumeration, most of which burned before being microfilmed.

Since the early years of the computer age, the Census Bureau and, later, teams of researchers explored making samples of these records machine readable. While the bureau focused on the then-current census, historians and social scientists worked with records of past censuses. Giant samples, nearly all numbering in the hundreds of thousands or millions of cases, have been drawn from all the extant censuses, 1850–1990. Some of these data collection and processing efforts are still underway, so that, for example, the 1860 and 1870 samples are much smaller than the 1850 and 1880 samples. Since we use the 1850, 1860, and 1880 samples repeatedly in the first two chapters in particular, this point should be borne in mind.

In the past few years a further enhancement has been undertaken by scholars at the University of Minnesota. They have rearranged the fields in which the items of information are found and rearranged the coding of each item so that samples are now broadly compatible despite the differences over time in the questions asked and in the classification of the answers. When a question was not asked in a given year (or a classification not used), the census for that year simply shows the field as blank (or the classification of an item as empty).

This enhancement of uniformity across the data sets will not concern the reader, but the reader should nonetheless appreciate how very much easier it is to carry out the explorations on these samples now than when we began our project a decade ago. Many more data sets are now available, and using them is much easier.

Our National Samples of American Teachers, 1860 and 1880

These samples were also drawn from census manuscript schedules. Every other reel of microfilm (in numeric order) was selected and every teacher on a systematic sampling of manuscript pages to appear in those microfilm reels was selected. These samples produced far more teachers than would have been available from the comparable IPUMS data sets (which in any case were not available when we selected out teacher samples). All data from the household in which a teacher lived were recorded. These national teacher sample data sets are described in further detail in Joel Perlmann and Robert A. Margo, "Who Were America's Teachers? Towards a Social History and a Data Archive" *Historical Methods* 22 (Spring 1989): 68–73.

In selecting the teacher samples, we used as inclusive a definition of the occupation "teacher" as we could. Unless otherwise indicated, when we present data from the teacher samples, the small number of people listed explicitly as school administrators, professors, and teachers of arts are excluded. The omission is numerically inconsequential, especially in rural areas. On the other hand, note that the teachers in our teacher sample (and in our tables based on those samples) include private as well as public school teachers. The two are typically not distinguished in the census manuscript schedules.

Evidence on Size of Place in the Census

The IPUMS indicate whether a place is urban or rural, using the census definition of an incorporated place of 2,500 residents as urban. Beyond that, only the 98 largest cities of the country are listed by population size in the early (1850–80) IPUMS. In our teacher samples, we relied on published census lists of incorporated places of 4,000 residents and over. Everyone in places of this size and larger was coded by size of place.

When we compared rural places (in chap. 2) using both our national teacher sample for 1860 and the IPUMS for 1850 and 1860, we defined rural in the IPUMS as the places other than the cities. We did so because, in the New England area in particular, incorporated places include what elsewhere are called townships (as opposed to towns). We did not want to exclude all townships with a population of 2,500 because so many would have been excluded. Nevertheless, most relevant analyses were made in both ways (eliminating all urban, eliminating only the 98 largest cities), and there was in fact no difference consequential to the conclusions.

The actual definition of places that are urban or rural in census data is notoriously complicated. For a description of the census efforts to classify places, and the complexity behind the seemingly simple classification of 2,500 and over as urban, see United States Bureau of the Census, *Current Population Reports*, series p-23, no. 1, "The Development of the Urban-Rural Classification in the United States: 1874–1949" (Washington, 1949). Our coders were provided with a list of the 137 cities that had populations of at least 25,000 in 1900. All other place names were copied as they read and made machine readable. Later, we coded all these place names by size, using an 1880 list of all incorporated places with a population of at least 4,000 which included the 1870 and 1880 population of each place (United States Census Office, *Statistics of the Population of the United States at the Tenth Census* [Washington, 1883], table IX, pp. 447–56). We traced each place name to that list. Places not on that list were coded as rural. Note that the population criterion of 4,000 is based on the 1870 enumeration, not on 1860, probably making the coding more restrictive than an 1860 list would have. Both national samples for 1860 (the national sample of teachers and their households, and the national sample of all households) were coded as described here.

THE URBAN TEACHER LISTS

We describe these lists in the text and notes of chapter 5 and in the first part of the related appendix 5, below.

APPENDIX 2

Female-to-Male Wage Ratio Data

WAGE RATIOS IN AGRICULTURE

Wages generally, and the female-to-male wage ratio in particular, reflected the impact of a wide range of factors; readers should bear in mind that the female-to-male wage ratio was therefore the outcome of highly complex processes, rather than a conceptually simple measure. We have a measure of the average wage paid in each county to women in a typical occupation (domestic service), and the average wage paid to men in two typical occupations (day labor, farmhand). We construct ratios using the wage for women's work as the numerator and one of the two wages for men's work as the denominator. We have evidence at the state level published for 1850 and for 1860 (thus, a total of four ratios for each state). The text restricts consideration to this state-level evidence.

Table A2.1 shows the four ratios *at the state level* on southern states that had high and low ratios, a classification central to our arguments in the text.

The two ratios for 1860 show the fourteen states of the South lining up in about the same order on each. And, in particular, we can divide these states into three groups: high, middle, and low. The figures for 1850 vary a bit from those of 1860, as a result of changes in the local economies over the decade, as well as simply with the crude nature of the data. Nevertheless, no southern state in the group of those with the highest ratios in 1860 was among those with the lowest in 1850 or vice versa.

The information on wages comes from a supplemental survey conducted at the local level (sometimes for counties; sometimes for smaller geographic areas and aggregated up to the county level). This information was collected in connection with the 1860 census, as part of a special enumeration of social statistics for counties. While the county-level data on wages were never published, the original manuscript schedules have been preserved on microfilm for

TABLE A2.1 Female-to-Male Wage Ratios in Agriculture, Southern States, 1850–60

Ratio	State	RATIODAY	RATIOFRM	RATIOD50	RATIOF50
Low	Delaware	0.25137	0.37398	0.27451	0.41411
	Virginia	0.31148	0.43220	0.34043	0.49348
	North Carolina	0.33333	0.45130	0.34524	0.52288
	Maryland	0.33621	0.52214	0.30272	0.48942
	Kentucky	0.34507	0.46942	0.36333	0.47233
	Tennessee	0.36158	0.46454	0.38760	0.49981
Middle	Georgia	0.44180	0.60558	0.50667	0.72942
	Mississippi	0.44118	0.58523	0.36715	0.59879
	Arkansas	0.40812	0.58082	0.51543	0.68078
	Texas	0.46296	0.67624	0.44444	0.72222
High	Florida	0.50877	0.70352	0.44853	0.79300
	South Carolina	0.51412	0.69364	0.48299	0.79706
	Alabama	0.49524	0.72630	0.47959	0.63514
	Louisiana	0.57732	0.85647	0.58676	0.87005

Note: RATIODAY (RATIOD50): The ratio of a female domestic's weekly wages to six times the value of a male day laborer's wages, both with board in 1860 (1850).

RATIOFRM (RATIOF50): The ratio of a female domestic's weekly wages (multiplied by 52/12) to a male farmhand's monthly wages, both with board in 1860 (1850).

a variety of states. The authors initially gathered some of the available county-level wage data for this project, and Margo gathered much more (also used here) in connection with other research on nineteenth-century wages. We rely on evidence for fourteen states, although it is often incomplete.

The evidence on the sex of the teacher comes from our national sample of teachers drawn from the manuscript schedules of the 1860 census; the analysis here is limited to teachers who were living in rural areas (i.e., in places with a population of less than 4,000). The 1860 national teacher sample included 1,232 rural teachers in 271 counties for which we were able to find county-level wage data.

THE QUALITY OF THE DATA

Is our indicator of the actual condition of wages good enough for our needs? Our evidence on wages derives from a different source than that used by Goldin and Sokoloff, and we have not tried to refine the raw data; however, the raw data have the tremendous advantage of being available for large numbers of counties in the same year. Enumerators working with the census of 1860 were asked to collect information on wages prevailing in their counties. Thus, for example, the enumerators recorded the wages for a farm-hand with board, for a day laborer both with and without board, and for a female domestic servant.

Exactly how the enumerators determined the prevailing wage is not clear;

also enumerators recorded the information they collected in a variety of ways. And even in the states from which the manuscript schedules have been preserved, schedules are missing or incomplete for a substantial minority of counties.[1]

The evidence on quality, namely the internal consistency of the evidence, is surprisingly heartening, considering all the sources for error. We were able to perform several tests of quality; in each, we used only the data pertaining to the counties from which we had selected teachers for the 1860 teacher sample, one observation per county. In this way we can check whether the wage ratio information to be used in the sample is reliable, a stronger test than whether all the county-level wage data available from states is reliable.

First, we exploit three items of information reported in the census of social statistics: wages paid to a day laborer with board, wages paid to a day laborer without board, and the price of board. How well do the wages with board, minus the price of board, predict the wages without board?[2] Parts 1–3 of table A2.2 show the correlation between DAYLABOR and TESTDAY for 1860, and part 4 shows the correlation between DAY50 and TESTD50 for 1850.

---

1. Use of the wage data required addressing various limitations in them. (1) New York state data were lost for the counties whose names begin with the letters A–L (this bias restricts the numbers of sample members on which we have complete data, of course, but should not otherwise matter). (2) In a number of states, wage information for some counties is available for small areas of enumeration, whereas in other counties it is available only at the county-level summary of this information is to be found in the manuscripts. Nor can we easily determine the relative population in each area of enumeration; as a result, the only way we could arrive at summary level figures for such counties was to determine an unweighted mean of the average for all areas of enumeration, thus treating the districts as though they included populations of equal size. (3) Enumerators made some obvious errors in recording data in a few counties, such as forgetting decimal points. These we corrected. (4) Finally, the enumerators were asked to record average monthly wages in some cases, average weekly wages in another, and average daily wages in still other cases. We converted days to weeks assuming six working days per week, and weeks to months by the multiplier 52/12. In addition to the wages described in the text, the census manuscripts also give us the wage for a carpenter; however we did not use this information.

2. Of course, the enumerators might have checked their own work for internal consistency, leaving us merely a record of their corrections and not evidence of the value of the data. However if they did check their work for internal consistency, they would have had to exert themselves a bit, since wages requested by the Census Office were daily wages and the price of board the office requested was for a week's board; the enumerators, therefore, could not simply have added two responses to check the third; at a minimum they would have had to do some multiplication or division as well as some addition to check the consistency of their figures. The cross-decade correlation discussed below strengthens our confidence in the measure.

TABLE A2.2 Testing the Quality of the County-Level Wage Ratio
Evidence: Correlation Coefficients

1. 1860, counties in 14 states (10 southern, 4 northern)

	TESTDAY	FARMHAND
DAYLABOR	0.77501	0.55684
	0.0001	0.0001
	195	271

2. 1860, counties in 4 northern states

	TESTDAY	FARMHAND
DAYLABOR	0.34887	0.29594
	0.1432	0.0032
	19	97

3. 1860, counties in 10 southern states

	TESTDAY	FARMHAND
DAYLABOR	0.77685	0.59855
	0.0001	0.0001
	176	174

4. 1850, 10 southern states

	TESTD50	FARM50
DAY50	0.80334	0.73068
	0.0001	0.0001
	94	94

5. 1850 and 1860, counties in 10 southern states

DAYLABOR/DAY50	FARMHAND/FARM50	FEMALEDM/FEMDM50
0.42433	0.52193	0.53851
0.0001	0.0001	0.0001
94	94	94

6. 1850 and 1860, counties in 10 southern states

	RATIODAY	RATIOFRM	RATIOD50	RATIOF50
COTTON	0.22396	0.33277	0.03105	0.05385
	0.0029	0.0001	0.7664	0.6062
	175	174	94	94

Note: First row: correlation coefficient (r).
Second row: statistical significance ($p <$).
Third row: number of counties included (N).
DAYLABOR (DAY50): Wages of a day laborer with board, 1860 (1850).
FARMHAND (FARM50): Wages of a farm hand with board, 1860 (1850).
FEMALEDM (FEMDM50): Wages of a female domestic with board, 1860 (1850).
TESTDAY (TESTD50): An estimate of the wages of a day laborer with board from wages without board and the cost of board, 1860 (1850).
RATIODAY (RATIOD50): FEMALEDM/DAYLABOR, 1860 (1850).
COTTON: A measure of cotton production in the county.
All measures are based on one observation per county in which county-level wage data are extant from 1850 or 1860 and from which a teacher was selected for the 1860 sample. Only teachers in rural areas (less than 4,000 residents) are included.
Differences in the Ns result both from the loss of the relevant manuscript data for some counties and from the fact that not all wage data were collected from all states in each year. The 14 states from which county-level wage data could be obtained were Massachusetts, New York, Pennsylvania, and Illinois in the North and Alabama, Florida, Georgia, Kentucky, Louisiana, North Carolina, South Carolina, Tennessee, Texas, and Virginia in the South.

We also expect that the wages of day laborers and the wages of farm-hands correlated highly across counties (again, in the South in both census years). Parts 1–3 of the table show the correlation between DAYLABOR and FARMHAND for 1860, and part 4 shows the correlation between DAY50 and FARM50 for 1850.

For the 10 southern states we can also perform two further tests. First, we can relate the 1850 and 1860 surveys of wage data (we did not collect 1850 information from the four relevant northern states). In part 5 of the table the three measures of wages for 1860, DAYLABOR, FARMHAND, and FEMALEDM are each correlated with the corresponding measure for 1850.

And, finally, following the observations of Goldin and Sokoloff, we expected that in counties which cultivated cotton intensively, female wages would be high, relative to male wages—because cotton could be cultivated by women and children (not requiring the strength some other crops did). In part 6 of the table, the correlation between COTTON on the one hand and RATIOD60 (and RATIOD50) and RATIOF60 (and RATIOF50) on the other is shown. Many of the counties are typified by no cotton production, so that the corre-lation is of limited value, but the relevant relationships can also be seen as well by looking at the two ratios within three levels of cotton production: for low, middle, and high levels of cotton production (in both 1850 and 1860; see table A2.3).

The single test that results in no confirmation of our expectations is the association between the 1850 wage ratios and the 1860 levels of cotton produc-tion (table A2.2, part 6). Of course, a decade had passed between the taking of the two sets of measures; still the passage of time had not affected the other 1850/1860 comparisons nearly as much (e.g., table A2.2, parts 4 and 5, and table A2.3).

In any case, all of the correlations are in the expected direction, many are reasonably strong (.4 or higher), and nearly all are statistically significant. We have some grounds, then, for expecting to observe associations between the wage ratios and the percentage of teachers who were women, if the former is really influencing the latter.

TABLE A2.3 Wage Ratios in the South, by Levels of Cotton Production

Level of Cotton Production[a]	N of Counties	RATIODAY	RATIOFRM	N of Counties	RATIOD50	RATIOF50
Low	116	.37	.52	62	.40	.52
Medium	26	.49	.68	14	.51	.76
High	32	.53	.73	18	.54	.74

Note: See notes to table A2.2.

[a] Cotton in bales/arable land in acres in 1860: low .006; medium .08; high .26.

THE COUNTY-LEVEL EVIDENCE

We explore the issues in our 1860 national sample of teachers. Only those teachers living in counties for which county-level wage data were available are included in the regression analysis (table A2.4). Thus, 1,232 teachers from fourteen states are included. We regress the odds that the

TABLE A2.4 Variables Included in the Logit Regression Analysis: Means and Standard Deviations

Variable	N	Mean	Std Dev
14 states	1,232		
FEMT		0.57224	0.49495
AGE19		0.19627	0.39734
AGE2529		0.17924	0.38371
AGE3039		0.13463	0.34147
AGE40		0.08921	0.28517
RATIODAY		0.32737	0.12109
SOUTH		0.34063	0.47411
4 northern states	813		
FEMT		0.67528	0.46856
AGE19		0.23616	0.42498
AGE2529		0.15621	0.36328
AGE3039		0.11193	0.31548
AGE40		0.07258	0.25959
RATIODAY		0.27943	0.05002
NY		0.26199	0.43999
PA		0.36408	0.48147
IL		0.20664	0.40515
PWFS		0.47579	0.01640
PWFIL		0.55155	0.09417
10 southern states	419		
FEMT		0.37232	0.48400
AGE19		0.11905	0.32423
AGE2529		0.22381	0.41729
AGE3039		0.17857	0.38345
AGE40		0.12143	0.32701
RATIODAY		0.42016	0.15866
PWFS		0.46062	0.06064
PWFIL		0.59018	0.08995

Note: The data set is the sample of teachers collected from the 1860 census manuscript schedules.

Variable definitions (other than those listed in notes to table A2.2):

AGE19: sample member is 19 or younger (0 = no; 1 = yes).

AGE2529: sample member is 25–29 years of age (0 = no; 1 = yes).

AGE3039: sample member is 30–39 years of age (0 = no; 1 = yes).

AGE40: sample member is 40 years of age or older (0 = no; 1 = yes).

PWFS: percentage of females among white school attenders in the schoolteacher's county of residence, ages 5–19.

PWFIL: percentage of females among adult white illiterates in the schoolteacher's county of residence.

teacher was a woman on the age of the teacher (measured in dummy variables), RATIODAY, geographic variables for state or region, and (crude) county-level education variables, measuring the proportion of girls among children in school and the proportion of women among the illiterate. In model A1, controlling only the age of the teacher, and measured across all fourteen states, the coefficient on RATIODAY is highly significant and in the predicted direction (table A2.5). But as soon as we distinguish South from North, in model A2 (with a dummy variable SOUTH), we see that what is operating on gender of the

TABLE A2.5 Logit Regression Analysis: Female Teachers and the Wage Ratio (likelihood that a teacher was female regressed on age, state, or region, and the female-to-male wage ratio in the county, 1860)

A. Analysis Carried out on Teachers in All 14 States for Which County-Level Wage Data Are Available (N cases = 1,232)

Variable	Model A1		Model A2	
	Parameter Estimate	Standard Error	Parameter Estimate	Standard Error
INTERCPT	1.3215	0.1961	0.9329	0.1992
AGE19	0.9437	0.1883	0.8941	0.1917
AGE2529	−0.4075	0.1656	−0.3487	0.1696
AGE3039	−0.7218	0.1852	−0.6725	0.1894
AGE40	−1.3681	0.2356	−1.3423	0.2401
RATIODAY	−2.7206	0.5404	−0.4359	0.6138
SOUTH			−1.0565	0.1553
χ^2 for covariates (−2LL)	151.1 with 5 DF		198.5 with 6 DF	

B. Analysis Carried out on Teachers in the 4 Northern States for Which County-Level Wage Data Are Available (N cases = 813)

Variable	Model B1		Model B2	
	Parameter Estimate	Standard Error	Parameter Estimate	Standard Error
INTERCPT	1.6904	0.4534	2.2378	0.5348
AGE19	0.8103	0.2290	0.7826	0.2343
AGE2529	−0.1875	0.2210	−0.2128	0.2279
AGE3039	−0.7278	0.2419	−0.6694	0.2493
AGE40	−1.6387	0.3071	−1.6915	0.3169
RATIODAY	−3.0731	1.5670	−1.9322	1.6674
NY			−0.3430	0.2948
PA			−1.1952	0.2692
IL			−1.3648	0.2924
χ^2 for covariates (−2LL)	75.0 with 5 DF		116.0 with 8 DF	

TABLE A2.5 *continued*

C. Analysis Carried out on Teachers in the 10 Southern States for Which County-Level Wage Data Are Available (*N* cases = 419)

	Model C1		Model C2		Model C3	
Variable	Parameter Estimate	Standard Error	Parameter Estimate	Standard Error	Parameter Estimate	Standard Error
INTERCPT	−0.3644	0.3183	−0.8548	0.8708	−1.8088	0.8899
AGE19	1.0738	0.3469	0.9607	0.3507	0.9865	0.3521
AGE2529	−0.5591	0.2820	−0.5396	0.2857	−0.5434	0.2865
AGE3039	−0.5295	0.3031	−0.5882	0.3047	−0.5716	0.3056
AGE40	−0.8292	0.3697	−0.8522	0.3722	−0.8385	0.3732
RATIODAY	0.0345	0.6597	0.3662	0.6931	0.6079	0.7098
PWFS			0.8765	1.7694		
PWFIL					2.1104	1.2916
χ^2 for covariates (−2LL)	28.8 with 5 DF		26.0 with 6 DF		28.5 with 6 DF	

Note: Variables are defined in tables A2.2 and A2.2. The dependent variable in each model, FEMT, is female teacher (0 = no; 1 = yes). The omitted category for dummy variables are AGE2024 (for the age of the teacher), NOTSOUTH (i.e., the 4 northern states) in model A2 and MA (i.e., the fourth northern state) in model B2. Replacing RATIODAY with RATIOFRM (substituting the wages of male farm laborers for the wages of male day laborers in the denominator of the wage ratio) yields no consequential interesting differences in the models.

teacher is something shared by all counties covered by the SOUTH variable, and that the apparent influence of RATIODAY was due to the fact that across the regions, South/non-South, RATIODAY also differed sharply. But once controlling for region, virtually all of the impact of RATIODAY disappears. The implication is that within each region, South and non-South, RATIODAY has no effect. If we now turn to the models in parts B and C, we find that expectation confirmed. In the North, the ratio may be operating in the expected direction, but once Pennsylvania and Illinois counties are distinguished from those in Massachusetts and New York, we again find the impact of RATIODAY across counties to be minimal. In the South, within which the ratio varies considerably, the impact of RATIODAY on the gender of the teacher is minimal. Nor does controlling for either literacy variable have any impact on this conclusion.

WAGE RATIOS OF TEACHERS IN THE SOUTH

With the exception of Calvin Wiley's detailed reports of North Carolina in the 1850s, few relevant reports were published in the antebellum period. After the Civil War, the United States commissioner of education began publishing summaries of state reports (in 1870); and these present the wages of male and female teachers. These reports are far from perfect: they

TABLE A2.6 Ratio of Female-to-Male Teacher Wages in the South,
1870–1900

State	1860	1870	1875	1880	1885	1890	1895	1900
DE	.251	n.a.	n.a.	.804	n.a.	.931	.931	.931
VA	.311	n.a.	.857	.844	.867	.849	.821	.822
NC	.333	.902	n.a.	1	1	.893	.881	.901
MD	.336	1	1	1	1	.804	.842	n.a.
KY	.345	n.a.	1	1	1	1.03	.824	.844
TN	.361	n.a.	1	1	1	.849	1	n.a.
AR	.408	.750	n.a.	.800	n.a.	n.a.	.948	.755
MS	.441	n.a.	1	1	1	.906	.826	.829
GA	.441	n.a.	n.a.	.600	n.a.	n.a.	n.a.	n.a.
TX	.462	n.a.	n.a.	.824	n.a.	.799	.820	n.a.
AL	.495	n.a.	.975	1	1	n.a.	n.a.	.871
FL	.508	n.a.	n.a.	1	1	n.a.	.958	.903
SC	.514	n.a.	.923	.947	.890	.842	.877	.894
LA	.577	.679	1	1	.912	.902	.901	.802

Note: n.a.: not available.

TABLE A2.7 Female-to-Male Wage Ratio in Teaching (FMWRT) Outside
the South in 1870, 1875, 1880, and 1885

State	1870	1875	1880	1885
CT	0.49642	0.53319	0.62821	1.26702
ME	0.43384	0.48649	0.65757	0.49392
MA	0.39928	0.40002	0.45292	0.36324
NH	0.57447	0.59939	0.65445	0.59169
RI	n.a.	0.79357	0.61204	0.54494
VT	n.a.	0.56225	0.62644	0.67427
NJ	0.57180	0.55802	0.58939	0.57829
NY	0.99432	n.a.	n.a.	1.08309
PA	0.77577	0.83005	0.87824	0.77108
IL	0.77358	0.69114	0.75859	0.78398
IN	0.76757	0.61538	0.94624	1.00000
MI	0.51038	0.54962	0.69018	0.67533
OH	0.59788	0.73333	0.69643	0.74074
WI	0.64955	n.a.	0.67071	0.67545
IA	0.73485	0.77236	0.84339	0.81337
KS	0.78176	0.80194	0.80012	0.74125
MN	0.66205	0.69898	0.77982	0.76333
MS	0.77228	0.77632	0.85714	n.a.

Note: n.a.: not available.

are simply missing for many southern states in the first years after the war, and often when they are presented, the figures for mean wages of men and women are precisely identical, which could suggest either equal wages or sloppy reporting. Also, in the early years some state data show a good deal of volatility. Perhaps the quality of reporting differed between urban areas (with graded school systems) and rural areas in some years but was more balanced in other years. In any case, these postbellum reports show clearly that women were indeed paid nearly as much as men for teaching in the South, nearly always at least 0.8 as much as men and often 0.9 as much or more. This conclusion derives from the figures we have *other than* those that show precisely equal average wages going to men and women. If the latter are taken seriously (and our hunch is that they should not be taken seriously), then the ratios would be still closer to unity (tables A2.6 and A2.7).

Many changes were occurring in late nineteenth-century schools: the proportion of men in teaching, the qualifications for teachers, the proportion of high school teachers were all shifting. Thus there would be reasons to expect that the wage ratio might move either up or down in a given state as these changes occurred. However, the regional difference remains clearly visible, and the absence of a difference between the "low" and "high" groups of southern states sorted by the wage ratio in the wider economy also persists.

APPENDIX 3

SOCIAL CHARACTERISTICS OF ILLINOIS COUNTIES
AND THEIR ROLE IN THE REGRESSION ANALYSIS
*Social Characteristics Controlled for Each
Illinois County*
Crops and Livestock

Differences in agricultural production between northern and
southern Illinois are shown in table A3.1, for the year 1860.[3] As discussed in
the text, our interest here was to determine whether the economic differences
across the state—in agriculture or manufacturing—might have produced differences in the competing demands for women's time, a midwestern variant
of the Goldin-Sokoloff formulations discussed in chapter 2. However, we had
no firm hypothesis about a specific crop-mix difference, only the general concern that the demand for women's time in work other than teaching might
have varied across the state in a way that would influence who would be hired
to teach.

Accordingly, we have explored how every major crop and livestock difference between northern and southern Illinois was associated with the prevalence
of female teachers. We do so because we are trying to control whatever makes
it more difficult to demonstrate that settlers' cultural origins explain the variations in the prevalence of female teachers.

Other Aspects of Agriculture

We approach other aspects of farm life in the same way. In
the north, farm machinery was more widely used; it averaged $143 per farm

3. Maps prepared by the agricultural historian John Falconer in the 1920s suggest similar
conclusions; see Bidwell and Falconer, *History of Agriculture.*

TABLE A3.1 Agricultural Patterns in the Northern, Central, and
Southern Tiers of Illinois Counties

Agricultural Product	Average Production by Tier of Counties		
	North	Central	South
Cows	29.21	5.60	15.94
Cattle	7.78	6.17	4.29
Butter	2.43	1.68	1.73
Cheese	1.02	0.08	0.11
Sheep	4.21	6.04	6.26
Wool	79.23	36.90	59.92
Wheat	2.14	1.38	1.63
Corn	3.92	11.12	9.50
Swine	12.03	19.93	17.54
Potatotes	0.38	0.34	0.31
Sweet potatoes	0.15	0.02	0.17

Source: U.S. Census Office, *Agriculture in the United States in 1860*, Washington, D.C., 1864.

Note: 98 counties, weighted in terms of number of teachers in each; Chicago's Cook County excluded. Figures for livestock are number/number of farms; figures for crops are number of units produced (pounds, bushels, etc.)/number of acres of improved land.

in the northern tier, $79 in the southern tier. Also, a strikingly higher proportion of farm land had been improved in the northern tier, 75 percent as against 38 percent in the southern tier.[4] While the average farm averaged 137 acres in the north, and 143 acres in the south, improved acres per farm averaged 102 acres in the northern tier of the state, 54 acres in the southern tier. A third such difference, although not one that survived the process of sifting variables described below, was the production of home-manufactured goods. Based on the many accounts of farm life, we might speculate that weaving, garment making, and other such work often required no great strength and could be undertaken between other household chores.[5] Home-manufactured products were indeed more common in the southern tier of the state, with the average value of such products at $14.46 on the farms of the southern tier, $6.77 on the farms of the central tier, and only $2.67 on the farms of the northern tier (perhaps because of less well-developed trade with the Northeast).

4. The value of farms was higher in the northern part of the state (mean value per farm acre being $22.52 in the northern tier of counties and $12.08 in the southern tier). On the other hand, the reason for the difference seems to have been the higher proportion of improved land in the north. The average price of an acre of improved land was nearly identical across the north-south gradient, $30.57 in the northern tier of counties, $31.03 in the southern tier. The average farm price was therefore not included in the multiple regression models shown in the tables here; other models confirmed that it was not an important control variable.

5. Bidwell and Falconer, *History of Agriculture*, 252–54.

Manufacturing

We can explore the percentage of adult males in manufacturing occupations, the percentage of adult females in such occupations, the percentage of capital invested in manufacturing (of all capital in manufacturing and agriculture), and the average value of manufacturing establishments.

Concentration of Population

In 1840, much of Illinois had still been very thinly settled. By 1860, this was no longer the case; only one county met Turner's criterion of a frontier area, with fewer than six people per square mile. Nevertheless, Chicago was the state's only major city, with a population of about 100,000 (we have excluded it from all analyses). There were two other cities of over 10,000, Peoria and Quincy, neither of which could boast 15,000 residents. Another 28 towns included 2,500–10,000 residents. Yet together these towns included less than 9 percent of the population, and Chicago's population did not quite reach 6 percent of the state's total. The other 85 percent of Illinois inhabitants lived in communities of under 2,500 residents.

Still, it is useful to distinguish among the smaller communities. The census may not be too reliable a guide to village life—no clear definition guided its tables of "Cities, Towns, etc." in 1860—but it does offer some guidance. We have distinguished the percentage of county residents living in these "Cities, Towns, etc." of 250–999 and those living in communities of over 1,000. Very high percentages of the residents of the northern counties lived in these villages, and very much lower percentages of those in the south did so.[6]

We include controls for the percentage of population in villages of 250–999 and in towns of over 1,000. We also included the density of population per square mile (a measure of overall concentration, not only in villages and towns). And finally we included two other related measures: (1) the ratio of farms to families in the county (which, in the absence of large holdings or many landless farm workers, should serve as a measure of the percentage of families living on farms); and (2) the ratio of 1860 to 1850 population, speculating that rapid population growth might have made the less expensive female teachers more attractive.

Sifting among These County-Level Variables

We first conducted a preliminary analysis to pare down to manageable size the many measures that are most closely associated with socio-

6. In order to save time and effort, we estimated the number of residents from the counts of towns rather than copying them directly from the tables of population; however, since the range of population in each category is narrow, the estimates of village population cannot be far off.

economic structure—the agricultural, industrial, and urbanization measures. The preliminary analysis can be described in terms of three steps (see table A3.2), although we tested a great many combinations of the twenty-three agricultural, industrial, and population density measures in order to be sure that we did not miss any important connections among them. In step 1, the correlation (r) between every measure and the percentage of female teachers was computed. If the correlation was not statistically significant, the variable was dropped from further consideration. The measures of population concentration were all important, and they are theoretically meaningful. Therefore in step 2, a series of regressions was run in which the percentage of female teachers was regressed on these population measures and on one additional "test" variable, a variable that had proven to be significantly correlated with the percentage of female teachers in step 1. In these regressions, the coefficients on several of the test variables were found to be insignificant, strongly suggesting that their prior correlation with the prevalence of female teachers was spurious (the coefficients on all the variables dropped at step 2 all had low t ratios). In step 3, all the remaining variables were entered simultaneously. The variables whose coefficients did not reach t levels of 1.0 were dropped; the rest of the variables were retained for inclusion in the analysis presented in table A3.2 (which also includes the FMWRA as well as measures of education, fertility, and settlers' origins). This procedure reduced the number of structural variables from twenty-three to nine, permitting meaningful analysis with ninety-eight data points.[7]

Several comments are in order before we take final leave of the other variables. That most crop-mix variables, as well as some other characteristics of agricultural life, were of trivial impact we cannot find startling since we had no strong theories about their importance in the first place. That the measures of industrial development were inconsequential is no doubt due both to the fact that industry was neither very developed in Illinois nor was its development very closely associated with the north-south gradient.

As our preceding comments and the description of our method of choosing the nine structural measures indicates, we do not have strong theoretical claims to make about the agricultural measures we retained from our preliminary analysis—corn, wool, butter, cheese, and the percentage of improved land. All are associated both with settlers' origins and with the prevalence of female teachers, and it is quite possible that some or all of these associations are in fact spurious. This is the danger inherent in such an avowedly

---

7. Also, none of the nine structural independent variables retained for the major phase of the analysis were so highly correlated as to create problems of multicollinearity, the highest correlation among them being under $r = .6$.

TABLE A3.2 Exploratory Analysis of County Characteristics

	Step 1		Step 2	Step 3	
Variable	r	p	p	p	t
Butter	0.29	Y	Y	Y	
Cheese	0.30	Y	Y	Y	
Wool	−0.02	N	Y	Y	
Corn	−0.45	Y	Y	N	1.30
PCTIMPLD	0.64	Y	Y	N	1.89
Wheat	0.23	Y	Y	N	<1
VAVHMFG	−0.47	Y	Y	N	<1
Sheep	−0.25	Y	Y	N	<1
Swine	−0.25	Y	N		
VAVFIMP	0.43	Y	N		
AVMFGCAP	0.29	Y	N		
PMFGFEM	0.22	Y	N		
Cows	0.08	N			
Cattle	0.14	N			
Potato	0.13	N			
SWPOT	0.13	N			
PMFGMALE	0.10	N			
PMFGCAP	0.14	N			
TO999P	0.20	Y		N	1.86
OV1000P	0.55	Y		Y	
FRMTOFAM	−0.37	Y		Y	
DENSITY	0.46	Y		N	<1
GROWTH	0.21	Y		N	1.34

Notes: Step 1: Was the correlation (r) with PFT (percentage of females among public school teachers in the county) significant? Step 2: When the percentage of women among teachers was regressed on this variable and the population concentration measures (TO999P, OV1000P, FRMTOFAM, DENSITY, GROWTH) was the coefficient on this variable significant? Step 3: PFT regressed on all variables for which the answer in step 2 was positive, as well as all population concentration measures. Those with t values over 1.0 retained.

Abbreviations (see also notes to table A3.1):

VAVHMFG: Average value of home-manufactured products, crops, and livestock: amounts produced (see table A3.1).

PCTIMPLD: Percentage of improved farm acreage.

VAVFIMP: Average value of farm implements per farm.

PMFGMALE: Percentage of males 15–59 in manufacturing.

AVMFGCAP: Average value of capital per manufacturing firm.

PMFGCAP: Percentage of capital in agriculture and manufacturing.

PMFGFEM: Percentage of females 15–59 in manufacturing.

TO999P: Percentage of county population in communities of 250–999.

OV1000P: Percentage of county population in communities of 1,000 or more.

FRMTOFAM: Ratio of farms to families in the county.

DENSITY: Population/area.

GROWTH: 1860 population/1850 population.

exploratory procedure. We can at least say that nothing *else* about the agricultural context (that we could measure) mattered *more* than these agricultural measures.

Finally, a comment about the association between the percentage of the population that lived in villages (population 250–999) and the percentage of female teachers is necessary. It is possible that the association is spurious, because Yankees were more likely to live in these villages and to choose female teachers. It is also possible that the Yankee communities were more likely to define themselves as villages, and the southern communities not to do so, even when there was little practical difference in the nature of population concentration between many of these small northern and southern communities. The association between the percentage of county residents living in towns of 1,000 or more residents and the percentage of female teachers is strong. It is worth noting here that most of these towns include fewer than 2,500 residents, and that indeed the relationship is clearly a result of patterns in those towns and not in the few larger centers.[8]

Estimating Settlers' States of Origin

Beginning in 1850, census takers ascertained each individual's state of birth. However, before 1870, data on state of origin were tabulated only at the state level (not the county level). It is true that we now also have public use samples drawn from these sources (the IPUMS files), however the number of native-born migrants into each county from out of state is too few for serious analysis. In 1870, county-level tabulations for some common states of birth were published. For Illinois, countylevel data include the number of all native-born residents as well as the number born in Indiana, Ohio, Pennsylvania, Kentucky, and New York. In addition, state-level tabulations report the number of Illinois residents born in every state.

Our interest is in those born throughout the South and those born in New York and New England. We have no choice but to use the 1870 information as a proxy for the 1860 period. In defense of this proxy we should recall not only that there is no alternative, but also that we are not, strictly speaking, trying to study the origins of the 1860 population; rather, we are interested

8. Indeed, when a related measure was substituted for the percentage living in towns of over 1,000—namely the percentage living in towns of 1,000–2,499—it was as strong as the measure used here. A separate measure for the percentage of county residents in towns of over 2,500 residents produced an insignificant coefficient. There were only about thirty counties that had such a town (a dummy variable was used to distinguish the counties with over 2,500, while a continuous variable measured the population in these larger towns). The relationship with the dependent variable was statistically negligible and the sign on the coefficient fluctuated.

in the domination of particular migrant origins in each part of the state. 1860 would be a better proxy than 1870, but it is not the state composition at one particular moment in time that we are after in any case.

This is how we constructed our estimates of the relative numbers of Yankees (those who had been born in New England and New York) and of Southerners (those who had been born in the states listed in the note to table 1.1) who had come to each county.

1. At the county level,

$$AllNB - (KY + NY + PA + IN + OH + IL) = OthNB,$$

where AllNB = the number of all native-born in the county, OthNB = the number of other native-born in the county, and state abbreviations = the number of those in the county born in each of the states shown.

2. At the state level, the published data show[9]

$$Sth + NEng + NY/OthNB = 0.72.$$

That is, at the state level, of all native-born not from the states listed in step 1, 72 percent had been born in New England or the South.

3. At the county level, we estimated

$$Sth/OthNB = KY/(KY + NY) \times 0.72 \times OthNB,$$
$$NEngNY/OthNB = NY/(KY + NY) \times 0.72 \times OthNB.$$

That is, in order to estimate the proportion southern-born and Yankees among the 72 percent estimated to be from the South in the county's OthNB population, we used as a proxy the numbers from Kentucky and New York in each state (since, of the states listed in step 1, the only one from New England and New York is New York and the only one from the South is Kentucky).

4. These county-level assumptions lead to a serious statewide overestimate of the number of New Englanders (by a factor of 1.47) and a serious underestimate of the number of Southerners (by a factor of 0.71).[10] We therefore multiplied the number of estimated New Englanders in every county by 1/1.47 and the number of Southerners by 1/0.71.

All these calculations were efforts to refine a cruder procedure, in which

9. Nearly all of the other 28 percent in the category of other native-born were from Missouri or the states of the northern Midwest (Michigan, Wisconsin, and Minnesota)—some 54,000 or 76,000. These residents too were probably distributed in much the same way as the Southerns and Yankees respectively, with most from Missouri in the southern part of the state, most from the upper Midwest in the northern part, and those in the central tier distributed much as Kentuckians and New Yorkers were distributed. Consequently, while the assumption that 72 percent of the other native-born in each county were from New England or the South is no doubt incorrect, a good case could be made that most of the other individuals in the other native category might in any case usefully be included.

10. The reason for the serious overestimate is that the ratio of New York–born to Kentucky-born is much larger than the ratio of New England–born to those born in other southern states.

we would have simply used the Kentucky-born as a proxy for all Southern-ers and the New York–born as a proxy for all Yankees. The proportions of Yankees and Southerners for each county that we arrived at in step 4 cor-relates extremely well with the proportions calculated by using only the New York and Kentucky numbers without any refinement ($r = .77$ and $.94$, re-spectively). This result is hardly surprising since our four steps of estimation still rely heavily on the New York and Kentucky figures. The estimates arrived at in step 4 correlate slightly more strongly with the prevalence of female teachers (the dependent variable in our regressions) than do the Kentucky-born and New York–born proxies ($r = .78$ for all southern born vs. $.65$ for Kentucky-born only, and $r = .71$ for all Yankee-born vs. $.69$ for New York–born only).

In general, the crudeness of our proxies and estimations of settlers' origins should increase random imprecision and random error and thus reduce rather than increase the likelihood that the regression analysis will support a connec-tion between the dependent variable and settlers' origins. We cannot think of reasons why our methods of estimation would introduce error systematically biased in favor of an association between the dependent variable and settlers' origins.

The Female-to-Male Wage Ratio Data for Illinois

The county data for the female-to-male wage ratio in agri-culture (FMWRA) come from the same source for Illinois as for the other states on which we collected it, the manuscript schedules of the census of social statistics for 1860. The ratio does not vary systematically across the north-south gradient within the state. On the other hand, the female-to-male wage ratio for *teachers* in Illinois counties—FMWRT—comes from the published state school records of the 1850s. This ratio does vary systematically across the north-south gradient (low in the north, high in the south) and therefore (1) is strongly negatively correlated to the proportion of women among teachers in the county and (2) is not correlated with FMWRA. The simplest explanation for these outcomes is poor data in the FMWRA measure. We can bring to bear only one slender piece of evidence on this point and it does not support the idea that the data are especially poor. We collected three items of informa-tion for each Illinois county: the wages of female domestics, male day labor-ers, and male farm laborers. We can thus compute the FMWRA using either of the two male wage rates in the denominator; they are highly correlated ($r = .68; p = .0001$), as they should be if the data do not contain especially large errors.

More subtle explanations would include a situation in which the female domestic workers in the FMWRA measure and the teachers were noncompeting groups so that the wages of the women in the FMWRA measure have no bearing on the wages of the women in the FMWRT measure. The reason to doubt this now (as in chap. 2) is that the demands on women's time in farming should have been so pervasive as to affect both sets of women's wages, *even if* the domestics and the teachers had little to do with each other (an assumption which is in fact far from certain in the world in which young midwestern farm people, who had received little or no education beyond that provided in the local district school, could teach). A third possibility is that there was an age difference involved, such that female teachers in the southern part of the state were notably older than those in the north or that male teachers in the southern part of the state were notably younger than in the north. Such a difference might make hiring women teachers in the southern counties more costly. But our skimpy sample of some hundred teachers in Illinois in our 1860 teacher sample does not support this possibility.

Whatever the explanation for the patterns of ratios, we could test the importance of the wage ratios to the general point of the chapter by substituting FMWRT for FMWRA. If the demand for women's time in the agricultural economy explains the prevalence of female teachers across the counties of the state, the fact should be reflected to some degree in the average wage paid to female teachers across the counties. And indeed, as already noted, it is ($r = -.71$). As appendix tables A3.3–A3.5 show, our structural controls do a pretty good job explaining both the cross-county variation in FMWRT and in the correlation between FMWRT and PFT. Moreover, the crucial point here is that PBS has a strong independent impact on PFT even when the structural controls *and FMWRT* are included in the model.

TABLE A3.3 Basic Regression Analysis: Percent Female Teachers in County Regressed on Other County Characteristics

Variable	Model 1		Model 2		Model 3		Model 4		Model 5	
	Parameter Estimate	Standard Error	Parameter Estimate	Standard Error	Parameter Estimate	Standard Error	Parameter Estimate	Standard Error	Parameter Estimate	Standard Error
INTERCPT	0.42841	0.05238	0.44513	0.02465	0.22971	0.08021	0.18583	0.24139	0.26159	0.26970
FMWRA	0.02322	0.15960			0.01300	0.09637	-0.03793	0.09694	-0.03629	0.09434
Butter					0.03352	0.00956	0.02816	0.00960	0.01251	0.01253
Cheese					0.03954	0.01317	0.03866	0.01307	0.02078	0.01594
Corn					0.00473	0.00240	-0.00420	0.00243	-0.00264	0.00264
Wool					0.00016	0.00006	-0.00017	0.00006	-0.00015	0.00006
PCTIMPLD					0.24139	0.06329	0.16907	0.07814	0.07038	0.08298
FRMTOFAM					0.21221	0.07687	-0.17646	0.08175	-0.20098	0.08001
TO999P					0.06938	0.04308	0.07656	0.04262	0.03933	0.04295
OV1000P					0.12911	0.03418	0.11182	0.03429	0.09205	0.03347
GROWTH					0.01873	0.00996	0.01733	0.00985	0.01169	0.00976
KMRATIO							-0.07097	0.05062	-0.03548	0.06130
PWFLIT							0.52162	0.28919	0.45051	0.27929
PWFS							0.13827	0.22247	0.17162	0.21511
PBS			-0.30341	0.05061					-0.17498	0.05822
PBY			0.23224	0.05562					0.06224	0.11480
Adj. R^2	-0.0102		0.6432		0.6799		0.6938		0.7195	

Note: Model 5 is summarized in the text table 3.5, based on the computations in table A3.4.
PFT: Percentage of females among all public school teachers in the county.
KMRATIO: Ratio of children to women of childbearing age.
PWFS: Percentage of females among white school attenders (ages 5–19) in the county.
PWFIL: Percentage of females among adult white illiterates in the county.
PBS: Percentage of state's settler population born in selected southern states (1870).
PBY: Percentage of state's settler population that was Yankee (born in selected New England states and New York, 1870).
For other variable definitions see notes to table A3.2.

TABLE A3.4 Computing the Impact of Variables from the Full Model's Coefficients

Variable	Tier1	Tier3	Diff	Coef	Diff×Coef
PFT	0.549	0.237	0.312	n.a.	n.a.
FMWRA	0.303	0.28	0.02	−0.0363	−0.001
Butter	2.43	1.74	0.69	0.0125	0.0086
Cheese	1.02	0.112	0.908	0.021	0.0191
Corn	3.92	9.5	−5.58	−0.0028	0.0156
Wool	79.23	59.9	19.33	−0.0001	−0.0019
PCTIMPLD	0.753	0.404	0.349	0.052	0.0181
FRMTOFAM	0.471	0.574	−0.103	−0.201	0.0207
TO999P	0.254	0.061	0.193	0.039	0.0075
OV1000P	0.569	0.09	0.479	0.092	0.0441
GROWTH	2.33	1.7	0.63	0.012	0.0076
KMRATIO	2.44	2.97	−0.53	−0.035	0.0186
PWFLIT	0.442	0.418	0.024	0.541	0.013
PWFS	0.469	0.456	0.013	0.172	0.0022
PBS	0.021	0.579	−0.558	−0.175	0.0977
PBY	0.471	0.091	0.38	0.062	0.0236
Total					0.2937
County economic characteristics (first 6 measures)					0.0587
Population concentration (next 4 measures)					0.0799
Both kinds of measures taken together (first 10 measures)					0.1386
Fertility rate and education (next 3 measures)					0.0338
Economic population, fertility, and education (first 13 measures)					0.1724
Settlers' origins (last 2 measures)					0.1213

Note: Based on table A3.3, model 5. n.a. = not available.

TABLE A3.5 Supplemental Regression Analyses (percent female teachers in county regressed on other county characteristics, unless otherwise indicated)

	Model 6	
Variable	Parameter Estimate	Standard Error
INTERCPT	0.44351	0.28526
FMWRA	−0.05929	0.09403
Butter	0.01491	0.01244
Cheese	0.02231	0.01575
Corn	−0.00317	0.00262
Wool	−0.00015	0.00006
PCTIMPLD	0.07422	0.08194
FRMTOFAM	−0.19187	0.07915
TO999P	0.03799	0.04240
OV1000P	0.08741	0.03315
GROWTH	0.01079	0.00965
KMRATIO	−0.01396	0.06171
PWFLIT	−0.01853	0.38183
PWFS	0.14826	0.21275
PBS	−0.14845	0.05939
PBY	0.04793	0.11361
PWIL	−0.21211	0.11946
Adj. R^2	0.7266	

TABLE A3.5 *continued*

Models 7–8: Dependent Variable: FMWRT2
(the female-to-male wage rate in teaching)

Variable	Parameter Estimate	Standard Error	Parameter Estimate	Standard Error
INTERCEP	0.61999	0.04409	0.85550	0.07591
FMWRA	0.00323	0.13432		
Butter			−0.03723	0.00977
Cheese			−0.03660	0.01355
Corn			−0.00178	0.00249
Wool			0.000014	0.00006
PCTIMPLD			−0.26896	0.06548
FRMTOFAM			0.20144	0.07941
TO999P			−0.04526	0.04464
OV1000P			−0.04437	0.03487
GROWTH			−0.01142	0.01013
Adj. R^2	−0.0104		0.5138	

Variable	Model 9 Parameter Estimate	Model 9 Standard Error	Model 10 Parameter Estimate	Model 10 Standard Error	Model 11 Parameter Estimate	Model 11 Standard Error
INTERCEP	0.95692	0.05411	0.41008	0.25022	0.36326	0.27458
FMWRT	−0.83915	0.08588	−0.24638	0.09966	−0.15186	0.10567
Butter			0.02032	0.00973	0.00990	0.01253
Cheese			0.02963	0.01314	0.01765	0.01590
Corn			−0.00471	0.00235	−0.00325	0.00263
Wool			−0.00017	0.00006	−0.00015	0.00006
PCTIMPLD			0.11688	0.07820	0.05564	0.08264
FRMTOFAM			−0.12628	0.08120	−0.16686	0.08238
TO999P			0.06314	0.04141	0.03692	0.04231
OV1000P			0.10403	0.03299	0.09072	0.03290
GROWTH			0.01416	0.00940	0.01082	0.00955
KMRATIO			−0.06171	0.04877	−0.03100	0.05958
PWFLIT			0.35977	0.28012	0.36188	0.27658
PWFS			0.15818	0.21463	0.18311	0.21187
PBS					−0.14007	0.06219
PBY					0.06594	0.11170
Adj. R^2	0.4934		0.7140		0.7259	

Note: PWIL: Percentage of white adults who were illiterate. For other variable definitions, see tables A3.2 and A3.3.

PRIOR USE OF IOWA TEACHER WAGES BY HISTORIANS

Thomas Morain's paper was innovative in itself and sparked additional intriguing suggestions by Tyack and his collaborators. Here we show, however, that the Iowa evidence cited there cannot sustain the arguments based on it. Morain's only systematic evidence was a table presented in a footnote to demonstrate a marginal point (that teachers were much more numerous than those obtaining certificates). His other concrete evidence is not merely anecdotal but in fact does not deal directly with the issue of causality in the process of feminization. That evidence consisted of observing (1) that male wages fell and then rose in the late 1870s and early 1880s while male applicants to teaching fell steadily; (2) that various legislation was passed to raise certification standards in the period; (3) and that 1880 figures for age and certificate levels of teachers are consistent with the possibility that "those males who did not seek a career in teaching tended not to enter the profession at all." In general, he believes that "the decline in the percentage of male applicants for certification documents the decreasing male interest in teaching." But in fact the trend is just as consistent with the alternative possibility that males increasingly knew school boards preferred females.

Morain in fact did not make the point that the lengthening school year drove out the men; he did say that requiring teachers to attend teacher institutes held before the school term amounted to lengthening the school term. On the other hand, Tyack and Strober's extension of the argument to cover also the nineteenth-century school term offers an idea very similar to Morain's: whereas Morain tended to stress unremunerated time and expenses of attendance at the institutes, Tyack and Strober add the expenses associated with being asked to teach longer terms that were remunerated, but were not remunerated at a rate high enough to compete with other job opportunities— opportunities that did not conflict with the shorter school terms but did conflict with the longer school terms. It should be stressed, however, that Morain's evidence was not only anecdotal—it was also limited entirely to the issue of rising standards for teaching, rather than to the length of the school term.

RURAL SCHOOL ORGANIZATION AND THE FEMINIZATION OF TEACHING

This appendix presents our empirical tests of the Tyack-Strober thesis discussed in the section "An Alternative Explanation," chapter 4. In tables A4.1–A4.3 below, the strategy of analysis is similar to that already presented in the intensive analysis of Illinois counties in 1858 (chap. 3, and app. tables A3.1–A3.5). The dependent variable is the proportion of female teachers in each county; the evidence is for Illinois counties in 1858 (as in chap. 3) and also for Illinois and Iowa counties for 1881. As before, we regressed the dependent variable on social characteristics of the counties. However, this time we add several measures of school organization (relevant to the Tyack-Strober thesis) to the list of regressors: the length of the school year, the existence of teacher institutes in the county, and the duration of the institutes. The controls we impose in studying Illinois in 1858 have already been discussed in connection with tables A3.1–A3.5; the controls for the 1881 Illinois and Iowa data sets are similar. However, we lack the crop-mix variables included in earlier Illinois analysis.[11]

Background Information

In 1881, ungraded schools still vastly outnumbered graded schools in Illinois and Iowa. Illinois was considerably more urbanized in 1880 than Iowa: by the census criterion of 2,500 residents for an urban area, 31 percent of the Illinois population was urban, and only 15 percent of the Iowa population was urban. But more than half of Illinois's urban residents lived in Chicago; in the rest of the state, 17 percent of Illinois residents lived in urban areas. In the urban areas, the schools were graded, and graded schools were far more likely to have women teachers.

In 1881 Illinois, 57 percent of teachers in ungraded schools were women, and 79 percent of teachers in graded schools were women; in Iowa the comparable figures were 68 percent and 92 percent. In 1881, the Illinois teachers who taught in ungraded schools numbered nearly 17,000. In the northern tier of counties, 69 percent of them were women; in the central tier, 52 percent; and

---

11. In the Iowa data set, we used the percentage of all adults employed in manufacturing rather than the proportion of women workers in manufacturing, since the former was more closely associated with the percentage of women teachers. Also, we omit the percentage of foreign-born as a regressor, since it involves problems of collinearity with the measure of Yankee origins.

in the southern tier, 38 percent. Also, the correlation between the percentage of southern-born settlers in a county and the percentage of its female teachers in that year stood at an incredible −.80, essentially the same as it had been in 1858 ($r = .77$); not surprisingly, therefore, county rankings on the dependent variable for 1881 and 1858 were also very highly correlated ($r = .77$). At the same time, feminization had been proceeding across the state, and the proportion of female teachers in 1881 was about fifteen points higher than it had been in 1858, within each tier. The true gain was greater, because the earlier figures do not exclude the teachers in graded schools (who were more likely to have been women).

Because Iowa lay further north and west than Illinois, Southerners had been much less prominent in its settlement than in the latter state.[12] Even in Iowa, a close observer could find latitude differences across the state's hundred counties—in regional origins, other social characteristics, and the proportion of female teachers. However, these differences were much more muted than in Illinois. In the northern tier of Iowa counties, women made up on average 70 percent of the teachers; in the central tier, 68 percent; and in the southern tier, 65 percent—a 5-point spread compared to the 31-point spread in Illinois. Indeed, the standard deviation of the percentage of female teachers across Iowa counties was only 6 percentage points, in Illinois 16 points.

Illinois School Reports for 1858 include the average length of the school year in each county, and whether a county held a teacher institute. Both varied with latitude. The school year averaged 7.3 months in the northern tier of counties, 6.6 months in the central tier, and 6.5 months in the southern tier. About a third of the counties held a teacher institute—63 percent of the northern tier counties, 31 percent of the central tier counties, and only one (4 percent) of the counties in the southern tier.

By 1881, the mean length of the ungraded school year in Illinois was 6.8 months and the standard deviation 0.7 months; in Iowa the comparable figures were 7.0 and 0.5 respectively. In Illinois, the average teacher institute lasted 19 days and standard deviation was 9 days; in Iowa the comparable figures were 21 and 7 respectively.[13] In Iowa, then, we have an opportunity to explore

12. In the case of Iowa, the 1879 census did not publish the number of settlers from any southern state. We therefore relied on the county-level data on states of origin published in the 1880 census: among native-born migrants to Iowa's northern tier of counties in 1880, 47 percent were from New York or Wisconsin, and 2 percent from Kentucky, Virginia, and Missouri; in the central tier of counties the comparable numbers were 22 percent and 5 percent, and in the southern tier of counties, 8 percent and 14 percent.

13. In Iowa only 1 county failed to hold a teacher institute; in Illinois, 28 counties failed to do so. The mean and standard deviation for Illinois institutes are based on the counties that held the institutes. Including also the counties that did not hold an institute (length) = 0 days), the mean length would be 10 days, the standard deviation 9 days; calculated either way, county-level variation in Iowa was similar to what it was in Illinois.

the impact of school organization in a context of less difference in the social characteristics of counties than in Illinois.

Before turning to the regressions, something more must be said about the character of the teacher institutes; the Tyack-Strober thesis stresses the economic disincentive teachers experienced when they were required to attend these institutes. However, from historian Wayne Fuller's description of the teacher institutes of the Midwest we can appreciate that there were also gains to those who attended (quite apart from the teaching job itself). The institutes were exciting events that offered young people a reason to come to the county seat, see new sights, meet new people—and learn pedagogical techniques from especially gifted and experienced teachers. Moreover, the review of subject content, rather than merely the teaching of pedagogic technique, was an important part of the institutes, and the lecturers at the institutes were carefully chosen to be impressive. The institutes, then, were also a form of continuing education for those whose formal schooling may not have gone far (if at all) beyond the local rural school. And for this reason, many people who did not in fact become teachers appear to have attended the institutes. Indeed, Fuller's description of the institutes reminds one of Jurgen Herbst's description of the normal schools of the same region: a means of higher education for the local population, the local variant of secondary or collegiate training.[14]

Multivariate Analysis

Across the three data sets the regressions deal with ten different associations—between the percentage of female teachers in a county on the one hand and the length of school term, teacher institutes, and duration of institutes in the county on the other. Yet the most important conclusion from these many regression analyses can be stated in a single sentence: not one of the ten associations unambiguously supports the hypothesis that aspects of school organization and the gender of the teacher were tightly linked. Some associations are in the right direction and some are also statistically significant—before controls are imposed. In the Illinois of 1881, the prevalence of female teachers was also positively (and significantly) associated with the holding of a teacher institute, even when controls were imposed. However, the duration of the institute was unrelated to the prevalence of female teachers. And it is difficult to see how the Tyack-Strober theory could explain why holding an institute was influential while the length of the institute was not influential—since the predicted economic disincentive of attending an institute should rise with the length of attendance. Other than that single case we find many weak and inconsistent results.

14. Fuller, *The Old Country School*, 170ff., and Jurgen Herbst, *And Sadly Teach: Teacher Education and Professionalization in American Culture* (Madison, Wis., 1989), chap. 5.

The magnitudes of the associations are generally also unimpressive, even if we were foolish enough to ignore the results of statistical significance tests. With controls imposed, each additional day in the length of a teacher institute in the Iowa of 1881 was associated with an increase of a tenth of a percentage point in the prevalence of female teachers. A two-week difference in institute length (a great difference indeed) could be expected to produce an increase of two percentage points in the prevalence of female teachers in the county. Yet during the last quarter of the nineteenth century, Iowa's teacher force shifted from 61 percent women to 83 percent women.

One other issue deserves attention. Is the apparent connection (when no controls are imposed) between the length of the school year and the prevalence of female teachers simply spurious, created by the fact that Southerners happened to favor both shorter terms and male teachers? Or did the length of the school year also influence the prevalence of female teachers directly—such that when Southerners opted for shorter terms they increased the likelihood that they would keep male teachers? The evidence before us very strongly favors the first interpretation; we focus on Illinois in 1881 to make the point (table A4.4 below). In order to simplify the issue we present a simplified set of models, in which the percentage of female teachers is regressed first on the percentage of southern-born settlers in a county, then on the length of the county's school year, and finally on both variables. Whether we focus on the R^2 or on the parameter estimates, the conclusion is the same: there is no association between length of school year and percentage of female teachers that is independent of settlers' origins, whereas the Tyack-Strober theory would predict such a relationship. On the other hand, there is a strong relationship between settlers' origins and the percentage of female teachers independent of length of school year.[15]

15. The absence of an association between length of school year and percentage of female teachers that is independent of settlers' origins could be understadable only in one circumstance: if within counties with the same percentage of settlers of southern origin the remaining variation in length of the school year and/or prevalence of female teachers was too small for the two measures to vary together much. However, this circumstance did not characterize the Illinois counties (part 3 of table A4.4). Within countries with the same percentage of settlers of southern origin, the standard deviation for length of school year still averaged 0.55 months, or 75 percent of what it was in the state as a whole, and the standard deviation for percentage of female teachers averaged nearly 10 points, or 60 percent of what it was in the state as a whole.

TABLE A4.1 School Organization and the Percentage of Female Teachers: Illinois, 1858

A. Means and Standard Deviations of County Characteristics (101 counties)

Variable	Mean	Standard Deviation
PFT	0.38	0.15
INST1	0.33	0.47
LENGTH	6.75	0.62
FMWAGE	0.66	0.13
Butter	1.85	0.97
Cheese	0.27	0.74
Sheep	5.59	4.03
Wool	49.47	185.69
PCTIMPLD	0.59	0.18
TO999P	0.21	0.21
OV1000P	0.38	0.29
FRMTOFAM	0.51	0.11
PWFS	0.46	0.04
PWATSC	0.53	0.15
PWFIL	0.17	0.17
PBS	0.31	0.25
PBY	0.19	0.18

B. No Controls

Variable	Parameter Estimate		t
INTERCEP	−0.287835		−2.333
LENGTH	0.104784		5.890
R^2		0.2654	
INTERCEP	0.394045		23.779
INST1	0.089909		3.697
R^2		0.1246	

C. Multivariate Analysis

PFT = Variable	Parameter Estimate		t
INTERCEP	0.288086		1.822
INST1	0.001723		0.108
LENGTH	0.003206		0.206
FMWAGE	0.066471		0.880
Butter	0.015350		1.269
Cheese	0.027235		1.766
Sheep	−0.001901		−0.991
Wool	−0.000143		−2.616
PCTIMPLD	0.072665		0.937
TO999P	0.069953		1.682
OV1000P	0.051634		1.704
FRMTOFAM	−0.225251		−2.904
PWFS	0.053866		0.229
PWATSC	0.153191		2.151
PWFIL	−0.132145		−2.029
PBS	−0.150586		−2.535
PBY	0.085265		1.059
R^2		0.7772	

Note: Abbreviations:
INST1: Whether or not the county held a teachers' institute (yes/no).
LENGTH: Length of the school year (in months).
PFT and all other variables: for definitions see table A3.2.

TABLE A4.2 School Organization and the Percentage of Female Teachers: Illinois, 1881

A. Means and Standard Deviations of County Characteristics (101 counties)

Variable	Mean	Standard Deviation
PFTU	0.52	0.16
UGLENGTH	6.79	0.73
TRINDAYS	7.80	9.49
INST1	0.72	0.45
INSTLEN	9.73	9.77
NOPRIVY	0.15	0.20
PFRAME	0.82	0.13
FMWAGE	0.74	0.10
FEMMFG	0.00	0.01
OV1000P	0.20	0.14
FRMTOFAM	1.78	0.51
POWNFARM	0.69	0.07
PFB	0.12	0.08
PFS	0.48	0.02
PATSC	0.68	0.13
PBS	0.30	0.25
PBY	0.19	0.18

B. No Controls

Variable	Parameter Estimate	t	Parameter Estimate	t	Parameter Estimate	t
INTERCEP	−0.25	1.94	0.50	17.85	−0.24	1.81
UGLENGTH	0.12	6.31				
INST1			0.11	2.91	0.08	2.22
INSTLEN			−0.00	1.44		
TRINDAYS					0.00	0.01
R^2		0.29		0.08		0.06

C. Multivariate Analysis

Variable	Parameter Estimate	t	Parameter Estimate	t	Parameter Estimate	t
INTERCEP	1.063	2.939	0.992	2.773	1.189	3.420
UGLENGTH	−0.028	−1.221	0.025	−1.087	−0.047	−2.037
INST1	0.041	1.700	0.054	2.381	0.054	2.494
INSTLEN	0.001	0.998				
TRINDAYS			−0.000	−0.067	0.000	0.128
NOPRIVY					−0.199	−3.076
FMWAGE	−0.149	−1.566	−0.148	−1.546	−0.133	−1.451
FEMMFG	1.092	0.963	1.352	1.194	1.366	1.264
OV1000P	0.050	0.441	0.042	0.376	0.049	0.457
FRMTOFAM	−0.007	−0.265	−0.010	−0.340	−0.012	−0.437
POWNFARM	−0.101	−0.652	−0.102	−0.639	−0.000	−0.006
PFB	0.177	0.858	0.153	0.734	0.116	0.584
PFS	−0.471	−0.712	−0.320	−0.494	−0.471	−0.758

TABLE A4.2 *continued*

	C. Multivariate Analysis					
Variable	Parameter Estimate	t	Parameter Estimate	t	Parameter Estimate	t
PATSC	0.124	1.613	0.102	1.384	0.072	1.007
PBS	−0.367	−5.793	−0.365	−5.677	−0.351	−5.713
PBY	0.127	1.329	0.122	1.235	0.097	1.026
R^2	0.7223		0.7191		0.7470	

Note: Abbreviations:
PFTU: Percentage of females among teachers in ungraded schools (the dependent variable in the regression analysis).
UGLENGTH: Length of the ungraded school year.
TRINDAYS: Number of days the average teacher spent at institutes.
INSTLEN: Average number of days the teacher institutes lasted.
INST1: Whether or not (yes/no) the county reported holding an institute.
PFRAME: Percentage of schoolhouses of frame construction.
NOPRIVY: Percentage of school sites without an outhouse.
FMWAGE: Female-to-male wage ratio.
FEMMFG: Percentage of adult women employed in manufacturing (near zero in most counties).
OV1000P: Percentage of the population in towns of 1,000 or more.
FRMTOFAM: Ratio of farms to families (families = population/5.5).
POWNFARM: Percentage of farms owned.
PFB: Percentage of foreign born.
PFS: Percentage of girls among school attenders in 1870.
PATSC: Percentage of 5–19-year-olds in school in 1870.
PBS: Percentage of settlers from southern states.
PBY: Percentage from New England and New York.

TABLE A4.3 School Organization and the Percentage of Female Teachers: Iowa, 1880

A. Means and Standard Deviations of County Characteristics (99 counties)

Variable	Mean	Standard Deviation
PFTU	0.68	0.06
UGLENGTH	7.04	0.49
INSTLEN	21.21	6.96
TRINDAYS	11.13	5.08
PFRAME	0.92	0.09
FMWAGEUG	0.82	0.08
HANDSMFG	0.06	0.06
OV1000P	0.15	0.15
FRMTOFAM	1.52	0.40
POWNFARM	0.76	0.05
PFS	0.47	0.03
PATSC	0.75	0.18
PBS	0.07	0.05
PBY	0.24	0.16

TABLE A4.3 *continued*

B. No Controls

Variable	Parameter Estimate	t	Parameter Estimate	t	Parameter Estimate	t	Parameter Estimate	t
INTERCEP	0.725	7.353	0.678	33.589	0.691	46.902	0.661	10.790
UGLENGTH	−0.006	−0.466						
INSTLEN			0.000	0.022				
TRINDAYS					−0.001	−0.888		
PFRAME							0.019	0.296
R^2	0.0022		0.0000		0.0081		0.0009	

C. Multivariate Analysis

Variable	Parameter Estimate	t	Parameter Estimate	t
INTERCEP	0.734	2.978	0.767	3.085
UGLENGTH	0.012	0.728	0.010	0.594
INSTLEN	0.001	1.589		
TRINDAYS			0.000	0.537
PFRAME	−0.028	−0.319	−0.023	−0.260
FMWAGEUG	−0.091	−0.926	−0.091	−0.910
HANDSMFG	0.017	0.093	0.032	0.167
OV1000P	0.052	0.671	0.065	0.834
FRMTOFAM	−0.059	−1.446	−0.065	−1.565
POWNFARM	0.059	0.398	0.026	0.175
PFS	−0.106	−0.446	−0.040	−0.169
PATSC	−0.012	−0.321	−0.007	−0.199
PBS	−0.097	−0.515	−0.114	−0.599
PBY	0.149	2.127	0.137	1.912
R^2	0.2689		0.2500	

Note: Abbreviations:
PFTU: Percentage of females among teachers in ungraded schools (the dependent variable in the regression analysis).
UGLENGTH: Length of the ungraded school year.
INSTLEN: Average number of days the teacher institutes lasted.
TRINDAYS: Number of days the average teacher spent at institutes.
PFRAME: Percentage of schoolhouses of frame construction.
FMWAGEUG: Female-to-male wage ratio in ungraded schools.
HANDSMFG: Percentage of adults employed in manufacturing.
OV1000P: Percentage of the population in towns of 1,000 or more.
FRMTOFAM: Ratio of farms to families (families = population/5.5).
POWNFARM: Percentage of farms owned.
PFS: Percentage of girls among school attenders in 1870.
PATSC: Percentage of 5–19-year-olds in school in 1870.
PBS: Percentage of settlers from southern states.
PBY: Percentage from New England and New York.

TABLE A4.4 Did Southern Distinctiveness "Work through" School Organization? A Test Case from Illinois, 1881

A. Means and Standard Deviations (101 counties)

Variable	Mean	Standard Deviation
PFTU	0.52	0.16
UGLENGTH	6.79	0.73
PBS	0.30	0.25

B. Regression Analyses: The Impact of Settlers' Southern Origins and the Length of the Ungraded School Year on Feminization

Variable		Parameter Estimate	t	R^2
1. UGLENGTH =	INTERCEP	7.420	110.760	0.43
	PBS	−1.905	−8.644	
2. PFTU =	INTERCEP	0.678	58.026	0.64
	PBS	−0.506	−13.175	
3. PFTU =	INTERCEP	−0.252	−1.936	0.29
	UGLENGTH	0.117	6.308	
4. PFTU =	INTERCEP	0.644	4.906	0.64
	UGLENGTH	0.004	0.262	
	PBS	−0.498	−9.727	

C. Analysis of Results

a. Percentage of the total impact of PBS on PFTU remaining when UGLENGTH is controlled (based on models 2 and 4): .498/.506 = 98%
b. Percentage of the total impact of UGLENGTH on PFTU remaining when PBS is controlled (based on models 3 and 4): .004/.117 = 4%
c. Standard deviation of UGLENGTH at any given level of PBS: 75% of the entire standard deviation, or .55 months.[a]
d. Standard deviation of PFTU at any given level of PBS: 60% of the entire standard deviation, or 9.6 percentage points.[a]

Note: Abbreviations:
PFTU: Percentage of females among teachers in ungraded schools.
UGLENEGTH: Length of the ungraded school year in months.
PBS: Percentage of settlers born in the South, 1870.
[a] Calculated as the square root of $[1 - R^2]$ in models 1 and 2.

Supplemental Tables for Chapter 4

Table A4.5 Impact of the Civil War on Feminization: Percentage of Female Teachers in 13 States before and after the War

Year	CT	IN	IA	ME	MA	MI	NH	NJ	NY	OH	PA	RI	WI
1841										44			
1845									56				
1846	56												
1847					66		64			48			
1849						65							
1850				59	72		70			37			
1851												55	
1852	52										33		
1855		21		62	78	68	74	39			34	59	
1856	68								59	47			
1858			47										
1860	69	20	49	63	78	67	72			47	37	71	60
1861								48					
1862									71				
1865	82	47	68	76	86	85	85	61	83	68	61	78	71
1870	82	40	63	75	88	75	83	68	77	58	54	81	71
1870	78	40	61	76	87	74	85	68	77	57	57	80	
1875	76	42	64	69	87	74	86	71	75	45	57	82	
1880	77	43	66	73	87	71	83	72	74	52	55	80	71
1885	83	49	75	79	89	75	88	77	81	56	63	82	78
1890	87	49	79	84	90	78	90	82	83	57	66	87	80
1895	90	52	79	82	91	79	91	86	85	59	67	89	81
1900	91	54	83	84	91	80	91	87	85	60	68	91	82
1905	93	61	88	90	91	84	91	88	88	67	75	92	86
1910	94	64	90	89	91	86	93	88	88	69	77	91	88
1915	94	68	90	89	90	86	91	86	89	75	78	92	89

Sources: The percentages for years prior to 1870, and for the first percentage from 1870, were taken from state school reports. The second percentage for 1870, and percentages for 1875–1915, were taken from the U.S. commissioner of education's annual report. The percentages from state records are reasonably consistent with those from the commissioner's reports, judging by the two percentages from 1870.

Except for the cases noted below, the figures from the state reports are based on a single number for all male teachers and a single number for all female teachers. In the following cases, the figures from state reports are based on the sum of males teaching in winter and summer sessions, and the sum of females teaching in winter and summer sessions: CT, all years; MA, 1850; NY, 1845; ME, 1865–70; NH, 1855. Also, in NH, figures were only available for the winter sessions prior to 1855; the percentages for 1847 and 1850 in the table were calculated by assuming that the summer session included half the teachers, and that 97% of these were female teachers (as was the case in 1855).

TABLE A4.6 Percentage of Female Public School Teachers in Southern
States, 1870–1915

Year	AL	AR	FL	GA	KY	LA	MD	MS	NC	OK	SC	TN	TX	WV	VA
1870		24	34			49	55		27		38			21	
1875	33	32			29	48	59	40			38	26		23	36
1880	36	22	38	35	35	54	57	39	29		41	26	25	25	38
1885	34	23	44		47	53	66	43	34		44	31	31	33	51
1890	37	32	52	47	50	55	72	50	41		50	38	39	37	59
1895	37	38	56	50	54	60	76	54	48	60	53	42	47	40	63
1900	70	40	63	56	55	52	78	56	51	57	57	46	51	42	69
1905	57	48	68	67	57	79	82	66	65	66	57	58	62	50	77
1910	65	53	74	76	58	79	83	69	72	74	77	63	69	52	80
1915	71	55	78	80	66	80	85	74	77	70	80	68	72	57	84

Source: U.S. Commission of Education, *Report,* 1870–1915.

TABLE A4.7 Community Size, Graded Schools, and Female Teachers:
Illinois, 1881

	Teachers in Graded Schools	Teachers/1,000 Pop.
a. All Illinois	5,163	–
b. Chicago	886	1.76
c. 6 other towns, >7,500: avg. pop. = 13,200	225	2.84
d. EST. for 15 other towns, pop. >7,500: avg. pop. = 12,000	509	2.84
e. Estimate for 171 other towns, 1,000–7,500	1,443–2,165	4–6
f. Subtotal: estimate for all places >1,000, lines b through e	3,063–3,785	–
g. Estimate for places of <1,000, line a less line f	2,101–1,378	–
h. Percentage of teachers in graded schools working in places of <1,000 (estimate)	41–26	

Sources: Line a from *School Report,* Illinois, 1881; lines b–c from U.S. commissioner of education *Report* for 1880; line d, population of towns from 1880 census (places of over 4,000 and minor civil divisions); line d, estimated number of teachers in graded schools based on assumption of 4 teachers per 1,000 population. Remaining lines by addition and subtraction.

TABLE A4.8 Size of Place and Percentage of Female Teachers: Graded
Schools Only, Iowa 1881

Size of Place	Percentage of Female Teachers	Number of Teachers	Number of: Schools	Number of: School Districts	Estimate: Teachers/ School[a]
Unknown, but < 4,000	83	72	31		
Under 500	90	230	148		1.6
500–999	88	326	105		3.1
1,000–2,499	92	489	68		
2,500–3,999	93	163	14		
4,000–9,999	93	274	12		
10,000 and over	98	366		69	5.3
All	92	1,920			

Source: Table F of the Iowa *School Report* for 1880.
[a] The school report lists school districts in which graded schools existed. In the smaller communities these apparently were single schools; if some districts had two or more such schools, the ratio of teachers per school would be even lower. In the middle-sized communities, it is clear that the districts involve more than one school, and in the larger cities, individual schools were listed under each district.

APPENDIX 5

The Urban Teacher Lists: The Regression Analyses

THE DATA SET: RELEVANT DETAILS

The interpretation of most variables is straightforward, with the exception of marital status and education. The lists do not report marital status per se; instead, we sometimes observe a "Mrs." in reference to a female teacher. The use of "Mrs." was most common in the Houston teacher lists; because the Houston school district had a marriage bar prohibiting the employment of married teachers (except during the teacher-scarce years of World War I), it is probable that use of "Mrs." indicates the teacher was a widow. The reporting of marital status was so sporadic, however, that we make no consistent use of this variable in our analysis.

The quality of the education variable deserves some comment. The most detailed reporting of education—essentially a complete identification of the institution the teacher attended—occurs in the Houston teacher lists. In the Grand Rapids and Paterson lists, the institution was generally identified only if it was a normal (teacher training) school, college, or university. In other cases, the location of the teacher's education was reported; we can presume, with confidence, that in these cases the teachers had completed high school and had taken education courses in a normal institute attached to the high school. The Portland lists report education after but not before 1896, and salaries before but not after 1896. Since we are examining variation in salaries and the probability of holding an administrative position, we cannot include education as a factor in our analysis of salaries in Portland prior to 1897—but we can include education as a factor in the analysis of administrative positions in that city, provided we restrict our attention to the period after 1896.

In computing the sample means shown in table 5.1 (text) we have combined the lists from each year. Thus if a teacher were employed in the Grand Rapids public schools for, say, seven years—we refer to this variable throughout the chapter as the teacher's "tenure" in the system—she would appear seven times in the sample.[16] For variables that do not change with tenure—for example, years of prior teaching experience on entry into the school system—an alternative way of computing the sample mean would be by the individual; that is, not to weight each observation by tenure in the system. This approach, however, would not work for variables that changed over a career—salary and position. In any case, gender differences would not be affected since, as we shall see, mean years of tenure were quite similar for male and female school personnel.

CHANGE OVER TIME

We explored change over time by estimating a series of regressions, in which the dependent variable—for example, years of teaching experience—was regressed on a time trend, a female dummy variable, and an interaction term between the female dummy and the trend. The coefficient of the female dummy variable measures the gender difference at the start of the period (when the time trend equals zero). If the coefficient of the interaction term is significantly different from zero, the gender difference in the dependent variable was changing over time (the direction of change depends on the sign of the female dummy variable and the sign of the interaction term). The results of this regression analysis are summarized in table A5.1.

With respect to the salary ratio and the percentage of administrators, the interaction terms generally have positive and statistically significant coefficients, which indicate a narrowing of the gender gap over time.

THE GENDER GAP IN SALARIES

For the sake of clarity, we present a full discussion of the regression models here, although several sentences from this discussion are also presented in the text.

We begin the analysis by estimating regressions of the form

$$LSAL = B_0 + B_1EXP + B_2EXP2 + B_3TEN + B_4COL + B_5NORM + B_6T + f,$$

where LSAL = log of the annual salary, in dollars of 1900; EXP = total years of experience in teaching; TEN = years of experience in school system; COL = 1 if the person attended or graduated from college, zero otherwise; NORM = 1 if the person attended or graduated from a normal school, zero otherwise; T = a time trend; and f = random error.

In terms of the specification of the experience and tenure terms, the regres-

16. We do not, however, attempt to adjust the sample means for the fact that some teachers had not completed their tenures at the end of the sample period; the samples are "censored" in this sense.

TABLE A5.1 Regressions on Time Trend: Coefficients of Female Dummy Variable and Female-Time Trend Interaction

	Portland	Grand Rapids	Paterson	Houston
Log(salary)				
Female	−0.991*	−0.922*	−0.865*	−0.588*
Female × time	0.036*	0.017*	−0.002	0.001
Administrator				
Female		−0.357*	−1.030*	−0.545*
Female × time		0.006**	0.015*	0.005*
Education				
Normal				
Female				−0.253*
Female × time				0.007*
College/univ.				
Female			−0.284*	−0.257*
Female × time			−0.005*	−0.005*
Total experience				
Female		−5.006*	−11.649*	−12.345*
Female × time		0.163**	0.177*	0.309*
Tenure				
Female		−1.437*	−2.984*	−4.501*
Female × time		0.225*	0.132*	0.207*

* Significant at the 5 percent level.
** Significant at the 10 percent level.

sion closely resembles Goldin's analysis of the earnings of male and female office workers.[17]

Because there is no reason to believe the coefficients will be independent of gender, separate regressions were estimated for male and female teachers.

We expect that B_1 will be positive and B_2 will be negative. More teaching experience raises one's salary ($B_1 > 0$) but at a rate that decreases with years of experience ($B_2 < 0$). The implied curvilinear shape is consistent with much modern and historical research on earnings and also with the typical salary schedule adopted by school boards.[18] Both B_4 and B_5 should be positive: education increases earnings. If B_6 is positive, teacher salaries were increasing over time, adjusting for changes in the price level.[19]

The coefficient of TEN, B_3, measures the value of experience specific to a school district, relative to experience gained elsewhere. If B_3 is negative for a

17. Goldin, *Understanding the Gender Gap*, 109.

18. The typical schedule had the largest percentage increases in salary during the first few years of experience. Increases gradually became smaller as experience rose and, in many cases, gradually became zero when a maximum salary was reached. The inclusion of experience and, in particular, experience squared captures the shape of the typical schedule.

19. The Bureau of Labor Statistics Consumer Price Index (U.S. Department of Commerce 1975, series E-135, p. 211) was used to deflate salaries to the 1900 base.

given amount of total experience (EXP), teachers who acquired more of their experience in the specific school system (a higher value of TEN) were paid less than teachers who acquired their experience elsewhere. If B_3 is positive, tenure in a school system was rewarded, at the margin, more highly than experience elsewhere. We expect that the difference between the male and female coefficients of EXP, TEN, and the education variables will be positive. Males were rewarded more, at the margin, for such characteristics than females.

The regression results are displayed in table A5.2. The results generally conform to our expectations. Both men and women benefited from additional years of experience, but at a decreasing rate ($B_2 < 0$). Except in Houston, the returns to experience were higher for men than for women. For men employed in the Paterson or Grand Rapids schools, the location of the experience did not matter. Holding constant years of experience, the coefficient of tenure was insignificantly different from zero. In the Portland and Houston schools, however, tenure brought greater rewards at the margin for males than experience elsewhere did.

In three of the four regressions—Portland is the exception—the female coefficient of tenure is negative. Women gain less, at the margin, from experience in a given system than general experience—this, despite the fact, noted in the previous section, that the average female teacher in all four systems had acquired relatively more of her experience in the form of tenure than the average male. Since the male coefficients in all of the regressions were either positive or insignificantly different than zero, it follows that men gained more, at the margin, from tenure than women did. Even in Portland—the one system where the female coefficient of tenure was positive—the returns to tenure were greater for males than females. Consistent with our expectations, both men and women benefited from college or normal school educations. In Paterson and Grand Rapids, the returns to education were greater for men but the opposite was true in Houston. With two exceptions (males in Grand Rapids and Portland) the coefficients of the time trend were positive, indicating that salaries rose over time in real terms.

The regressions in table A5.2 do not control for position held in the school system. In light of our earlier discussion, we next ask whether the gender differences in returns to experience, tenure, and education were a consequence of the greater likelihood that males would hold an administrative position as they progressed through their tenure in a school system. Accordingly, table A5.3 shows the regressions results when a dummy variable for administrators (ADM) is included.[20]

Holding constant other characteristics, and regardless of gender, adminis-

---

20. The dummy variable for administrators takes the value 1 if the person held an administrative position (e.g., principal), zero otherwise.

TABLE A5.2 Regressions of Teacher Salaries

	Grand Rapids	Houston	Portland	Paterson
		Male		
Constant	6.210	6.332	6.743	6.127
	(98.401)	(157.243)	(58.014)	(89.963)
EXP	0.076	0.021	0.051	0.041
	(9.250)	(11.308)	(4.419)	(6.329)
EXP2 $\times$ 10^{-2}	−0.190	0.024	−0.112	0.056
	(7.595)	(11.564)	(3.749)	(3.722)
TEN	0.008	0.010	0.019	−0.004
	(1.650)	(4.636)	(3.531)	(0.100)
COL	0.402	0.138		0.220
	(8.779)	(5.092)		(5.186)
NORM		0.075		0.266
		(2.537)		(4.346)
Time	−0.0032	0.002	−0.018	0.015
	(0.897)	(1.602)	(4.091)	(9.966)
R^2	0.457	0.306	0.451	0.548
N	299	1,084	128	199
		Female		
Constant	5.617	5.776	6.213	5.636
	(830.610)	(433.785)	(311.443)	(672.028)
EXP	0.065	0.046	0.032	0.041
	(60.708)	(28.630)	(9.542)	(20.094)
EXP2 $\times$ 10^{-2}	0.150	−0.062	−0.040	−0.063
	(40.770)	(16.891)	(3.292)	(13.950)
TEN	−0.004	−0.005	0.011	−0.003
	(5.617)	(4.829)	(5.186)	(1.990)
COL	0.310	0.262		0.406
	(21.774)	(23.747)		(9.377)
NORM		0.109		0.091
		(19.633)		(4.128)
Time	0.016	0.0001	0.004	0.013
	(41.237)	(1.441)	(3.323)	(43.419)
R^2	0.650	0.299	0.393	0.700
N	5,767	6,498	1,257	2,440

Source: See text.
Note: EXP: Years of teaching experience.
TEN: Share of total experience in city school system.
COL: College graduate.
NORM: Normal school graduate.

trators earned significantly more than school employees. It is also clear that including ADM reduces the gender gaps in the coefficients of experience and tenure. The effect of including ADM on the gender gap in returns to experience, however, is greater than the effect on the gap in returns to tenure. Consider, for example, the Grand Rapids regressions. If ADM is excluded, the

TABLE A5.3 Regressions of Teacher Salaries: Includes Administrative Dummy

	Grand Rapids	Houston	Portland	Paterson
	Male			
Constant	6.222	6.360	6.755	5.903
	(108.186)	(75.815)	(57.888)	(86.937)
EXP	0.058	0.012	0.047	0.030
	(7.407)	(6.847)	(3.832)	(4.990)
EXP2 × 10^{-2}	−0.160	−0.012	−0.100	−0.035
	(6.767)	(5.951)	(3.266)	(2.541)
TEN	0.004	0.006	0.018	−0.006
	(0.929)	(3.258)	(3.487)	(1.562)
COL	0.340	0.123		0.180
	(8.779)	(5.044)		(4.686)
NORM		0.026		0.141
		(0.984)		(2.478)
ADM	0.352	0.303	0.052	0.375
	(7.808)	(16.181)	(1.036)	(7.270)
Time	0.0004	0.002	−0.019	0.021
	(0.143)	(2.163)	(4.217)	(13.378)
R^2	0.549	0.441	0.451	0.644
N	299	1,084	128	199
	Female			
Constant	5.611	5.781	6.210	5.633
	(869.923)	(439.814)	(324.737)	(709.009)
EXP	0.064	0.045	0.033	0.039
	(62.441)	(28.572)	(10.373)	(20.176)
EXP2 × 10^{-2}	−0.150	−0.060	−0.050	−0.067
	(43.548)	(47.178)	(4.356)	(15.770)
TEN	−0.006	−0.004	0.009	−0.001
	(8.032)	(4.949)	(5.154)	(0.937)
COL	0.322	0.243		0.296
	(23.553)	(22.260)		(7.135)
NORM		0.112		0.074
		(10.036)		(3.554)
ADM	0.192	0.282	0.278	0.438
	(24.153)	(13.292)	(10.583)	(16.756)
Time	0.016	0.0001	0.004	0.013
	(45.320)	(1.382)	(3.285)	(47.012)
R^2	0.683	0.317	0.442	0.730
N	5,767	6,498	1,257	2,440

Source: See text.
Note: ADM = 1 if administrator. For definitions of other variables, see table A5.2.

TABLE A5.4 Decomposition Analysis of Gender Gap in Salaries

Sample Mean, Log	Grand Rapids	Houston	Portland	Paterson
Salary				
Male	6.887	6.886	7.152	6.978
Female	6.189	6.326	6.582	6.125
Hypothetical male	6.664	6.788	6.981	6.664
Percent due to discrimination	68.1	83.6	70.0	63.2

Source: See text.

gender difference in the tenure coefficient (male-female) is 0.012; if ADM is included, the gender difference is 0.010. This controlling for position held explains about 17 percent of the gender difference in the tenure coefficient. The percent explained is much larger for the difference in returns to experience. If ADM is excluded, the gender difference in the coefficient of EXP is 0.011; if ADM is included, the gender difference is negative. Similar qualitative findings hold for the other cities. The implication, which is examined in greater detail in the next section, is that total experience in the teaching profession was an important determinant of the probability of holding an administrative position.

The regressions discussed thus far provide insights into the determinants of salaries, but we have yet to answer the question: how much of the gender gap in salaries is attributable to gender differences in characteristics (i.e., experience, tenure, and education)? To answer this question, we make use of a technique applied to a similar problem by Goldin.[21] We use the male regression to calculate the average salary a male teacher would earn if he had the same average characteristics as a female teacher. The difference between the average male salary and this hypothetical salary captures the portion of the gender gap in salaries that is due to the gender gap in characteristics. The remainder of the gap is conventionally assigned to wage discrimination. For the purposes of the calculation we use the regressions in table A5.2, which exclude the dummy for administrative positions.

The results are shown in table A5.4. Because the coefficients of the time trends in the salary regression are generally different between males and females, it is necessary to select a point in time to perform the calculations. This point in time is the average value of the time trend for females which, it should be recognized, differs across the cities.

Gender differences in the characteristics of teachers were important determinants of gender differences in salaries. In each city, had women had the same experience, tenure, and education as males, their average pay would have been higher. The bulk of the gender gap in salaries was due to "wage discrimi-

21. Goldin, *Understanding the Gender Gap*.

TABLE A5.5 Logistic Regressions of Position Held: Probability of an Administrative Position

A. Logistic Coefficients				
	Grand Rapids	Houston	Portland	Paterson
Male				
Constant	−3.109	−3.015	−1.354	0.478
	(5.892)	(8.687)	(1.760)	(0.560)
EXP	0.328	0.145	0.203	0.303
	(4.876)	(9.990)	(2.794)	(3.514)
EXP2 × 10⁻²	−0.668	−0.190	−0.795	0.564
	(3.537)	(11.560)	(3.725)	(2.701)
TEN	0.066	0.058	0.313	0.086
	(1.905)	(3.720)	(4.573)	(1.387)
COL	0.992	0.368	−0.295	0.688
	(3.227)	(1.638)	(0.774)	(1.261)
NORM		0.933	1.858	2.802
		(3.831)	(1.737)	(3.245)
Time	−0.060	−0.007	−0.082	−0.138
	(2.731)	(0.763)	(1.369)	(5.842)
χ^2	104.54	283.82	55.46	91.11
Female				
Constant	4.333	−5.549	−1.641	−6.766
	(20.641)	(18.700)	(5.650)	(9.621)
EXP	0.284	0.123	0.278	0.387
	(10.584)	(4.553)	(5.643)	(4.481)
EXP2	−0.552	−0.122	−0.640	−0.459
	(7.242)	(2.259)	(5.858)	(2.816)
TEN	0.057	0.001	0.107	−0.038
	(5.014)	(0.792)	(2.717)	(0.940)
COL	−0.886	1.494	−1.379	0.480
	(2.040)	(9.791)	(1.360)	(5.370)
NORM		−0.391	0.337	0.176
		(1.697)	(0.816)	(2.806)
Time	−0.055	0.0003	−0.099	−0.077
	(6.740)	(0.732)	(2.631)	(4.297)
χ^2	700.99	225.78	46.11	113.04

B. Predicted Probabilities of an Administrative Position Using Male Equations and Female Sample Means Predicted				
Probability	0.213	0.359	0.812	0.648
Administrators (%)				
Male	0.378	0.477	0.750	0.789
Female	0.213	0.039	0.040	0.016
Percent of gender gap explained	58.2	26.9	–	18.3

Note: Panel A: Absolute values of t-statistics in parentheses.

Panel B: Percent explained is calculated in two steps. First, the value of the logit using the male coefficients and the female sample means is computed, call this L^*. The predicted probability, p^*, is the solution to $\ln[p^*/(1 − p^*)] = L^*$. Second, the difference between the sample mean proportion of males with administrative positions (from the logistic regression sample, row 2 of panel B) and p^* (row 1 of panel B) is computed. This difference, divided by the difference between the actual male and female proportions (rows 2–3, panel B) is the percent explained (row 4 of panel B). – means the percent explained was less than zero.

nation." The levels of wage discrimination in these four school systems—ranging from 63 to 84 percent—far exceed wage discrimination ca. 1900 in manufacturing, which was a major sector in terms of employment of women. In terms of wage discrimination, in other words, teaching was unusual at the turn of the century. The levels, however, are comparable to those observed among office workers ca. 1940—an occupation, like teaching, in which education was important and in which internal labor markets were common.[22]

Gender and Administrative Positions

The framework for our analysis is essentially the same as above. We estimate regressions of the form

$$p(\text{ADM}) = B_0 + B_1\text{EXP} + B_2\text{EXP2} + B_3\text{TEN} + B_4\text{COL} + B_5\text{NORM} + B_6\text{TIME},$$

where $p(\text{ADM})$ is a dummy variable equal to 1 if the person held an administrative position, zero otherwise.

The other variables in the regression are defined in the same way as in our analysis of salaries. Because the dependent variable is a dummy variable, we use logit analysis to estimate the regression rather than ordinary least squares. Separate regressions were estimated for male and female school personnel. The logit coefficients are shown in table A5.5. The χ^2 statistics, which are a measure of goodness of fit, are all significant at the 0.0001 level.

Table A5.5 shows the impact of gender differences in characteristics on the gender gap in administrative positions. The methodology is the same as in the previous section. The probability that a man with average female characteristics would hold an administrative position is computed, and the difference between this predicted probability and the percentage of men holding administrative jobs gives the percentage of the gender gap explained by characteristics.

---

22. Goldin estimates that wage discrimination probably accounted for between 15 percent and 25 percent of the gender gap in pay in manufacturing. The comparable figure for the clerical sector in 1940 was 61 percent (*Understanding the Gender Gap*, 104, 110).

INDEX

Massachusetts Board of Education, 20
McCurry, Stephanie, 55
McPherson, James, 77
men's work, 31
Michigan: effect of Civil War on feminization of teaching in, 87, 168t; feminization of rural teachers in, 96–99, 97t; feminization of teaching in, 91, 97–99, 97t;
fertility rates in, 54; proportions of female teachers in, 22t, 53, 74–75, 75t;
school board fiscal concerns in, 108
Middle Atlantic, schools in, 8, 71, 90–91,
90t. *See also* New York; Pennsylvania
Middlekauf, Robert, 19–20 n. 14
Middlesex County, 18, 19
middling orders, southern, 45–49, 48t
Midwest: demands of child care in, 53; and
increasing wages of female teachers,
105–6; marriage patterns in, 50–51, 51t;
opportunities for female teaching in, 48;
proportion of female teachers in, 51;
women in labor force in, 47–49, 48t
Midwest, schooling in: feminization of
teaching in, 90t, 91; and increasing
wages for increased duties, 103–6; Massachusetts pattern of, 99; in the post–Civil
War period, 90; proportion of female
teachers in, 8, 22, 22t, 35, 74–76, 75t,
76t, 90–91, 90t; as replication of regional
difference, 2, 75–76; and rise in female
teacher salaries, 105; school organization
in, 94
migration, and educational hiring patterns:
Illinois as case study for, 77–85, 79t; in
the Middle Atlantic, 71–74, 72t; in the
Midwest, 74–76, 75t, 76t
Minnesota, 22t, 75t
Mississippi, 93 n. 7
Missouri, female teachers in, 74–75, 75t, 91
Morain, Thomas, 101 n. 15, 103, 104, 158,
159
Murphy, Geraldine, 12, 13, 14

New England, schooling in: age distribution
of students attending, 36–37, 36t; age-
specific sex distribution of teachers, 37–
38, 37t; centralized organization of, 40–
41, 69; dame schools within, 15–16;
division of towns into separate school
districts, 16; effect of population dispersal on, 16, 19; feminization of teaching

in, 88, 90–91, 90t; gendered seasonal division of teaching, 20, 21, 27; and hiring
of teachers, 69; historiography of, 11–
13; intraregional differences in, 12; Latin
grammar schools in, 13; number of teachers within, compared with the South,
34–35; and payment of Latin teachers,
14; proportion of female teachers in
rural schools, 8; reading and writing
schools within, 13; seasonal patterns of
teaching in, 18, 20–21 (*see also* summer
session schools; winter session schools);
two tiers of town-supported schools, 17,
18, 21, 22, 35 (*see also* dame schools;
two-tier school system; writing schools)
New England rural schools, proportion of female teachers in, 8
New Hampshire, feminization of teaching
in, 87, 92, 168t
New Jersey, 22t, 35
New Mexico, Spanish subculture of, 91 n. 2
New Orleans, 7
New York, 71–72, 72t; absence of antebellum reform movement in, 73; administrative organization of schooling in, 73;
antebellum nature of public support for
schooling in, 72–73; comparative number of teachers in, 35; feminization of
teaching in, 90–91, 90t; proportion of
female teachers in, 8, 22t, 28t, 32 n. 25
North Carolina: effect of Civil War on feminization of teaching in, 89; male-female
teacher salary differential in, 89; perceptions within, of utility of female teachers, 38–39; tradition of female teachers
in, 89
Northeast, women in labor force in, 47–49,
48t
northern Midwest: fertility rates in, 53; percentage of female teachers, 22t, 75, 75t;
settled by Northerners, 75
Norwich, 18

office workers, wage discrimination among,
115
Ohio: intrastate split in hiring of female
teachers, 75–76, 76t; intrastate split in
settlers' region of origin, 75–76, 76t; proportion of female teachers in, 75
old field schools, arrangements concerning,
35, 41